OVERSHADOWED

OSPREY
PUBLISHING

OVERSHADOWED

US MARINES IN WORLD WAR II: EUROPE, THE CARIBBEAN, AND SOUTH AMERICA

ISAAC LAMBERTH

OSPREY PUBLISHING
Bloomsbury Publishing Plc
Kemp House, Chawley Park, Cumnor Hill, Oxford OX2 9PH, UK
Bloomsbury Publishing Ireland Limited,
29 Earlsfort Terrace, Dublin 2, D02 AY28, Ireland
Bloomsbury Publishing Inc.
1359 Broadway, 12th Floor, New York, NY 10018, USA
E-mail: info@ospreypublishing.com
www.ospreypublishing.com

OSPREY is a trademark of Osprey Publishing Ltd

First published in Great Britain in 2026

A catalog record for this book is available from the British Library

ISBN: HB 9781472872722; eBook 9781472872715; ePDF 9781472872746;
XML 9781472872739

26 27 28 29 30   10 9 8 7 6 5 4 3 2 1

Page 2: Marines aboard USS *Texas* man a 40mm antiaircraft gun at a position just off the
coast of France, June 6, 1944. (USMC, photo by Cpl William R. Gibbon)
Page 3: World War II-era Eagle, Globe, and Anchor. (USMC, photo by Sgt James
Stanfield)

Cover, page design, and layout by Stewart Larking
Maps by www.bounford.com
Index by Alan Rutter
Printed by Repro India Ltd

Osprey Publishing supports the Woodland Trust, the UK's leading woodland
conservation charity.

To find out more about our authors and books visit **www.ospreypublishing.com**. Here
you will find extracts, author interviews, details of forthcoming events and the option to
sign up for our newsletter.

For product safety related questions contact productsafety@bloomsbury.com

DEDICATION

To the Marines who served far from the Pacific – in the snow of far-off northern lands to the sunny tropics – this one is for you. Your stories may have faded from memory but your service deserves to be remembered.

CONTENTS

American Marines on maneuvers in Northern Ireland, May 1943. (USMC, photo by SSgt Weldon Keating)

PREFACE

Every year on June 6, many American soldiers are proud to talk about Operation *Overlord*, and rightfully so. The American landings at Omaha and Utah Beaches, and the air insertions by the 101st and 82nd Airborne Divisions, would prove to be critical events for the war in Europe. Also on every June 6 is the near certainty of soldiers poking fun at Marines about their absence during the largest amphibious landing of the European Theater. Many Marines will lament the fact and scratch their heads silently, wondering how in the world the Army pulled off the landings if the service best suited for amphibious assaults was concentrated on the other side of the world in the Pacific.

While there is no denying the American land component of Operation *Overlord* was carried out by soldiers, this is not to say there were no Marines on the beaches of Normandy, or even in Europe, during the war. In fact, research compiled for this book shows that in all, several thousand Marines served outside the Pacific Theater during the war. Not only did Marines fight the Germans in Europe, but they also fought them in Africa, guarded naval bases in South America, at Caribbean outposts, and on the East Coast of the United States, and landed with the US Army in Africa, all the while receiving numerous valor awards fighting alongside US soldiers and sailors.

Almost a century later, we often look back at the black-and-white photos, videos, maps, and paintings of World War II and imagine a time long forgotten. The great battles of Operation *Overlord*, Operation *Market Garden*, the Battle of Britain, the Battle of the Bulge, Iwo Jima, Saipan, Guadalcanal, and Pearl Harbor often receive much of the attention. However, areas where Marines helped fight the Germans, such as during the Battle of the Atlantic, Operation *Torch*, Operation *Dragoon*, Operation *Shingle*, or Operation *Union II* are all but given a glancing view, with the Marine portions forgotten to all but a few.

Research for this book took years to compile, scouring internet message boards, searching and following leads, emailing people around the world who I hoped would have information and be kind enough to pass it my way, reading dozens of books, and spending numerous hours at the US National Archives in College Park, Maryland. Surprisingly, a fair amount of people who are also interested in Marine Corps history discouraged me from writing on it.

The results of the FLEX experiments were profound in how they prepared the Marine Corps for World War II. The exercises outlined the need for increased gunfire skill in support of landing forces, improved communication for air and ground units, the creation of landing craft specifically designed to efficiently ferry troops from ships to shore and quickly offload them, the creation of reconnaissance units for pre-landing scout activities, and elevated the importance of streamlining logistics movements, enabling the quick unloading of supplies on beachheads to resupply troops already ashore while having supplies on hand for follow-on forces.

Following the Navy's lead of publishing official doctrine in the *Fleet Training Publication 167: Landing Operations Doctrine* in 1938, the Army published one soon thereafter. In June 1941, the US Army published its own amphibious operations manual entitled *Field Manual 31-5, Landing Operations on Hostile Shores*, which largely copied the Navy's document verbatim.

One key doctrinal difference between the Navy and Army was the Navy's focus on controlling smaller territories to extend naval dominance, in contrast to the Army's emphasis on conducting prolonged land campaigns. Another divergence was in how the services sustained their assault forces after the initial landing. To address this, the Marine Corps established Pioneer Platoons – specialized units tasked with logistics and engineering functions. As the war progressed, these platoons expanded in both size and importance, eventually evolving into Pioneer Companies and, later, full Pioneer Battalions. While the name "Pioneer Battalion" may have faded into history, its legacy endures in the Marine Corps' modern Combat Engineer Battalions.

In 1939, War Department planners abandoned the original color-coded plans in favor of the Rainbow plans – plans that accounted for the US fighting wars in the Pacific and Atlantic simultaneously. The newly evolved plans dubbed War Plan Rainbow refined aspects of the prospective future wars, with various versions of Rainbow being assigned numbers.

Developed in 1939, Rainbow 1 focused on defensive actions in the event of an attack on the US, particularly by Germany or Japan. It envisioned the US defending the Western Hemisphere and protecting its possessions in the Pacific and the Caribbean, relying on naval strength. Also developed in 1939, Rainbow 2 saw a shift in strategy to the possibility of simultaneous German aggression in Europe and Japanese aggression in the Pacific. The plan called for the US to support Great Britain if it was drawn into war with Germany. The plan also saw the protecting of American interests in the Pacific without immediately entering the conflict.

Army, Navy, Marines Plan Joint Exercises

Tacoma Times, **Washington State, January 18, 1941**

Washington – The army, navy and marine corps will hold joint training exercises in Puerto Rican waters, beginning about Jan. 21 and extending into February according to Frank Knox, secretary of the navy and Henry L. Stimson, secretary of war.

The exercises are held annually either in the Caribbean area or in the Pacific.

Knox said he did not believe the bases in the Caribbean recently acquired from Great Britain will be involved in the exercises.

2,900 Marines At Quantico Base Ordered to Cuba

Contingent in 'Training' Will Be Near Canal And South America

By the Associated Press.

Amid far-reaching plans to strengthen United States defenses in the Caribbean, the Navy is ordering 2,900 Marines to Guantanamo Bay, Cuba, for intensive training maneuvers.

The contingent—the 1st Marine Brigade of Quantico, Va.—would be in a position to reach Central or South America quickly, should any trouble requiring their presence arise.

The Navy already has undertaken conversion of four fast American ships into "destroyer transports" so the brigade could be moved swiftly.

The action comes shortly after the adoption at the Havana Pan-American Conference of a resolution expressing opposition to the transfer to other non-American nations of foreign possessions in this hemisphere. The conference voted to let one or more of the American republics establish a provisional administration over any possession affected.

Transfer of the Quantico brigade, Navy officials said, is "for the purpose of preliminary training of this force in view of extensive maneuvers planned during the winter in the Caribbean area."

The maneuvers—similar to those conducted each year—involve landings and other operations. Guantanamo provides a base from which ships may operate in carrying out one of the Navy's missions; keeping any enemy aircraft carrier from getting within 1,000 miles of the Panama Canal.

As the world stage became more complex, Rainbow 3 was developed in 1940. It assumed a two-front war, with the US assisting Britain against Nazi Germany and defending against Japanese threats in the Pacific. This plan also emphasized increased defense spending and the expansion of US forces to prepare for eventual involvement in the war.

Developed simultaneously with Rainbow 3, Rainbow 5 had evolved into the most detailed and comprehensive strategy, anticipating the US would need to engage in a full-scale two-front war with Germany and Japan. Rainbow 5 assumed the United States would be allied with the United Kingdom and France, with the US first concentrating its efforts in Europe and Africa to assist the Allies before turning its full attention to Imperial Japan in the Pacific. During this time, the US would wage a containment strategy in the Pacific to prevent the Japanese military from further spreading. Rainbow 5 would lay the foundation for the later strategies of combined Allied operations throughout World War II.

The work done between the Navy and Marine Corps in the years leading up to World War II would greatly assist and shape how the Army carried out amphibious operations throughout the war. While not perfect, the experiments and manuals helped rectify many major issues on how to carry out amphibious operations before the United States' entrance into the war and allowed American planners to focus on minute details for operations such as *Torch* and *Overlord*.

Prepared for Any Nazi Threat, Marines Move Up Trip to Cuba

A hand-picked force of 2,900 United States Marines will sail this month for Guantanamo Bay, from which it could strike swiftly to take over imperiled Caribbean possessions of conquered European nations or aid Latin American republics in downing any Nazi-inspired uprising.

Ostensibly bound for maneuvers the 1st Brigade of the Fleet Marine Force, stationed at Quantico, Va., will leave three months ahead of schedule for its customary winter operations in that area. The brigade is well-equipped with planes, tanks, artillery, anti-aircraft weapons and was organized as a hard-hitting fighting team, complete in itself, even as to transportation. Two for-

mer Grace liners, renamed the McCawley and Barnett, are to be commissioned at Brooklyn and Hoboken as Marine transports.

The Marines would be available also for their historic duty of guarding United States defense outposts—this time the new Atlantic bases leased from Britain. It was considered unlikely, however, that the brigade would be dispersed along the new frontier stretching from Newfoundland to British Guina. Marines from other organizations are expected to be used to guard the bases.

Although there was no official indication the Marines were being

(See MARINES, Page A-5.)

LEFT The *Evening Star,* Washington DC, August 10, 1940. (Library of Congress, hereafter LoC)

RIGHT The *Evening Star,* Washington DC, September 8, 1940. (LoC)

The maneuvers on cactus-studded beaches at Guantanamo Bay, Cuba, begin as US Marines climb down the nets of a transport into a landing boat, February 1941. Soldiers from the US Army crowd the decks to watch the Marines. (United States Marine Corps, hereafter USMC)

TOP Even before the landing boat hits the beach, the Marines are into the water in realistic landing maneuvers at Guantanamo Bay, February 1941. Leading his men, carrying a pistol on the left, is First Lieutenant Joseph L. Herson. On the far right is First Lieutenant Alfred L. O'Connor. (USMC)

CENTER These US Marines, normally stationed at San Juan, Puerto Rico, are in the "chow" line at a camp area in the Caribbean National Forest, February 1941. Mess gear in hand, they are ready for a big meal after a tough 15 miles of hiking. The 15 miles was part of a 90-mile hike in six days and periodic maneuvers for Marines stationed in the Caribbean. (USMC)

BOTTOM After a 90-mile trek over the rough terrain of Puerto Rico, these Marines stop to refill their canteens, February 1941. As the original caption reads, "One dog, pictured in the center, followed the Marines over the whole course and really looks 'dog tired' as one of the boys stops to give him an encouraging pet." (USMC)

Although some of the information contained within this book is available publicly, much of it is scattered across the internet, books, and inside various private collections. *Overshadowed* concentrates much of what is available about the topic into one concise location. This book unearths the work Marines accomplished outside of the Pacific and their impact, and brings credit where credit is due – to the Marines who fought in those locations, and to the Marine combat correspondents and combat cameramen with them. Marines played a very small part in the war outside of the Pacific, but their part should not be forgotten.

Overshadowed was written with the assumption that readers already possess a general understanding of World War II. Major events involving the Marines – such as Operation *Overlord* and the Battle of the Bulge – are mentioned with little additional context. In contrast, smaller engagements like Operation *Leader* and Operation *Husky* are given some background, but only to clarify the Marines' involvement rather than to provide a full historical account. The book's primary goal is to recognize and honor the contributions of Marines whose actions have long been forgotten over time but had an incalculable impact on the war outside of the Pacific.

Semper fidelis,
Isaac Lamberth

Colonel W. Garland Fay, USMC, Commander at the Charleston Navy Yard, awards "Ponselet" Private First Class chevrons, April 9, 1943. Ponselet was the mascot for the Marine garrison. (US Navy)

CHAPTER 1

BECOMING THE AMPHIBIOUS FORCE

Contrary to popular belief, leaders in the US Army did not keep the Marine Corps from participating in the Atlantic on a large scale. In fact, the Marine Corps being located almost exclusively in the Pacific is a result of several strategic-level decisions from the White House, military planners, and diplomats before the US even fully entered World War II. Additionally, Marine Corps infantry units peaked at six divisions by the end of the war, whereas the Army had 91 divisions, with about 21 serving in the Pacific (these do not include aviation units). The Marine Corps was imperatively needed in the Pacific due to its expertise in amphibious operations. These skills were used to seize and defend advanced naval bases in support of the US Navy

After World War I, the United States largely accepted a foreign policy stance of isolationism. Many Americans had no desire to become involved in what was perceived as another European war, regardless of whether a war would cause the fall of a close ally. Despite this period of isolationism, the US military quietly developed several color-coded war plans that detailed strategies for potential future conflicts. One of these was named War Plan Orange. It detailed a series of military plans to deal specifically with the Empire of Japan in the Pacific. The Marine Corps' contribution to this was by Major Earl H. "Pete" Ellis. He had been assigned to the Operations and Training Division in the early 1920s and is largely credited with pioneering the Marine Corps' development in amphibious warfare – something that would help transform the war for the Allies in Europe less than 20 years later.

Ellis's studies of the Pacific, and on the Japanese military, resulted in the creation of *Operational Plan 712: Advanced Base Operations in Micronesia* in July 1921. Beginning in the 1920s, the Marine Corps carried out several landing experiments with the Navy after the publication of the document to understand the necessary requirements for amphibious assault operations. One of these was conducted in April 1922 in Guantanamo Bay, Cuba, and Culebra, Puerto Rico. The exercises tested the viability of landing heavy equipment such as heavy tractors and artillery. Lessons learned included protecting equipment that had been landed and resolving communication issues between landing units, landing craft, and ships in the fleet.

In December 1923, over 3,000 Marines participated in a fleet landing exercise near the Panama Canal and Culebra. Knowing logistics was a friction point in past landings, a detachment of almost 30 Marines was assigned to USS *Sirius* (AK-18) to create procedures to properly load cargo, and then to allow the most efficient method to unload supplies. These exercises also experimented with customized landing boats, as previous iterations of exercises had proved difficult to disembark Marines under fire.

By 1925, then Commandant of the Marine Corps, Major General John A. Lejeune, ordered amphibious operation studies to be carried out for officers in formal schools, showcasing how important amphibious operations were expected to be in a future conflict.

In 1927, the Joint Army and Navy Board created the Joint Action Document, which assigned the Marine Corps responsibility for providing and maintaining forces to seize advanced naval bases for naval campaigns. The document outlined responsibilities between the services and called for the Marine Corps to receive special training in amphibious assaults to capture beaches before being relieved by follow-on Army units.

The operational plan from 1921 by Ellis, along with the *Joint Overseas Expeditions, Tentative* pamphlet published in November 1929, would help redefine and change the Marine Corps from a largely constabulary force for the US Navy to one that specialized in amphibious and expeditionary warfare. This new expeditionary and amphibious warfare organization was designed to assist the Navy in island-hopping campaign tactics across the Pacific should another large-scale war break out.

Building on Ellis's vision of a specialized amphibious force, the Navy and Marine Corps continued and grew experimentation and training in amphibious assault tactics. By the early 1930s, greater emphasis was placed on integrating the Army and Navy to facilitate smoother joint amphibious operations. The results of these efforts would become evident in the years ahead, as the Army had to master amphibious operations to achieve its strategic objectives while the Navy leveraged the Marines to accomplish its own goals. Through Ellis's work, Marines were tasked with seizing key land masses, enabling the Navy's operational maneuver by removing Japanese forces from key islands that supported its airfields and naval facilities. This shift – redefining the Marine Corps as an enabling and supporting arm of the Navy rather than primarily a policing force – was revolutionary and remains a defining feature of the modern Marine Corps. In essence, the Marines had evolved into the Navy's own Army rather than its private security detail with the occasional land operation.

Following the publishing of the formal and revised *Joint Overseas Expeditions* pamphlet in 1933, the Marine Corps published its own landing operations publication entitled *Tentative Landing Operations Manual* in 1934. The manual became the guiding document for the organization's amphibious ambitions and was revised on a number of occasions in the following years. In 1938, the Navy retitled it as *Fleet Training Publication 167* and it became official Navy doctrine.

The sea-going service put the theoretical doctrine to the test the next year during Fleet Landing Exercise 1 on March 15, 1935, in Puerto Rico. The Fleet Landing Exercise (FLEX) experiments would continue annually, in different locations, growing in scale, with the last FLEX being conducted in February 1941. A follow-on FLEX was planned for early 1942 but was canceled due to the United States' entrance to the already ongoing world war.

During the 1930s, amphibious assaults were widely regarded as a flawed and dangerous method of warfare. Historically, large-scale landings had produced mixed results, and their reputation suffered even further after World War I, particularly following the disastrous British Empire assault at Gallipoli in 1915. History was already filled with examples of major failed amphibious operations, such as the swift defeat of Ottoman forces by French troops at the battle of Abukir in 1799, and the destruction of the Spanish Armada by the Royal Navy in 1588 before it could deliver its invasion force.

Planners recognized the immense challenges involved: concentrating troops, transporting them from ship to shore, sustaining the landing force through logistics, maintaining effective command and control, providing accurate and deadly supporting fire from ships, and overcoming enemy defenses. Skeptical of how the Navy and Marine Corps could succeed in a form of warfare seen as futile, the US Army sent observers – and later, participants – to several of the FLEX, with some iterations involving hundreds of soldiers gathering notes and insights.

LEFT FLEX 7 off the shore of Cuba in 1941. (Dmitri Kessel/The LIFE Picture Collection/Shutterstock)

BOTTOM Marine Corps radiomen scout out for enemy troop movements during a training event with their radio reconnaissance car at Guantanamo Bay, Cuba, November 2, 1943. (USMC, photo by Sgt Sommers)

US Marines take part in squad-level scouting and patrolling exercises in Guantanamo Bay, August 9, 1941. (USMC)

INSET In July 1941, Brigadier General John T. Walker was sent to Cairo, Egypt, to serve as the assistant naval attaché and then later as naval attaché in London. While in Egypt, he acted as an observer to how the British forces were fighting the Axis in the desert. Walker was just one of dozens of Marines sent overseas during this time to gather knowledge and report back to Headquarters Marine Corps on how to make a more effective fighting force. He was sent to the Pacific shortly after the Japanese attack on Pearl Harbor. (USMC)

MARINE CORPS' INFLUENCE ON LANDING CRAFT

While only a few thousand Marines may have served in Europe and Africa, the Corps' influence was at every amphibious landing, whether soldiers realized it or not.

During the 1930s, the Navy and Marine Corps were on the lookout for a craft to efficiently move troops from ship to shore. In the late 1930s, Andrew J. Higgins had created the Eureka boat, a small craft designed to ferry heavy logs and explore for gas and oil in river and coastal areas. Seeing an impending global conflict on the horizon, Higgins unsuccessfully attempted several times to have his Eureka boat looked at by Navy planners. The Navy had already reached out to and had prototypes from several companies who were testing their boats with the Marine Corps. Although the Marine Corps lobbied Navy leaders to consider Higgins's boats, the Navy was developing its own requirements and designs and was uninterested in his version.

After several failed tests from the prototypes the Navy had contracted out to industry, Navy designers and leadership finally relented and allowed Higgins to showcase his Eureka boat to them. So impressed was the leadership that Higgins was awarded a small contract to begin building boats. He also received US Patent No. 2,144,111, protecting the Eureka boat's unique hull design which allowed the boat to land on a beach without the propellers getting stuck in the sand. Higgins would go on to expend development of the Eureka boat into the Landing Craft, Personnel (LCP) and Landing Craft, Personnel (Large), or LCP(L), for military use.

Original patent illustration submitted for the Eureka boat. (US Patent and Trademark Office, hereafter USPTO)

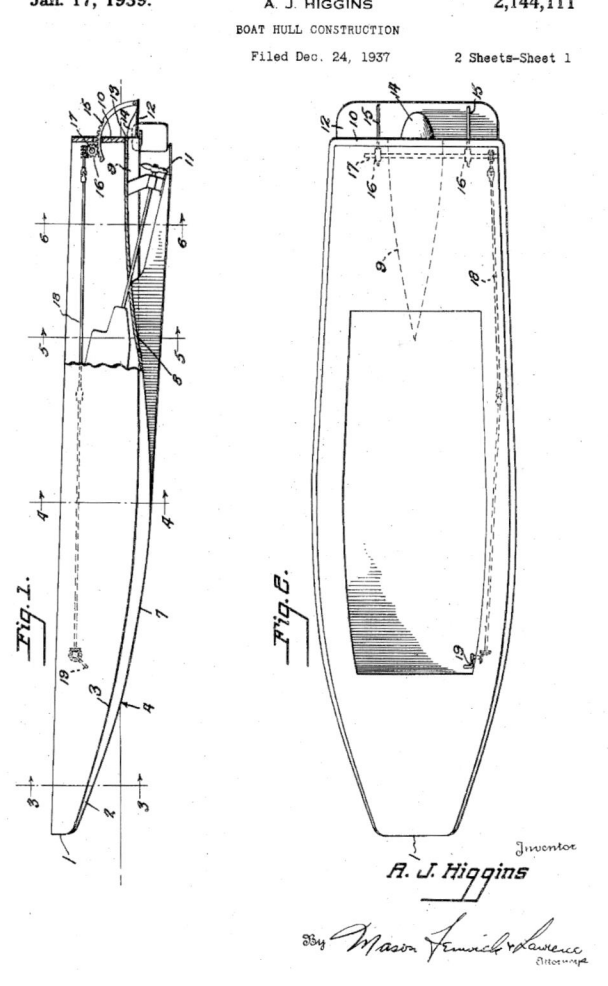

Marines with the 1st Marine Division land on Guadalcanal using Higgins's LCP(L), August 7, 1942. Notice the lack of bow ramp on the landing craft. During this time of the war, the now famous Landing Craft Vehicle, Person (LCVP) was only available in limited numbers. (USMC)

Original patent illustration for the LCVP with bow ramp. (USPTO)

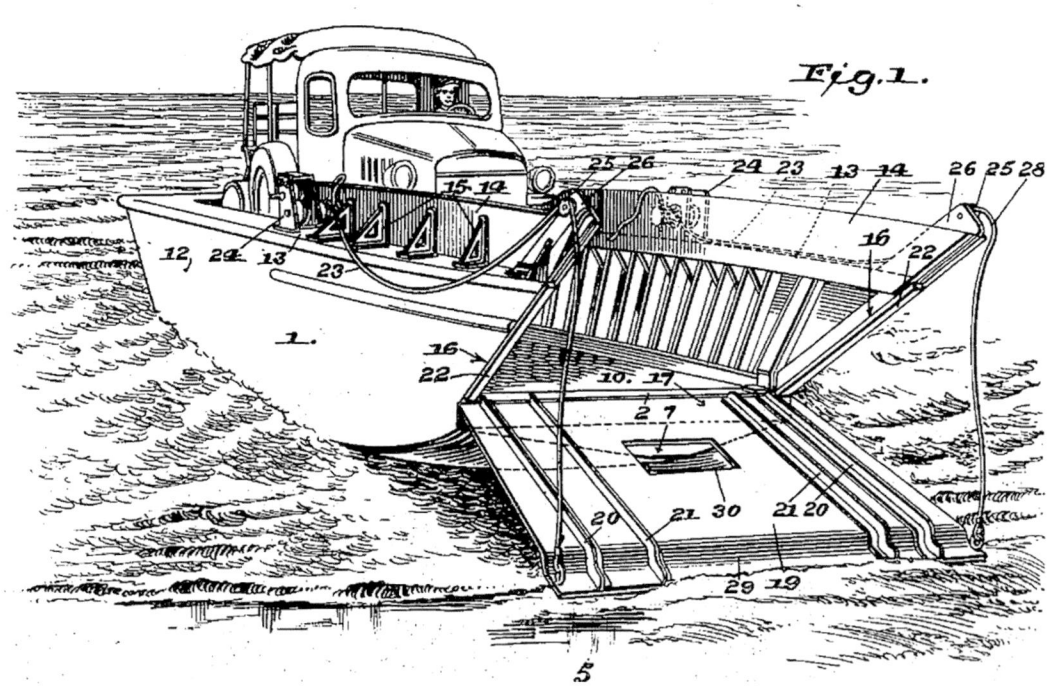

Feb. 15, 1944.   A. J. HIGGINS   2,341,866

LIGHTER FOR MECHANIZED EQUIPMENT

Filed Dec. 8, 1941   4 Sheets—Sheet 1

While the LCP boats solved the problem of transporting troops from ship to shore quickly, a new deficiency was discovered when Marines disembarking from the boat had to climb over the sides, exposing themselves to enemy fire and making unloading supplies and equipment cumbersome. Unknowingly to leadership, a solution already existed from a junior Marine officer.

In 1937, Marine Lieutenant Victor Krulak was in China as an observer to the Second Sino-Japanese War. During this time, he observed Japanese landing craft having a blunt bow with the bow becoming a ramp upon hitting the beach, enabling easy and fast unloading of troops. In the subsequent years, Krulak suggested such a device; his suggestions would eventually be listened to by Navy and Marine planners and ultimately made their way to Higgins. Higgins filed a patent for the ramp bow feature onto the Eureka boat the day after the Pearl Harbor attacks. The modified Eureka boat would be named the LCVP for Landing Craft Vehicle, Person.

The importance of the LCVP cannot be overstated enough. Eisenhower said, "If Higgins had not designed and built those LCVPs, we never could have landed over an open beach. The whole strategy of the war would have been different." The Marine Corps' mark was now cemented in nearly every amphibious assault of the war.

Marines with the guard detachment at Naval Air Station Patuxent River, Maryland, raise the flag during a morning colors ceremony, April 1, 1943. (US Navy)

MARINE DETACHMENTS EXPAND

By 1940, the Navy and Marine Corps had expanded in both size of manpower and locations. Retaining its role as a naval constabulary force, Marines were at nearly every location the Navy had a land presence, as base security was built into planned expansion considerations. Commercial contracts were awarded to expand Marine Corps presence in multiple locations, such as Cuba. The facilities there were extended to hold more than 2,000 men, with all necessary utilities, such as barracks, administration buildings, medical facilities, mess halls, storage buildings, laundry, and roads. In the spring of 1941, there were approximately 6,000 Marines stationed across the Caribbean, taking part in deterrence operations and safeguarding naval facilities.

During 1940 and 1941, numerous naval bases were set up in the Atlantic – all the way up from Newfoundland down to South America. St. Lucia, Antigua, Jamaica, British Guiana, and the island of Great Exuma in the Bahamas – all had secondary air bases built. Trinidad, Bermuda, and Argentia in Newfoundland were built into major air bases.

As described in *Building the Navy's Bases in World War II*, volume II, the major bases were "to be equipped with complete facilities for operation, storage, and supply, engine overhaul, and complete periodic general overhaul of all types of planes. A secondary air base was a smaller installation, having facilities primarily for the operation, routine upkeep, and emergency repair of aircraft." All of these bases had Marine detachments providing security in the event German saboteurs and spies decided to test their luck. The minor bases contained approximately 50 Marines for security, while the Marine barracks on major bases could have several hundred men assigned to them.

Additionally, during this time, the US embarked on a great diplomatic journey to show presence in South America and shore up its ties with nations to deter them from joining the Axis powers. Marine detachments from ships and shore establishments were used in parades and trained local militia-type groups in the basics of land warfare.

The American outposts in the Atlantic, the Caribbean, and on the East Coast of the United States scouted for German submarines, which preyed upon Allied supply shipments coming up from South America. Simultaneously, there were numerous times Marine detachments were called upon to assist with German crews who had been captured when their submarines had been sunk by Allied aircraft or warships or take any German spies into custody.

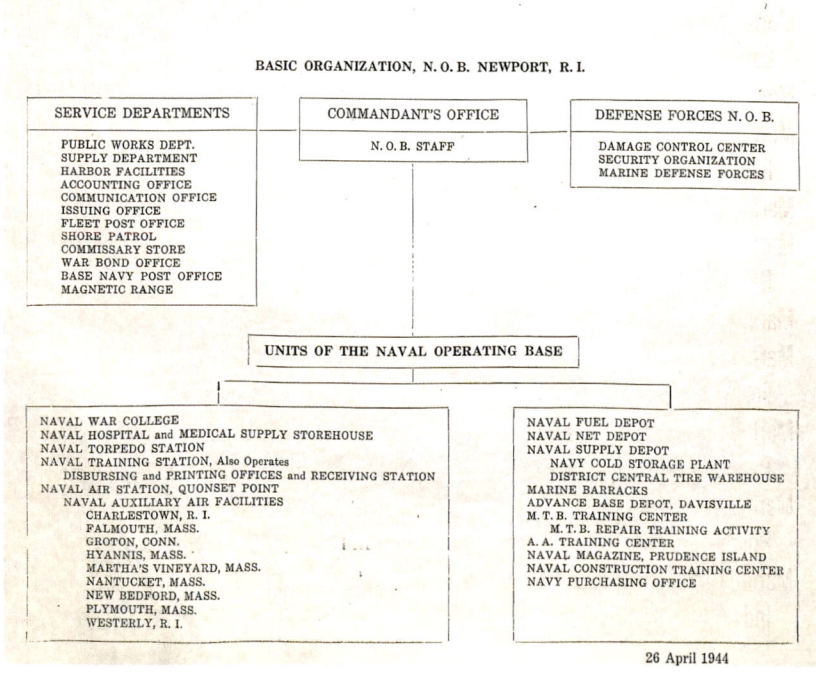

Organizational chart of Naval Operating Base (NOB) Newport, Rhode Island, from the base familiarization pamphlet, April 26, 1944. The Marine garrison is mentioned on the two right blocks of the chart. (US Navy)

BASIC ORGANIZATION, N. O. B. NEWPORT, R. I.

SERVICE DEPARTMENTS	COMMANDANT'S OFFICE	DEFENSE FORCES N. O. B.
PUBLIC WORKS DEPT.	N. O. B. STAFF	DAMAGE CONTROL CENTER
SUPPLY DEPARTMENT		SECURITY ORGANIZATION
HARBOR FACILITIES		MARINE DEFENSE FORCES
ACCOUNTING OFFICE		
COMMUNICATION OFFICE		
ISSUING OFFICE		
FLEET POST OFFICE		
SHORE PATROL		
COMMISSARY STORE		
WAR BOND OFFICE		
BASE NAVY POST OFFICE		
MAGNETIC RANGE		

UNITS OF THE NAVAL OPERATING BASE

NAVAL WAR COLLEGE
NAVAL HOSPITAL and MEDICAL SUPPLY STOREHOUSE
NAVAL TORPEDO STATION
NAVAL TRAINING STATION, Also Operates
    DISBURSING and PRINTING OFFICES and RECEIVING STATION
NAVAL AUXILIARY AIR FACILITIES
    CHARLESTOWN, R. I.
    FALMOUTH, MASS.
    GROTON, CONN.
    HYANNIS, MASS.
    MARTHA'S VINEYARD, MASS.
    NANTUCKET, MASS.
    NEW BEDFORD, MASS.
    PLYMOUTH, MASS.
    WESTERLY, R. I.

NAVAL FUEL DEPOT
NAVAL NET DEPOT
NAVAL SUPPLY DEPOT
    NAVY COLD STORAGE PLANT
    DISTRICT CENTRAL TIRE WAREHOUSE
MARINE BARRACKS
ADVANCE BASE DEPOT, DAVISVILLE
M. T. B. TRAINING CENTER
    M. T. B. REPAIR TRAINING ACTIVITY
A. A. TRAINING CENTER
NAVAL MAGAZINE, PRUDENCE ISLAND
NAVAL CONSTRUCTION TRAINING CENTER
NAVY PURCHASING OFFICE

26 April 1944

US EAST COAST MARINE DETACHMENTS

Marine Guard Detachment, Naval Disciplinary Barracks Portsmouth, New Hampshire

Marine Barracks, Naval Yard Portsmouth, New Hampshire

Marine Guard Detachment, Naval Ammunition Depot Hingham, Massachusetts

Marine Barracks, Naval Yard Boston Chelsea, Massachusetts

Marine Guard Detachment, Naval Air Station (NAS) Squantum, Massachusetts

Marine Barracks, NAS South Weymouth, Massachusetts

Marine Barracks, Naval Operating Base (NOB) Newport, Rhode Island

Marine Guard Detachment, NAS Quonset Point, Rhode Island

Marine Guard Detachment, Naval Training Center Newport, Rhode Island

Marine Barracks, Naval Submarine Base New London, Connecticut

Marine Barracks, NAS Lakehurst, New Jersey

Marine Guard Detachment, Naval Ammunition Depot Lake Denmark, New Jersey

Marine Barracks, NAS Wildwood, New Jersey

Marine Guard Detachment, Naval Ammunition Depot Iona Island, New York

Marine Barracks, Naval Yard New York, New York

Marine Guard Detachment, Naval Receiving Station New York, New York

Marine Guard Detachment, NAS New York City

Marine Guard Detachment, Naval Ammunition Depot Fort Mifflin, Pennsylvania

Marine Barracks, Naval Yard and Station Philadelphia, Pennsylvania

Marine Guard Detachment, Naval Receiving Station Philadelphia, Pennsylvania

Marine Guard Detachment, Naval Powder Factory, Indian Head, Maryland

Marine Guard Detachment, US Naval Academy, Annapolis, Maryland

Marine Guard Detachment, David Taylor Model Basin, Carderock, Maryland

Marine Barracks, Washington DC

Marine Barracks, Navy Yard Washington, Washington DC

Marine Guard Company, Navy Yard, Washington DC

Marine Guard Detachment, Naval Proving Ground Dahlgren, Virginia

Marine Barracks, Naval Yard Norfolk, Portsmouth, Virginia

Marine Barracks, St. Juliens Creek Naval Annex, Virginia

Marine Guard Detachment, Naval Receiving Station Norfolk, Virginia

Marine Guard Detachment, NOB Newport, Virginia

Marine Guard Detachment, Naval Ammunition Depot St. Juliens Creek, Virginia

Marine Guard Detachment, Naval Mine Depot Yorktown, Virginia

Marine Barracks, Naval Station Weapons Station Yorktown, Virginia

Marine Guard Detachment, Naval Ammunition Depot South Charleston, West Virginia

Marine Barracks, Naval Yard Charleston, South Carolina

Marine Guard Detachment, NAS Glynco, Georgia

Marine Guard Detachment, NAS Banana River, Florida

Marine Guard Detachment, NAS Vero Beach, Florida

Marine Barracks, NAS Miami, Florida

Marine Guard Detachment, NAS Sanford, Florida

Marine Barracks, NAS Jacksonville, Florida

Marine Barracks, NAS Key West, Florida

Marine Guard Detachment, NAS Vero Beach, Florida

Marine Barracks, NOB San Juan, Puerto Rico

TOP Thirty-three German prisoners were brought ashore at the Navy Yard, Charleston, South Carolina, by US Coast Guard cutter *Icarus* (WPC-110) after the sinking of German submarine *U-352* off the Atlantic coast on May 9, 1942. The executive officer of the German submarine repeats in German the instructions given to him by US Navy officers. Note the Marine guard on the left side with fixed bayonet. (US Navy)

ABOVE LEFT US Marines with fixed bayonets stand guard as the German prisoners from *Icarus* are lined up in front of the Coast Guard cutter in Charleston, South Carolina, on May 9, 1942. (US Navy)

ABOVE RIGHT Marching from *Icarus*, the German prisoners show rigid discipline as they follow their captain in perfect step. Note the 13 Marine guards around them. (US Navy)

TOP LEFT *U-805*'s crew are lined up for press photographers before boarding busses bound for Portsmouth Naval Prison, December 1942. Many of the crew carry the Red Cross survivors' packages they were issued aboard USS *Otter*. Marine guards armed with Reising Model 50 .45-caliber submachine guns stand to the left. (US Navy)

BOTTOM LEFT A Marine assigned to Marine Guard Detachment, NOB Norfolk, escorts Lieutenant Commander Klaus Heinz Bargsten on June 2, 1943. Bargsten was the sole survivor of German submarine *U-521*, which was sunk off the Atlantic Coast by the USS *PC-565*, a submarine chaser. (US Navy)

TOP RIGHT More Marines assist in escorting Bargsten. *U-521* was credited with sinking four Allied vessels during World War II. (US Navy)

CENTER RIGHT A Marine guard stands on the right with a Reising Model 50 .45-caliber submachine gun while watching over captured crew members of *U-858* aboard US Navy rescue tug *ATR-57* at sea, May 1945. (US Navy)

BOTTOM RIGHT Marine guards assist members of *U-858* debark from US Navy rescue tug *ATR-57* at US Army base Fort Miles, Delaware, May 1945. (US Navy)

TOP German officers and their crew from the surrendered *U-873* at the Portsmouth Navy Yard in New Hampshire, May 16, 1945. German officers, with their backs to the camera, stand on the deck of the tug that brought in the submarine. The Marine guards stand ready to take the prisoners ashore. The man in the white cap with his hands behind his back is Captain Steinhoff, the submarine's commanding officer. (US Navy)

CENTER This photograph shows four German submarines at the Portsmouth Navy Yard, which were surrendered off the coast of Portland, May 16, 1945. A US Marine from Marine Detachment, Portsmouth, stands guard over German sailors. (US Navy)

BOTTOM Marine Guard Detachment, NAS New York City, September 5, 1942. (US Navy)

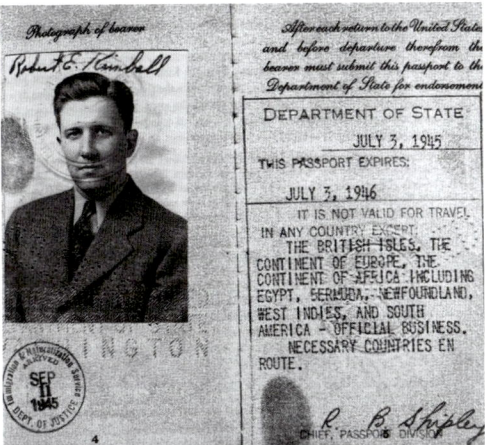

TOP Another lesser-known Marine Corps role during the war was using Marines as diplomatic document couriers, such as Gunnery Sergeant Robert E. Kimball. After serving in the Pacific with the 1st Marine Division, Kimball was home on leave when offered the courier position. Attracted by alternating travel and home time, he accepted eagerly. Based in Washington DC, his route included the United Kingdom, Portugal, the Caribbean, South America, and then back to Washington. (Robert E. Kimball's State Department passport, Leo. J. Daugherty III collection, used with permission)

CENTER First Lieutenant H. Feehan salutes the colors during an inspection at the Navy Nurse Indoctrination School in October 1943. It was not uncommon to have Marine detachments at Navy schools to help train sailors. (US Navy)

BOTTOM The Philadelphia Marine Detachment building still stands today and is now an administrative building for the Navy. (Author's collection)

VMS-3 "Devilbirds" Squadron insignia. (USMC)

13th Defense Battalion insignia. (Author's collection)

MARINES IN THE CARIBBEAN

Nearly forgotten now, the battle of the Caribbean saw United States Marines in sunny tropic scenes protecting naval installations and taking on the German and Italian navies.

The Caribbean Sea saw the US, British, and Dutch utilize the waters as shipping lanes transporting food, oil, and other raw materials from South America and outlying territories up to the US East Coast. Additionally, the region saw major throughput from US ships transiting from the East Coast and Atlantic to the Pacific via the Panama Canal. Nearly all Navy facilities contained a Marine guard unit in charge of protecting the installations in the event German and Italian submarines managed to land personnel with the intent of sabotage.

Beginning in the late 1930s, the US slowly began to enhance its presence in the area. A multitude of Navy installations were planned to provide bases for antisubmarine operations. Due to the Caribbean's logistic importance to the Allies, Hitler had directed constant pressure to be placed on the region.

As the war dragged on, fewer and fewer submarine encounters occurred as U-boat losses in the Atlantic caused Hitler to incrementally withdraw U-boats from the Caribbean and divert them to the Atlantic. During World War II, the Allies would lose more than 400 ships in the Caribbean, compared with the Axis navies' loss of 17 submarines from direct action from Allied antisubmarine efforts.

Alongside the Marine ground forces, Marine aviation had a small presence. Marine Scouting Squadron 3 (VMS-3) took part in numerous antisubmarine patrols throughout the duration of the war, while also providing search and rescue capabilities for crews of merchant ships that had been sunk. Several times during the war, the squadron dropped depth charges on Axis submarines when the vessels surfaced for fresh air and to recharge their batteries.

A unique mission given to the Marine Corps during the war was the task of guarding Navy communications and radio points sprinkled throughout Central and South America. These wireless transmissions points were put in place through a joint effort between the State Department and War Department and were utilized to collect information on Nazi spies. In turn, captured communication could also be used to help identify the whereabouts of Axis submarines in the area.

Marines of various job specialties assigned to Marine Corps Air Facility (MCAF) St. Thomas take part in refresher ground combat training events at the air station training area of the island on April 27, 1944. While their duty location may have been in the sunny tropics, the Marines, regardless of their jobs, were expected to keep a baseline of infantry proficiency in case they were shipped to the Pacific, which many of them were. (USMC)

MARINE DETACHMENTS IN THE CARIBBEAN AND CENTRAL AMERICA

Marine Barracks, NOB Bermuda

Marine Guard Detachment, Naval Air Facility Great Exuma, Bahamas

Marine Embassy Guard Detachment, Havana, Cuba

Marine Barracks, NOB Guantanamo Bay, Cuba

Marine Guard Detachment, NAS Jamaica

Marine Legation Guard Detachment, Guatemala City, Guatemala

Marine Guard Detachment, Naval Air Auxiliary Facility Corinto, Nicaragua

Marine Barracks, US Naval Station Coco Solo, Panama

Marine Barracks, US Naval Station Balboa, Panama

Marine Barracks, Naval Ammunition Depot Balboa, Panama

Marine Legation Guard Detachment, Ciudad Trujillo, Dominican Republic

Marine Guard Detachment, NAS San Juan, Puerto Rico

Marine Barracks, Roosevelt Roads Naval Station, Puerto Rico

Marine Barracks, MCAF St. Thomas, US Virgin Islands

Headquarters Squadron, MCAF St. Thomas, US Virgin Islands

Marine Scouting Squadron 3, MCAS St. Thomas, US Virgin Islands

Aircraft Engineering Squadron 31, MCAS St. Thomas, US Virgin Islands

Marine Guard Detachment, NAS Antigua

Marine Guard Detachment, NAS St. Lucia

Marine Barracks, Naval Air Auxiliary Facility Trinidad

Marines in the Caribbean

**By Private First Class A. George February 1943
Marine Detachment, Naval Air Station, New York**

There are few changes to report in the personnel here. Most important was GySgt Julis Grossman's transfer to Norfolk, Va. and Pfc. C. K. Holton got his transfer to glider school, among other personnel transfers that occurred.

Construction of a quarter-mile cinder track has been authorized by the Commanding Officer and work is well underway. It will afford the station means of staging meets with other military college teams in this section as well as facilities for conditioning all station personnel.

We finished tenth, 54 points behind the winning Coast Guard team from Manhattan Beach, in the championship rifle and pistol tournament of the Third Naval District.

TOP Marines at MCAF St. Thomas, US Virgin Islands, render honors for the crown prince and princess of Denmark as they depart the air facility, 1943. (USMC)

BOTTOM A detachment of US Marines march across a bridge on the island of St. Lucia in the British West Indies, June 16, 1943. The American base was established there in 1941. (USMC)

MARINES IN THE CARIBBEAN

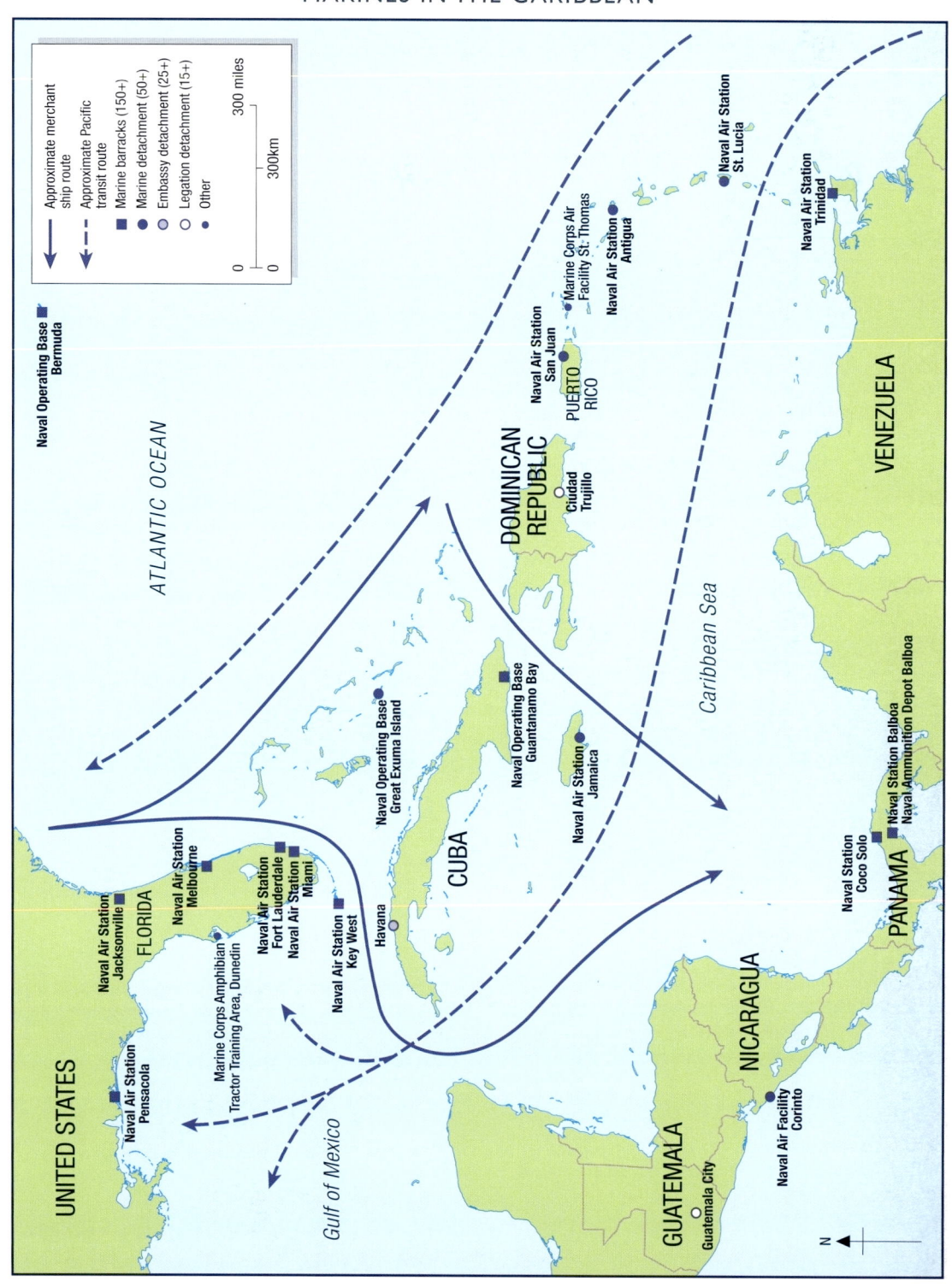

Legend:
- Approximate merchant ship route
- Approximate Pacific transit route
- Marine barracks (150+)
- Marine detachment (50+)
- Embassy detachment (25+)
- Legation detachment (15+)
- Other

0 — 300 miles
0 — 300km

Naval Operating Base Bermuda

ATLANTIC OCEAN

Naval Air Station St. Lucia
Naval Air Station Trinidad
Marine Corps Air Facility St. Thomas
Naval Air Station Antigua
Naval Air Station San Juan
PUERTO RICO

VENEZUELA

DOMINICAN REPUBLIC
Ciudad Trujillo

Caribbean Sea

Naval Operating Base Great Exuma Island

Naval Operating Base Guantanamo Bay

Naval Air Station Jamaica

CUBA

Havana

Naval Air Station Melbourne
Naval Air Station Jacksonville
FLORIDA
Naval Air Station Fort Lauderdale
Naval Air Station Miami
Marine Corps Amphibian Tractor Training Area, Dunedin
Naval Air Station Key West
Naval Air Station Pensacola

UNITED STATES

Gulf of Mexico

Naval Station Coco Solo
Naval Station Balboa
Naval Ammunition Depot Balboa
PANAMA

NICARAGUA

GUATEMALA
Guatemala City

Naval Air Facility Corinto

N

LEFT Marines with the 13th Defense Battalion practice gun drills with their five-inch naval gun at Guantanamo Bay, April 10, 1943. (USMC, photo by Sgt Andrew Knight)

BOTTOM Marines with the detachment at Guantanamo Bay salute during a visit from Secretary of the Navy Frank Knox, October 8, 1943. (USMC, photo by Cpl Chowaniec)

Marines in Great Exuma

By Sergeant Maurice Moran
February 1943

Great EXUMA, The Bahamas – After six months the Marines who helped build this Caribbean outpost own one complete victory – a rout with concentrated wisecracks of the loneliness which could have engulfed them.

These Leathernecks, young and tough as whipcord, today observed the six month anniversary of their occupation of this base.

When Marines landed here with supplies, they began a stretch of back breaking toil immediately after their feet touched solid earth.

It's difficult to glamorize such a prosaic thing as hard work and eternal watchfulness. But maybe Joe citizen back home will understand better if he recalls that hard work – and eternal warfullness – by another gallant band of Marines who saved Wake Island.

This island, some 150 miles from Nassau, that peacetime winter fairyland, looks now like Wake Island might have looked if those Marines had a little more time – and a little more help. It's secure.

There is historical significance to the Marines' presence in the Bahamas. The Corps' first success, in a 167-year-old history of successes, was scored in an invasion of Nassau in the Revolutionary War. This island is breath taking in its natural beauty – and overpowering in its remoteness from the hurdy-gurdy of America, which these Leathernecks love, left, and miss.

Great Exuma, about 35 miles long, and three to four miles wide, is part of the chain which rises like vertebrae from the ocean's back, beginning off the coast of Florida and extending south easterly into the Caribbean Sea. San Salvador, where Christopher Columbus landed, also is part of the chain.

Great Exuma is of coral rock, topped with a thin skin of sandy soil and a tangled thatch of scrubby growth. It nestles snugly in the lee of Stocking Island, famed in the bloody history of old free booters.

Exuma has stretches of excellent beaches, spread with blinding white sand. It has the prismatic unbelievable colors of sea, sky and land, and the picturesque pastels of resident homes. It has swaying coconut palms, soft breezes, and a healthy climate.

But it has nothing else – lizards, spiders and a harmless variety of boa constrictors constitute animal life. It is as if God had wrought an artistic masterpiece but had forgotten to breathe life into it – at least the life an American boy knows.

White persons are numbered by the handful; USO shows, and other types of state-side entertainment are only a pleasant dream.

Liberty – the Marines' term for a few hours of freedom to find entertainment in their own way – is only a figure of speech here.

The island houses about 12 settlements, populated by natives who are friendly and eager to please the Marines. An astonishing number of the island's 4000 native population bear the same surnames.

The nearest settlement is Georgetown, inhabited by a few hundred souls. Because of its proximity, it gets the greatest play from Marines and sailors on liberty.

There are a few dowdy snacks claiming the title of restaurant or grocery store. There is Solomon Glass establishment, a tavern so called because it is the only place on the island where liquid refreshments may be obtained.

To compensate for the lack of outside recreation, men and officers at the base have endeavored to provide entertainment within the reservation. They have succeeded admirably with limited resources.

There are nightly movies – if the dated film arrives and the weather permits – outdoor with the sky as a canopy. Most of the command uses the hard earth as seats.

The raw lumber recreation rooms house two pool tables and a ping pong table. Corporal

Henry Stephens, a Harvard graduate from Grosse Pointe Farms, Mich., voluntarily operates a library containing excellent volumes donated by himself.

The Post Exchange, whose steward is Corporal Mike Burak, a former *New York Daily News* circulation employee, supplies beer and some candy.

Sergeants Sidney Rosen, Long Island, NY, and Joe Gatto, of Brooklyn, NY, are excellent hosts if you can catch them in their free time. They'll show you around the island, boat and swim with you and best of all, assure you: "This isn't such a bad place. The fellow here are swell and you sort of get used to the loneliness."

They're right. The fellows are swell. From commanding officer to newest recruit, you never hear a complaint.

Caribbean Sea Frontier – Task Force 90

War Diary, September 16, 1942

Miscellaneous: A Marine Corps plane was reported missing since September 14th, at which time it was operating in the locality of 13-30 north, 61-00 west. Army, Navy, and Marine Corps planes have conducted continuous search for this plane without success. Two other Marine Corps planes have been lost while conducting search operations; an OS2N and a J2F, each with a crew of one officer and one enlisted man.

Author note

During the war, it is known that VMS-3 lost at least two Marines in the line of duty: Second Lieutenant Richard Dabbs, a pilot, and Private First Class Bert A. Shea, Jr., a mechanic. Dabbs's duties included flying patrols searching for Axis submarines in the Caribbean and locating survivors of sunk ships.

On September 15, 1942, Dabbs and Shea were assigned to temporary duty at nearby NAS St. Lucia. A Marine Corps plane operating between St. Lucia and St. Vincent was overdue, and Dabbs and Shea set out as part of the search and rescue force. They departed St. Lucia but never returned to base. Dabbs and Shea were reported missing in action the next day. Both Marines were officially declared dead on September 16, 1943, one year later.

Snapshot of US Marine Judson Stover standing in front of a Douglas SBD Dauntless dive bomber, with his hands holding onto the propeller blades. Judson was stationed in the Caribbean with his brother, Buford H. Stover, who was also a Marine. (Courtesy of the State Archives of North Carolina)

A formation of SBD-5 Dauntless dive bombers painted in the Atlantic Theater camouflage from VMS-3, August 1944. Based at MCAF St. Thomas (previously known as Bourne Field) during the entire course of its existence, the squadron logged hundreds of patrols from 1934 to its deactivation on May 20, 1944. Included among them were flights on May 11–14, 1942 to circumvent the expected escape attempt of the Vichy French Fleet for Guadeloupe, the constant scouting for German submarines, and the occasional dropping of explosive to either sink submarines or force them to surface. Originally, there were three Marine scouting squadrons prior to World War II; however, VMS-3 was the only squadron to retain the designation. It began the war flying Grumman J2F Ducks, later transitioned to the Naval Aircraft Factory/Vought OS2N Kingfisher, and then switched to the SBD Dauntless dive bomber.

In 1941, a series of upgrades expanded MCAF St. Thomas with additional barracks, recreational services and facilities, ammunition magazines, liquid fuel storage, and fresh-water storage capabilities. The expanded base included housing for 700 enlisted men in three barracks, one barracks for 40 officers, and 24 housing units for married non-commissioned and commissioned officers. The substantial expansion was to provide services and housing for all of the Marine pilots, mechanics, technicians, clerks, base security, and the small submarine base that had been built there. (USMC)

CONFIDENTIAL

U. S. AIRCRAFT — ACTION WITH ENEMY

C75

INSTRUCTIONS

(a) To be filled out by unit commander immediately upon landing after each action
or operation in contact with the enemy.
(b) Do not "gun deck" this report — if data can not be estimated with reasonable
accuracy enter a dash in space for which no data is available.

1. DATE 3 July 194 2 LAT 19-05 LONG 63-10 TIME 0710 ZN + 4

2. WEATHER Visibility — 3 miles

3. UNIT REPORTING VMS-3 TYPE PLANES J2F-5

4. NATURE OF OPERATION

Patrol

5. SPECIFIC OBJECTIVE

SUBMARINES

6. FORCES ENGAGED (include models and markings)
        Own   Enemy

1 J2F-5   SUBMARINE

7. TYPE OF ATTACK (Own/Enemy)(Scratch one)

Glide bombing

8. ENEMY TACTICS

Crash dive

9. BRIEF DESCRIPTION OF ACTION (include altitudes and range of contact. Altitudes
and directions of release and withdrawal.)

Glided to position above submarine and released depth bombs.

10. WEAPONS EMPLOYED
        Own   Enemy
325 lbs. depth bombs   None

11. EVASIVE ACTION EMPLOYED

12. AMMUNITION EXPENDED (include types and fuse settings. Indicate number of duds.)

Two depth MK. 17-1 bombs set at fifty feet. No duds.

13. RESULTS (Certain)

Unknown

156542   (Estimated)

Page 1 of an action report from VMS-3 after patrol planes engaged a German submarine on
July 3, 1942, when it dropped two glide bombs onto the submerging submarine. There was
plenty of fighting to be had in the Caribbean. Between 1942 and 1943, 12 German U-boats
were sunk between the Caribbean Sea, Gulf of Mexico, and Bermuda. (NARA)

SECRET

MARINE SCOUTING SQUADRON THREE
UNITED STATES MARINE CORPS AIR STATION
NAVAL OPERATING BASE
SAINT THOMAS, VIRGIN ISLANDS

Reg. No. M-2324
R.S. No.

1 March 1944

WAR DIARY

1944 APR 10
13
18

COMMANDER-IN-CHIEF
FLAG OFFICE
RECEIVED

1. Designation and Composition of Unit.
   (a) Designation:
       Marine Scouting Squadron Three,
       U. S. Marine Corps Air Station, NOB, St. Thomas, V.I.
       Puerto Rican Sector, Caribbean Sea Frontier.

   (b) Composition:
Personnel	Material
31 Officers	12 SBD-5
163 Enlisted	4 OS2U-3
	2 OS2N-1

2. Operation Plan:
              Com Task Group Two Six Three Op Orders
              5-42 para 3(e); as modified by C.C.S.F.
              letter, Serial 063, dated 25 May 1942.

3. Does not apply.

4. Day's Operations:
   (a) | Planes in Commission | Out of Commission |
       |----------------------|-------------------|
       | 8 SBD-5 | 4 SBD-5 |
       | 4 OS2U-3 | |
       | 2 OS2N-1 | |

6994

   (b) Brief of Operations:
       1. Operation plan (2. above), carried out.
          (a) Two patrols daily, one morning, one evening,
              are carried out with stand-by pilots and planes
              to cover emergencies and perform escort duty.
              Patrols range from St. Thomas to and including
              Virgin Passage and from St. Thomas to and incl-
              uding Anegada Passage, with occasional patrols
              made of Anguilla, St. Martins and St. Berthelemy.

          (b) One plane assigned to escort all vessels in our area.

          (c) Changes in formation and composition of unit: None.

          (d) Enemy Contacts: None.

          (f) Reference toother units: None.

          (g) Important information of own or enemy forces: None.

81571

The first page of a war diary report from VMS-3. (NARA)

Colors in the evening. Fish Point, Guantanamo Bay. Cuba.

TOP LEFT Marines at MCAF St. Thomas raise the American flag during a morning colors ceremony in 1940. (USMC, photo by Sgt Joseph Heiberger)

BOTTOM LEFT Corporal Clemon L. Hicks, stationed at the Marine Detachment in Jamaica, marches a squad of Marines, May 1, 1943. (USMC, photo by Sgt David Stick)

TOP CENTER Field Music Corporal Charles H. Kennedy, of Huttig, Arkansas, sounds colors, July 1943. (USMC, photo by Sgt Joseph Heiberger)

RIGHT US Marines raise Old Glory on Jamaican soil, July 1943. In the background are the ruins of a fort that once was the headquarters of Sir Henry Morgan, feared buccaneer and later Lieutenant Governor of Jamaica. (USMC, photo by Sgt Joseph Heiberger)

TOP LEFT Marine guards at the Kingston airport in Jamaica, August 1943. Not shown in the background are the pilot and crew of a Naval Air Transport Service plane getting weather information prior to takeoff for Coco Solo near the Panama Canal. (US Navy)

TOP RIGHT A Marine guard looks suspiciously at the photographer as he stands beside a PBM-3R at the Kingston airport, August 1943. (US Navy, photo by Lt (jg) Wayne Miller)

BOTTOM The 13th Defense Battalion passes in review at Guantanamo Bay in 1943. (USMC)

US Marine antiaircraftmen fire at a small sleeve target towed by a Navy plane, March 9, 1943 in Guantanamo Bay. (USMC, photos by Sgt Andrew Knight)

TOP Corporal Eugene L. Whatley, of Mobile, Alabama, receives the China Medal from Lieutenant Colonel W. W. Orr at Guantanamo Bay, August 5, 1943. (USMC, photo by Pvt Ostorich)

BOTTOM On training maneuvers, Marines stationed at San Juan, Puerto Rico, crossed streams in rubber boats, July 1943. Normally, these rubber boats carried seven persons, but the weight of the rifles and other equipment reduced the capacity to five. Light aluminum paddles were used to propel the craft. (USMC, photo by Sgt Joseph Heiberger)

Duty and beauty seem to go hand-in-hand as far as jungle scenery is concerned for this quartet of US Marines on guard on Vieques Island in the Caribbean, close to Puerto Rico, November 3, 1943. (USMC, photo by SSgt Byrd Ferneyhough)

TOP LEFT Marine Sergeant James Devaney exchanges addresses with four Puerto Rican women he met on a day's sightseeing trip from his base on the island, January 1943. (USMC)

TOP RIGHT Virgin Islands Home Guard being instructed by US Marines on a .22-caliber rifle range, March 1942. (US Navy)

BOTTOM Admiral Georges Robert leaves the French cruiser *Le Terrible* at San Juan, and steps ashore in civilian clothes, July 14, 1943. Admiral Robert, who resigned his post as high commissioner of the French island of Martinique, was replaced by French Nationalist Henri Hoppenot. Admiral Robert visited Puerto Rico to confer with Admiral John Hoover of the 10th Naval District. Marine Privates Frank G. Swagger, left, and Bernard L. Wright stand guard at the foot of the gangplank. (US Navy)

TOP LEFT When local roads became impassable because of mud left by heavy rains, Marines took to the open fields of Puerto Rico, as here during training maneuvers, June 18, 1943. Normally stationed at San Juan, the Marines remained in the field a week and hiked 90 miles in six days. (USMC, photo by Sgt Joseph Heiberger)

TOP RIGHT These Marines have pitched camp for the night. During the training maneuvers, they carried their full equipment. Photo dated June 17, 1943. (USMC, photo by Sgt Joseph Heiberger)

BOTTOM At the completion of the week's maneuvers in the field, Marines enter the main gate of their station in San Juan, June 23, 1943. (USMC, photo by Sgt Joseph Heiberger)

TOP Trinidad Marines guard the entrances to the base's sentry posts. Pictured is the control gate where Marine sentries checked the daily passage of thousands of local workers, May 13, 1943. Left to right are Private First Class George A. Salavati, of North Adams, Massachusetts, and Private First Class Richard M. Lawless, of Chicago, Illinois. Here, a Marine jeep is seen from nearby Port of Spain, the island's capital. Two-way radio contact supplemented telephone communication with Marine Headquarters and patrol jeep drivers in outlying districts of the base. (USMC, photo by Sgt Joseph Heiberger)

BOTTOM Marines in Bermuda take the new unit speed boat for a test ride, March 1943. (USMC)

THIS PAGE AND OVERLEAF
Marines with the Marine Detachment aboard the USS *Ranger* (CV-4) disembark from a landing craft at NAS Bermuda, October 1942. The detachment took advantage of the carrier docking in Bermuda to refresh their land combat skills. Their exercise saw them take part in a mock attack on an enemy force, eventually taking them all the way to West Whale Bay, Bermuda, on the other side of the island. (US Navy)

MARINES IN SOUTH AMERICA

Crucial to the Allied war effort were the raw materials sourced from South American nations, including oil, rubber, food, sugar, and other essential goods. These resources, vital to sustaining the war, began their journey in the Southern Hemisphere. Recognizing the importance of these shipments, the Axis powers deployed numerous spies to sabotage Allied efforts and gather intelligence on cargo ships and logistics bases in the late 1930s. In addition to sabotaging facilities, probing base defenses, intercepting communications, and providing merchant ship coordinates to Axis submarines, these covert operations aimed to undermine the goodwill the US had cultivated over years of sending Navy warships to the region. Propaganda campaigns were also employed to spread misinformation and further erode support for the Allied cause.

Although the US was importing significant resources, the military and economic benefits for South American nations were also substantial, particularly for Brazil. As wartime efforts intensified, trade between the US and other South American countries flourished. The United States forged key trade agreements with Colombia for platinum, Chile for copper, Peru for cotton, and Venezuela and the Guianas for bauxite (the ore from which aluminum is derived). Additionally, Brazil became a crucial supplier of rubber to the US after economic ties with Japan were severed following the outbreak of war.

In addition to Marines stationed at naval airfields, several small units of Marines were assigned to protect US Navy counter-espionage operations. These Naval Mission teams had the crucial responsibility of detecting and intercepting transmissions from German spies operating in South America. These spies were providing intelligence to German and Italian submarines about cargo ship movements and Allied antisubmarine efforts.

Marines were also involved in training South American militaries in a wide range of modern tactics, significantly enhancing their combat readiness. Brazil in particular made exceptional use of this training. In 1944 and 1945, Brazil deployed 25,000 troops to support the Allies in Europe, playing a sizable role in the Italian campaign. Their training in modern military strategies proved invaluable as Brazilian forces participated in operations alongside Allied troops, contributing to the eventual defeat of Axis forces in Italy. This collaboration underscored the growing importance of inter-American military partnerships and demonstrated the significant impact of US military expertise in strengthening Allied efforts during World War II.

Marines serving in the Caribbean and in South America, on ships and at installations, were awarded the American Campaign Medal. Marines serving on ship detachments on duty in the Atlantic also received this award. (Author's collection)

Key West Citizen, June 11, 1940

Press reports disclose concerted activities of Nazi "fifth columnists" in South America. Stories are emanating that even a picked force of marines are being held in readiness and ready to embark on two hours notice to be rushed to a neighbor country to the south when the Nazi's blitzkrieg there. Large German populations in Mexico, South and Central America make this doubly possible. We do have a large number of troops in the South and Southwest.

However, in 1941, US planners were uncertain about the reliability of an alliance with Brazil and feared the country might align with Germany due to its dictatorship and certain characteristics of its government that resembled fascist regimes, particularly those of Italy and Spain in the late 1930s. This political climate in Brazil fueled concerns that the country could join the Axis powers. In late 1941, US diplomats requested that President Getúlio Vargas permit the stationing of American troops at airports in northern Brazil to safeguard Allied flights en route to French West Africa and Sierra Leone. However, the Brazilian government initially refused, further deepening suspicions about Brazil's potential sympathy toward European fascism. Additionally, reports from the Office of Strategic Services (OSS) – the precursor to the CIA – indicated that roughly 70 percent of the Brazilian military had pro-Nazi sympathies. With the fall of France and the Axis powers' occupation of French territories in West and North Africa, the US feared Brazil's potential entry on the German side. This initial refusal to allow US troops to be stationed in Brazil almost prompted President Franklin D. Roosevelt to send the 1st Marine Division to take control of the country and prevent it from siding with the Axis.

In December 1941, Secretary of State Sumner Welles successfully persuaded President Vargas to allow the first wave of US troops into Brazil. One hundred and fifty Marines were deployed, divided into three platoons, and stationed at airfields in Recife, Natal, and Belém. Their mission was to ensure the security of the airfields and military aircraft, vital for the safe transport of Allied forces to Africa. To avoid alarm and suspicion, the Marines were initially deployed under the guise of aircraft mechanics rather than as uniformed troops. Simultaneously, President Roosevelt authorized the export of weapons and ammunition to Brazil, bolstering support for the Allied cause within both the Brazilian government and military. In January 1942, during the Pan-American States Conference, US diplomats urged Brazil and other South American nations to sever diplomatic ties with Germany. By the end of the conference, Brazil made the pivotal decision to join the Allied side,

MARINE DETACHMENTS IN SOUTH AMERICA

Marine Guard Detachment, US Embassy
   Bogota, Colombia

Marine Guard Detachment, US Naval Mission Ecuador

Marine Guard Detachment, US Naval Mission Peru

Marine Guard Detachment, NAS British Guiana

Marine Guard Detachment, Naval Air Facility
   Amapa, Brazil

Marine Guard Detachment, Naval Air Facility
   Belém, Brazil

Marine Guard Detachment, Naval Air Facility
   Sao Luis, Brazil

Marine Guard Detachment, Naval Air Facility
   Recife, Brazil

Marine Guard Detachment, Naval Air Facility
   Maceio, Brazil

Marine Guard Detachment, Naval Air Facility Aratu, Brazil

Marine Guard Detachment, Naval Air Facility
   Caravelas, Brazil

Marine Guard Detachment, Naval Air Facility
   Santa Cruz, Brazil

Marine Guard Detachment, US Embassy
   Rio de Janeiro, Brazil

marking a significant shift in the country's stance and strengthening the Western Hemisphere's commitment to defeating the Axis. This diplomatic breakthrough laid the foundation for a deeper alliance between the United States and Brazil, which would prove essential in the coming years of the war.

By May 1942, the Brazilian–American Defense Agreement was established, fostering military cooperation between the United States and Brazil and encouraging the latter to align with the Allies in the war effort. Three months later, in August, Brazil officially joined the Allies after nearly two dozen Brazilian merchant vessels were sunk by German and Italian submarines, marking a turning point in Brazil's involvement. In response, approximately 500 Marines remained stationed in Brazil throughout the war to protect key naval air facilities, while several thousand US Army troops were also deployed. Both the US Navy and Army stationed significant antisubmarine assets in the region to safeguard convoys departing from South America, which were transporting crucial raw materials to the United States. This strategic cooperation played a key role in securing the Western Hemisphere's supply lines and fortifying the alliance between US and Brazil.

MARINES TO GET FOUR DESTROYERS

'Minute Man' Expeditionary Force For Use In South America Seen

BY EDWARD E. BOMAR

WASHINGTON, July 21—(P)—The navy disclosed today that four destroyers were being fitted out for use of the marine corps, evidencing efforts to speed creation of a "Minute Man" expeditionary force ready for any hemisphere emergency.

The destroyers are World war warships, recently recommissioned after years of idleness. Naval circles understood they would be converted into high speed transports, specially armed and equipped to put ashore advance forces at any hemisphere point where hostilities threatened.

At the same time officials said the marine corps has rapidly been increased to a strength of approximately 28,000 officers and men, with the 34,000 goal in sight.

The fleet marine force, subject to first orders for overseas service, is being expanded one-third by the formation of two new heavily armed defense battalions.

In addition to the destroyer-transports, converted commercial vessels are to be made a part of the overseas force, informed congressmen understood. The liner Iroquois and the cargo-passenger ship Mormacpenn were acquired last week by the navy for undisclosed purposes.

The navy's intention, informed house members reported, is to maintain in a high state of readiness a seagoing version of Germany's fast moving armored land divisions. Ships would be fully equipped with artillery, tanks and special boats for quick landings so they could sail as soon as the marines marched aboard.

Any attempted "fifth column" coup in Latin America resulting in a call for United States intervention thus could be dealt with promptly, it was explained.

Third U. S. Ship Ordered to South America

The Navy has ordered a third cruiser to South American waters following increased reports of "fifth column" activities in Latin America, it was revealed today.

The 10,000-ton cruiser Phoenix, which has been operating with the battle fleet off Hawaii, was ordered direct from the islands to the west coast of South America. Acting Secretary of the Navy Compton announced. He said the Phoenix is making "a friendly visit to South American ports in accordance with the custom of making these periodic visits."

The first stop will be at Valparaiso, Chile, one of the southernmost ports on the west coast and not far from Cape Horn, which would be rounded if a ship was required to make a dash to east coast ports.

The Phoenix carries 6-inch guns and has a complement of 888 men and an undisclosed number of fleet marines.

Several weeks ago the cruiser Quincy was dispatched to Montevideo, Uruguay. Shortly thereafter a sister ship, the 10,000-ton Wichita, was sent to Rio de Janeiro, Brazil. It is understood unofficially the destroyer O'Brien and several other destroyers are in the vicinity.

ABOVE Newspaper clipping from the *Evening Star*, June 26, 1940. Marines are mentioned near the end. (LoC)

LEFT Newspaper clipping from the *Wilmington Morning Star*, July 23, 1940. (LoC)

MARINES IN SOUTH AMERICA

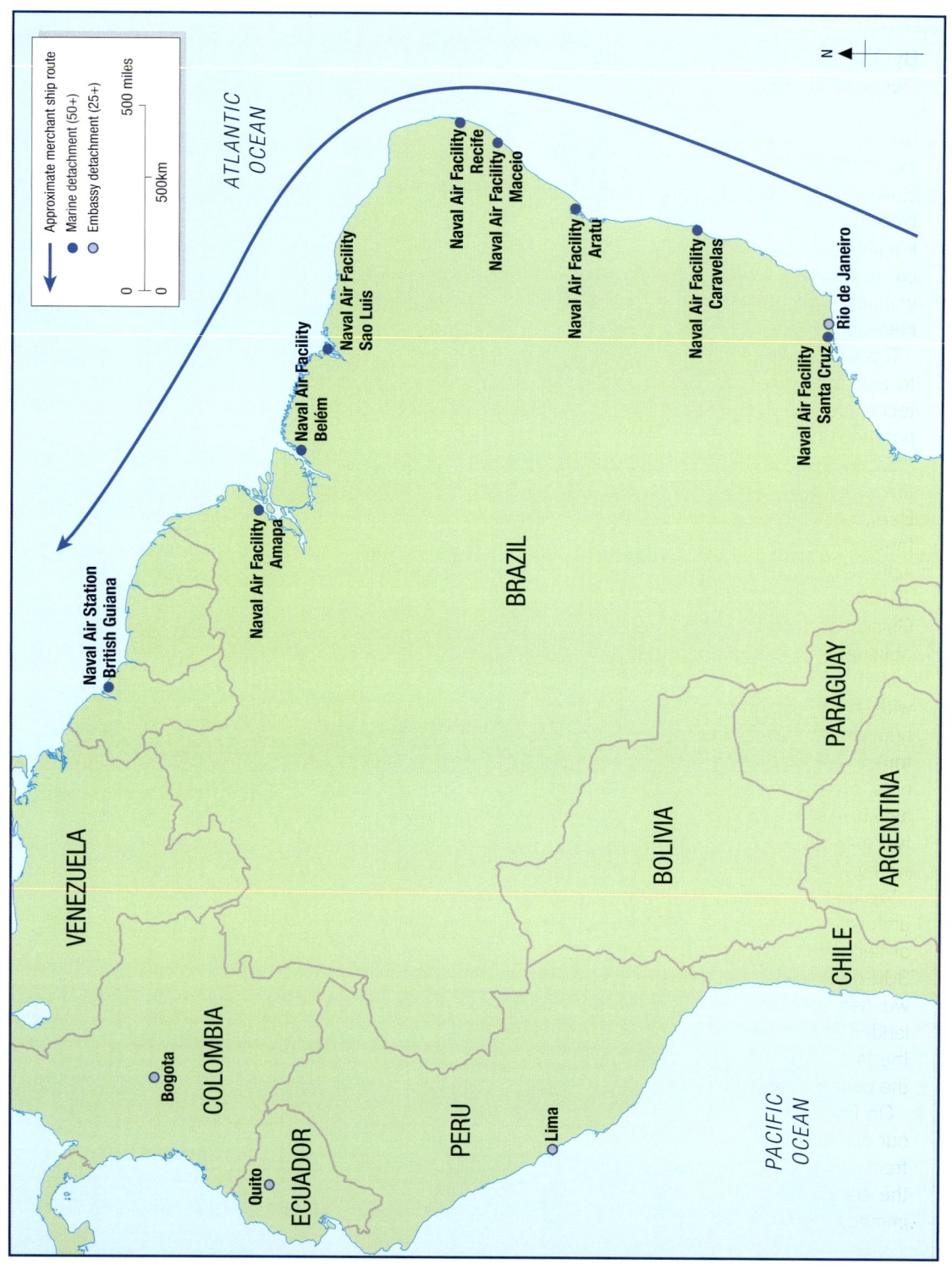

Marines Scout in Guiana

By Sergeant Jeremiah A. O'Leary, Jr.
December 1942

Marines here went on a 300-mile scouting expedition into the interior of primitive British Guiana. Into a land of impassable jungles, of bloodthirsty vampire bats, into a veritable kingdom of butterflies, aboriginal natives who carry blowguns and pointed darts, and the wonder of the greatest waterfall in the Western Hemisphere, Kaieteur.

The expedition allowed the Marines here time to exercise some and practice their patrolling techniques in case they get the opportunity to fight the Japs.

Six days passed before these men – of whom the writer was one – returned to their base at Bartica on the Essequibo River, unshaven, tattered, dirty, and hungry, but happy in their achievement.

There is an acute food shortage in British Guiana, and we knew there would be no food obtainable in the bush, as the inland jungle is called. We were compelled to carry all our food with us. This we did in two sea bags filled to the brim with canned goods, mostly beans. We also took seven cots and a like number of mosquito nets, files, pistols, bayonets, canteens, a first aid kit, rubber ponchos, an outboard motor and two milk cans filled with gasoline for the boats we had arranged to use.

We left the base at sunup. Dressed in old khaki uniforms, campaign hats, and boon dockers – or field shoes – we piled our dunnage into our 30ft river boat and shoved off. In 45 minutes, we had crossed the choppy Essequibo and landed at Bartica, an old mining town which is the last outpost of civilization until Manaus in the center of Brazil's "Green Hell."

On Friday – six days after the beginning of our expedition – we arrived back riding a lorry from a local. We barely beat a heavy rainfall into the sleepy little town mid-afternoon and went immediately to report in to our superior officer.

Marines with the Marine Detachment in British Guiana during a training expedition into the jungle, December 1942. (USMC, photo by Sgt Jeremiah A. O'Leary, Jr.)

Marines with the Marine Detachment, NAS British Guiana, take part in a field exercise at Kaieteur Falls, 1944. Now named Guyana, the country borders Venezuela, Brazil, and Suriname (formerly called Dutch Guiana). During World War II, the US Navy built a small airfield to use seaplanes and blimps to patrol for Nazi U-boats. (USMC, photos by Sgt Jeremiah A. O'Leary, Jr.)

LEFT A Marine with US Naval Mission Colombia helps load first aid supplies at the airport in Bogota for transport to Panama, June 1943. The items would eventually be grouped with other supplies and sent to the Pacific. (USMC, photo by Sgt Palmer)

RIGHT Colonel Byron F. Johnson, American naval attaché and naval attaché for air to Colombia and Panama, takes part in military and diplomatic ceremonies at the airport in Bogota, Colombia, July 20, 1943. (USMC, photos by Sgt Palmer)

RIGHT Colonel Miguel A. Lloma, Peruvian Air Corps; Colonel Ford O. Rogers, USMC, Chief of the US Naval Aviation Mission to Peru; General Fernando C. Melgar, Peruvian Minister of Aviation; Colonel Manuel P. Escalante, Peruvian Air Corps; and other Peruvian Air Corps officers are shown during an inspection tour immediately following their arrival in Chiclayo on May 26, 1943. The trip was made in a US Marine Corps plane flown by Colonel Rogers. (USMC, photo by Sgt Byrd F. Ferneyhough)

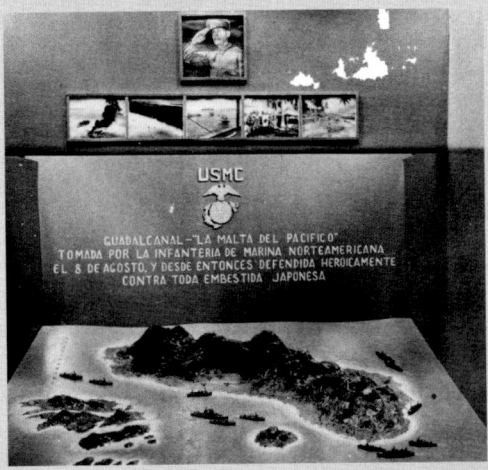

TOP LEFT Mrs. June, wife of Lieutenant Colonel Frank M. June, naval attaché at Guatemala City, Guatemala, and Marine Gunner William G. Mann, of Baltimore, Maryland, work on Christmas toys for Guatemalan children, December 1942. (USMC, photo by SSgt Wess Howland)

BOTTOM Marines with US Naval Mission Guatemala during a ceremony at the Guatemala Military Academy, May 29, 1943. (USMC, photo by SSgt Wess Howland)

TOP RIGHT A pictorial display showcasing part of the battle of Guadalcanal on display in Guatemala City, September 1943. Translated, it states, "The Pacific island taken by the North American Marine Corps on August 8 and since then heroically defended against any Japanese attack." (USMC, photo by SSgt Wess Howland)

Marines, US Army Military Police, and Brazilian Army Military Police take into custody 68 German spies and saboteurs who were arrested by Guatemalan police, October 1943. The prisoners were sent to the United States for further interrogation. (USMC, photos by SSgt Wess Howland)

TOP The tropical rains in Guatemala force the Marines to get the assistance of locals to get moving again, June 1943. (USMC)

BOTTOM Marines from various Marine detachments across Brazil joined to take part in a Victory over Europe parade in Rio de Janeiro, July 17, 1945. (US Army)

MARINE DETACHMENTS IN THE NORTH ATLANTIC

Marine Guard Detachment, Naval Operating Base
  Newfoundland

Marine Guard Detachment, Naval Air Station Argentia,
  Newfoundland

Marine Barracks, Naval Air Station Keflavik, Iceland

Marine Barracks, Naval Fleet Air Base, Iceland

Marine Barracks, Naval Operating Base Londonderry,
  Northern Ireland

Marine Barracks, Naval Operating Base Rosneath,
  Scotland

Marine Guard Detachment, US Embassy London,
  United Kingdom

MARINES IN NEWFOUNDLAND

From the outset of World War II, Britain faced steady losses of ships due to relentless German attacks on its fleet. As these losses mounted, the Royal Navy urgently needed to replenish its forces, especially with destroyers to escort convoys. A swift solution emerged with the "Destroyers for Bases" agreement, signed on September 2, 1940. Under this agreement, the United States provided Britain with 50 World War I-era destroyers to bolster its fleet. In exchange, the US was granted permission to establish military bases on British colonies and territories across the Caribbean and Atlantic. This deal allowed both nations to strengthen their strategic positions and safeguard vital maritime routes. A month later, engineers and surveyors began preliminary work on base construction, marking the beginning of a significant US military presence across the northern Atlantic region. On February 13, 1941, Marines officially raised the Stars and Stripes over the British colony of Newfoundland, signaling the first of many US military outposts that would play a role in defense and support the Allied war effort.

The US presence on Newfoundland would be substantial, with approximately 12,000 permanent personnel stationed on the island throughout the war. This strategic location would serve as a vital staging area for ships making supply runs across the Atlantic, enabling the US and its Allies to maintain crucial supply lines to Europe. Newfoundland also became home to key antisubmarine and convoy protection squadrons, ensuring the safety of Allied merchant vessels. In addition to providing repair facilities for ships, the island boasted a drydock and airfields for Allied antisubmarine aircraft.

Newfoundland hosted two detachments of Marines during World War II. One was stationed at NOB Newfoundland, which was officially commissioned on July 15, 1941, and the other at NAS Argentia, which opened on August 28, 1941. Each facility was guarded by approximately 100 Marines tasked with providing security. The strategic importance of these Marine guards was underscored a year later when German submarines attacked Allied ships in the surrounding waters and successfully landed spies ashore.

From 1942 to 1944, the battle of the St. Lawrence took place in the Gulf of St. Lawrence, the body of water separating Newfoundland from New Brunswick and Nova Scotia. This battle involved a series of engagements between British, Canadian, and German forces, with German U-boats sinking around two dozen merchant ships and several Royal Canadian Navy vessels. Despite the fact that the Allies did not succeed in sinking any German U-boats during this period, the battle was still considered a victory. The Allies effectively disrupted the U-boat operations and successfully captured all spies that had been landed during the attacks.

While the Marines in Newfoundland did not engage directly with German forces, their presence helped secure the naval installations. The Marines' security efforts ensured that the key bases in Argentia remained operational and secure throughout the battle, contributing to the overall Allied success in the region.

OPPOSITE Officers and men of the Marine Detachment that, on January 25, 1941, landed in Argentia. On February 13, 1941, this detachment, under command of Major H. E. Dunkelberger, raised the first US flag over a Lend-Lease base acquired from the government of Great Britain. (USMC)

MARINES IN THE ATLANTIC

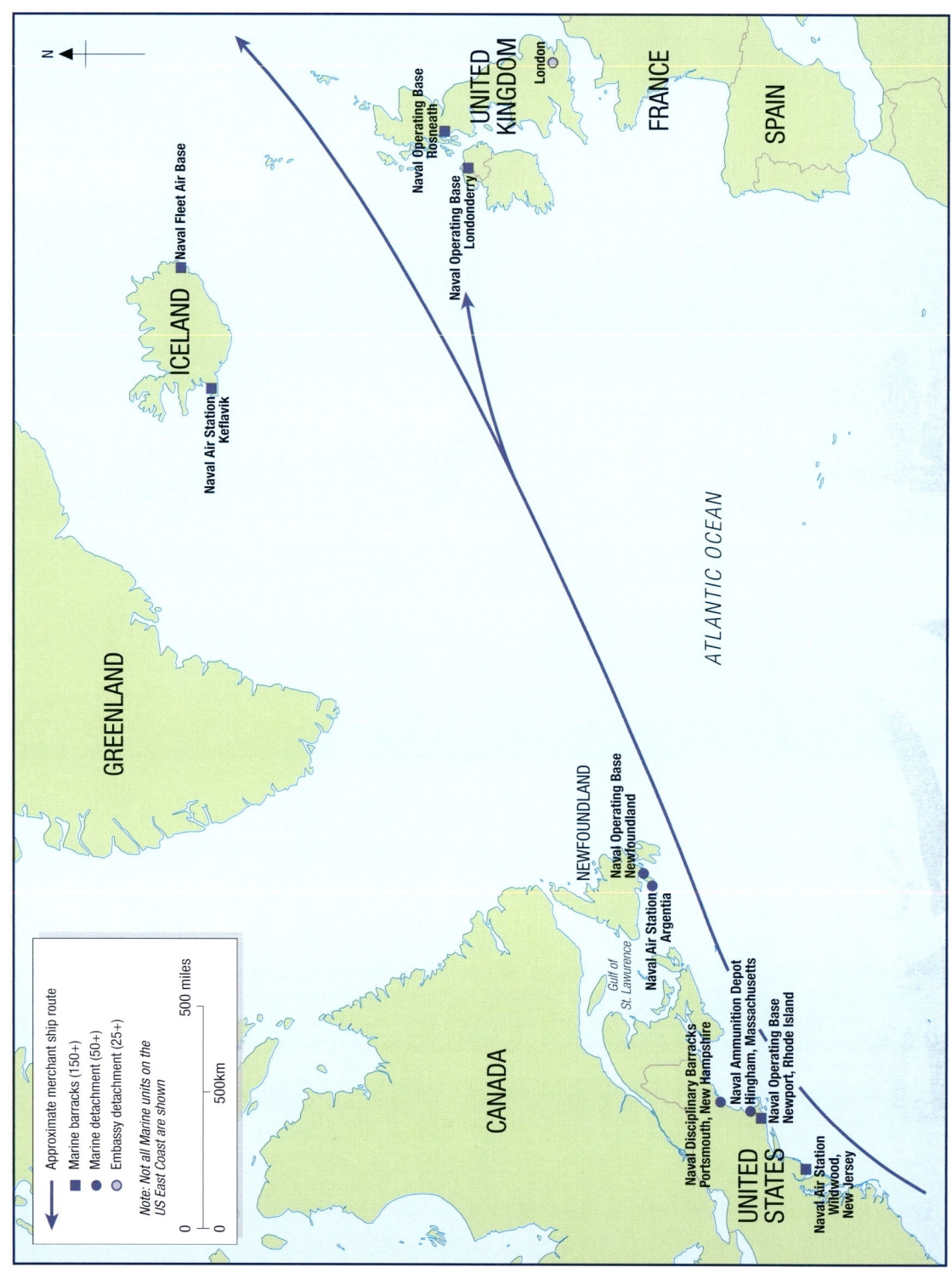

N

ICELAND

■ Naval Fleet Air Base

Naval Air Station
Keflavik

GREENLAND

Naval Operating Base
Rosneath

UNITED
KINGDOM

London ○

FRANCE

SPAIN

Naval Operating Base
Londonderry ■

ATLANTIC OCEAN

NEWFOUNDLAND

Naval Operating Base
Newfoundland ●

Naval Air Station ●
Argentia

*Gulf of
St. Lawrence*

CANADA

Naval Ammunition Depot
Hingham, Massachusetts ●

Naval Disciplinary Barracks ●
Portsmouth, New Hampshire

Naval Operating Base
Newport, Rhode Island ●

UNITED
STATES

Naval Air Station ■
Wildwood,
New Jersey

Approximate merchant ship route
■ Marine barracks (150+)
● Marine detachment (50+)
○ Embassy detachment (25+)

*Note: Not all Marine units on the
US East Coast are shown*

500 miles
500km
0
0

TOP Marines assigned to NAS Argentia take part in a morning colors ceremony, February 13, 1941. (US Navy)

LEFT A detachment of Marines stands at 'present arms' during the playing of the national anthem of the United Nations at the base in Argentia, July 1943. (USMC)

TOP Marines stand in formation at a dock at NAS Argentia, February 8, 1941. (US Navy)

BOTTOM Staff Sergeant Jack C. Harvey, USMC, of Flint, Michigan, poses with his wife, Margaret Walsh, on the steps of a Newfoundland church after their marriage ceremony, July 1943. (USMC)

MARINES IN LONDON

During the summer of 1941, a Marine Detachment of approximately platoon strength was established in London to help provide a guard unit at the US Embassy. Even before the United States formally entered the war, the Marines faced considerable danger as they crossed the Atlantic. Some members of the detachment saw combat when their transport ship was sunk by German U-boats, marking one of the first instances of Marines engaging in direct conflict in the Atlantic Theater.

As the months passed, the detachment's role expanded, and additional duties were assigned, causing the unit's ranks to swell. By December 1941, the detachment had grown to approximately 120 Marines. However, in October 1942, the detachment was temporarily disbanded when its personnel were sent to Rosneath, Scotland, to establish a Marine barracks there. Despite this shift, the detachment's role in London was quickly reinstated in January 1943, when it was reformed as the Marine Detachment, US Naval Forces, Europe. The detachment became a linchpin in support of naval and Allied efforts in the Atlantic and European Theaters of Operations.

Although officially designated as a guard detachment, the Marines stationed at the US Embassy in London played a much broader and more dynamic role. Administratively, the detachment was more akin to a battalion, having administrative control over hundreds of Marines throughout the European Theater of Operations, while only having several hundred on hand in London. In addition to their primary responsibility of securing the embassy against spies and saboteurs, the Marines were tasked with providing security at multiple naval headquarters buildings throughout the city. They also served as orderlies and drivers for flag officers, ensuring the smooth operation of high-level military leadership.

Beyond these duties, the Marines participated in Commando training alongside the Royal Marines, strengthening their combat capabilities and

Marines serving in Iceland and the United Kingdom were awarded the European–African–Middle Eastern Campaign Medal. Less then 1 percent of all Marines in World War II received this award due to the rarity of Marines serving outside the Pacific, especially in Europe. (Author's collection)

Harlem News, Montana, July 4, 1941

Incomplete account of the torpedoing of a detachment of US Marines to London has been disclosed this week. It is feared two Marines may have been lost. There were 17 Red Cross nurses aboard, it has been stated from one source, but all were safe. The Marines were bound for London to assist the American embassy in its expanded service, including fire prevention and communications.

Two District Marine Captains Report for Duty in Britain

LONDON, Nov. 26 (Delayed).— Marine Capt. Edward T. Johnson, 34, of Washington has reported for duty with the commander United States naval forces in Europe.

In his more than five years of service in the United States Marine Corps Capt. Johnson has served in New Caledonia, New Hebrides and Guadalcanal in the South Pacific.

Capt. Johnson.

Prior to combat duty he was a civilian engineer in charge of the construction of American airfields in British Guinea and Trinidad.

At Guadalcanal, where he was attached to a marine aviation unit, he was in charge of constructing an airfield. While there he became a member of the Century Club after spending more than 100 hours in foxholes with other marines.

He is a former student at George Washington University. His father, Ellwood Johnson, 3309 Runnymede place N.W., is superintendent of the Sanitary Department of the District of Columbia. Capt. Johnson's wife lives at 2401 Calvert street N.W.

Capt. John S. Hudson, 3348 Valley drive, Alexandria, Va., is at Marine Barracks, Londonderry, Northern Ireland. A native of Washington, D. C., he enlisted in the marines in May, 1939, while still an undergraduate at the College of William and Mary. He was commissioned in the Reserves in May, 1941 and in the regular Marine Corps in May, 1942.

Capt. Hudson.

After graduation from William and Mary in June, 1940, and prior to returning to active duty in February, 1941, Capt. Hudson was document and rare book librarian at his alma mater. He was married shortly before going overseas in the summer of 1942.

TOP Taken from the *Evening Star*, December 5, 1943 (LoC)

enhancing interoperability between US and British forces. They also took part in various ceremonial functions as required, showcasing their professionalism and versatility. When needed, they provided personnel for shore patrol security operations, helping to maintain order and discipline of American troops, and they operated as part of the motorcycle courier service, transporting classified documents between military and diplomatic offices in London.

As previously touched upon, the Marine Detachment in London also served as the administrative headquarters for Marines serving in the Office of Strategic Services (OSS). The OSS Marines would, on paper, be assigned to the detachment in London; however, their day-to-day duties would be in countries such as Yugoslavia, Italy, France, Belgium, or Morocco for extended periods of time.

In addition, a number of Marines on special assignments were also administratively attached to the Marine Detachment in London. These Marines held roles as observers, advisors, and Allied staff planners, and many played pivotal roles in shaping key operations throughout the war. Some were attached to British Army and Royal Navy units, while others were integrated into Allied staffs, contributing their expertise to the planning and execution of major Allied offensives, particularly those involving amphibious operations.

Notable figures such as Colonel Richard Jeschke, Colonel James Kerr, and Colonel Robert Bare, among many others, exemplified this collaboration. While they wore the uniform of the United States Marine Corps, much of their time during the war was spent working alongside Allied forces or within US Army units. Their contributions were critical in the development of joint strategies and the success of numerous operations, underscoring the Marine Corps' essential role in the broader Allied war effort.

Around 100 Marines, both officers and enlisted, were assigned to various Royal Air Force units in the UK and North Africa for extended periods during the war. While administratively under the command of the US Embassy in London, their primary mission was to gain expertise in nighttime fighter tactics and the effective use of radar. The British success in utilizing radar during the Battle of Britain was of significant interest to the Marine Corps, and these Marines were embedded into RAF nighttime fighter squadrons to gain practical experience by conducting nighttime combat air patrols against the German Luftwaffe. Several Marine pilots were shot down while serving with the RAF. With the exception of one, all of the Marines managed to make their way back to Allied lines and fight another day.

One notable Marine among these was Major Frank H. Schwable, who played a crucial role in this initiative. Schwable would go on to become the first commanding officer of Marine Night Fighter Squadron 531 (VMF(N)-531), the Marine Corps' first dedicated nighttime fighter squadron. The valuable tactics and techniques learned from the RAF's use of radar and night-fighting would prove indispensable when VMF(N)-531 was deployed to the Pacific in 1943. The newfound expertise would help counter the growing threat of Japanese night bomber and fighter attacks. The collaboration with the RAF not only provided critical skills to the Marines but also showcased the vital role of Allied cooperation in overcoming shared challenges during the war.

During the summer of 1941, Major Gerald C. Thomas and Captain James Roosevelt, the son of Franklin D. Roosevelt, had one of the most interesting assignments of the war. On special orders direct from Secretary of the Navy Frank Knox, the duo traveled to London and were attached as naval attachés to the US Embassy. From there they flew to India and then to Basra, Iraq. From Basra they flew on a British flying boat to Suez. Upon landing, they rode in a car to Cairo where they linked up with Marine Lieutenant Colonel Claude Larkin and Captain Perry Parmalee, both of whom were already in Egypt on assignment to observe the RAF.

After several days in Cairo, the pair traveled to Crete, Greece, to hand deliver a message to King George VI of the United Kingdom from President Roosevelt. Incidentally, they landed in the middle of a German air raid. Upon completing their mission, they flew to Jerusalem to meet several other high-ranking officials and were nearly killed from a strafing attack by German fighters, only surviving due to taking cover behind some nearby sandbags.

Upon leaving Jerusalem, they returned to Cairo and learned of the fall of Crete to German forces who had inflicted heavy casualties upon the defending British garrison. Shortly upon returning to the United States, both Marines were returned to regular Marine Corps duties, with Roosevelt taking a position of leadership in the newly created Marine Raiders and Thomas being assigned to the 1st Marine Division in time for the amphibious landings on Guadalcanal.

TOP The *Wilmington Morning Star*, June 30, 1941. (LoC)

BOTTOM RIGHT *Detroit Times*, July 7, 1941. (LoC)

BOTTOM LEFT The *Fort Worth Star-Telegram*, April 17, 1941. (LoC)

Fear U. S. Marine Lost On Torpedoed Vessel

WASHINGTON, June 29.— (P).— An authoritative source said today that a ship carrying a detachment of 10 American marines to England had been torpedoed and sunk in the Atlantic.

Advices on the sinking, this source said, reported that one American was missing, leading to the presumption that the others had been rescued.

The ship was said to be the Maarsden, a former Dutch vessel now in the service of the British.

At the Navy department there was no immediate confirmation of the report.

The department announced yesterday that three officers and 60 men of the Marine corps were being dispatched to London "to facilitate communications between the various United States offices located there."

U. S. MARINES IN LONDON

MARINES GUARDING THE U. S. EMBASSY IN LONDON

Marines to Guard U. S. Embassy at London

WASHINGTON, April 16 (P).— Secretary Knox said Wednesday the navy was preparing to send a force of one officer and 35 marines to London to guard the American embassy.

The Secretary of the Navy said only a formal request from Ambassador John G. Winant was awaited before the guard was sent. He described the move was "minor" matter and said the guard was "an ordinary embassy guard."

Marines now guard the embassy at Peiping, China, and were stationed at the London embassy in the World War.

James Roosevelt's original orders to serve in Europe, April 11, 1941. He is instructed to travel to Cairo "via such commercial transportation as may be most expedient." The orders conclude, "The travel herein enjoined is necessary in the public service." (NARA)

```
                                                          05477-1
                                                          AN-114-ebh

RESTRICTED              11 April, 1941

From:     The Secretary of the Navy.
To:       Captain James Roosevelt, Marine Corps Reserve,
            San Francisco, Calif.
Via:      The Major General Commandant.

Subject:  Orders.

     1.   On receipt of these orders, about 19 April, 1941, you
will proceed via such commercial transportation as may be most
expedient, to Cairo, Egypt, via Manila, P.I., and India.  On arri-
val at Cairo, you will report, by despatch, to the Naval Attache,
American Embassy, London, England, for duty as Assistant Naval Attache
and Assistant Naval Attache for Air to that country.

     2.   You are authorized to participate in such flights in
foreign belligerent aircraft as may be necessary in the performance
of your duties.

     3.   You will perform such travel abroad from time to time in
connection with your duties as may be required.  You will perform
the travel directed in this paragraph by air or by such other modes
of transportation as you may deem expedient, and you are authorized
to travel via conveyances of foreign registry.

     4.   Your dependents will not be permitted to accompany you
abroad under these orders.

     5.   The travel herein enjoined is necessary in the public
service.  For all travel abroad directed under these orders and
while away from your designated post of duty abroad, you will be
allowed a per diem of six dollars.

                                              FRANK KNOX

Copy to The Chief of NavOp.,
        The Director of NavIntel.,        CG, Dept of Pacific,
        The Quartermaster,                CG, MCB, San Diego,
        The Paymaster - 3,                CG, 2d Mar.Div., FMF,
        N.A., London, England,            Capt. Roosevelt - 10.

                                              RESTRICTED
```

TOP Captain James Roosevelt (left) and Major Gerald C. Thomas in Cairo, May 1941. It was one of the last stops on Roosevelt's intel-gathering mission. Later in the war, Roosevelt would climb the ranks and become the executive officer for the 2nd Marine Raider Battalion and, eventually, the commanding officer for the 4th Raider Battalion. Thomas would be assigned to the 1st Marine Division and participate in the landings at Guadalcanal. (Marine Corps History Division, hereafter MCHD)

CENTER Brigadier General Julian C. Smith (center) and Colonel H. D. Weir, British Royal Marines, and their staff officers, observe Royal Marines in Eastney, southern England, June 1941. (A 4506 Imperial War Museum)

BOTTOM For the first time in their history, the graduating class of the Royal Marine Officers School was addressed by a US Marines officer. Colonel William T. Clement addressed and reviewed the Royal Marine Military School in southern England. Adjutant Lieutenant J. F. Parson, Royal Marines (left), Lieutenant Colonel F. M. Brosall, Royal Marines, and Lieutenant Weldon B. James, USMC (rear) accompanied the colonel during the inspection. Photo dated February 5, 1943. (USMC, photo by SSgt James R. Kilpatrick)

Marines assigned to the Marine Detachment in London make their way through an assault course in London Park, August 12, 1942. The Marines smashed all of the course records, which were previously held by the Coldstream Guards up until that day. Officers of the Coldstream Guards asked that the Marines put on all future demonstrations on the course. (Associated Press/Alamy)

US Naval Rating Buried

Nottingham Evening Post, March 17, 1942

United States Marines fired a last salute over the grave of Florencio Casiano, the first American naval rating to be killed in this country, when he was buried at Gillingham (Kent) with naval honours today. Casiano, a Filipino, was an officers' cook, attached to the office of the Special Naval Observer in London. His body was found in a dry dock. British sailors completed the funeral party and the US Embassy was represented by a naval officer.

Marines with the US Embassy in London render honors during a combined joint service funeral for Steward Second Class Florencio Casiano, US Navy, March 17, 1942. Casiano was later reinterred at the Cambridge American Cemetery. (piemags/ww2archive/Alamy)

On Duty in London

London, England, June 16, 1944 – The strange roar of a Nazi raider flying low over this city one night recently gave American Marines on duty here a few anxious moments as a few Leathernecks viewed the new German "pilotless planes" for the first time.

Some of the Marines stationed here at the Naval headquarters witnessed some 300 German air raids in this country during the past three years, and they have taken the Nazi planes and bombs as a matter of course – that is until now.

"I've never heard a plane sound like that one," stated Marine Corporal John W. Linden, of 163-22 Sayers Avenue, Jamaica, Long Island, New York. "It sounded like a motorboat overhead with that put-put noise," he concluded after a wild dash down several flights of stairs to the ground floor of his billet.

"It looked like a Flying Fortress returning from a bombing raid with one of her engines on fire until I heard the explosion," added Sergeant Gilbert Cotton Jr. of 606 North Lincoln Avenue, Rockport Indiana, who watched it from the street.

Marines quartered in this billet move to various posts throughout the building during an air raid, while the rest of the Leathernecks go below to a shelter.

Five minutes after the warning last night the sound of the plane's engine brought Private First Class Carlton S. Ebling, of 6 Kingbury Avenue, Batavia, New York, out of his bunk with the mattress literally on his back.

"I thought the darn thing was going to crash on us," he admitted between gasps for breath on the ground floor. "That's the weirdest sounding plane I've heard since I've been in this country."

Sergeant Robert Kelly, of 1720 Kentucky Avenue, Detroit, Michigan, was on his way back to quarters after seeing a moving picture when he heard the plane.

"I was heading for home fast," he stated, "when a blonde bumped into me on her way to somewhere. The guns opened up about that time and I figured it would be a better idea to bump into a blonde some other night."

Private First Class Frank Perkins, of 5 Anita Terrace, Roxbury, Massachusetts, averred that "it was no fun patrolling those quarters on the top deck. That's one night I would like to have been below."

Hastily dressing as he raced down the stairs, Corporal Charles T. Brady Jr., of 260 Valentine Lane, Yonkers, New York, agreed that "It's the first real excitement we've had in some time."

A Marine from Broadpark Lodge, White Plaines, New York, Private First Class Harvey T. Bronkhurst, got a good look at one of the new weapons from the roof of the building.

"It was traveling very fast and appeared to be just another plane until I saw an exhaust of blue flame coming from its tail. It passed on and the guns banged away at it. Finally, I saw a big billow of smoke off in the distance where it hit," he said.

Marine Corporal Eugene Ferris, of New Brunswick, New Jersey, sums it up this way: "I definitely take a dim view of this Buck Rogers invention which they are throwing over here."

Although the majority of these Marines have served in this theater of operation for the past two years, Marine Private First Class Robert G. Wilfong, of Box 1141, Lakemore, Ohio, explains it this way: "We aren't fighting much of a material war at our base here, but we're batting pretty high in the war of nerves."

U. S. Marines on Duty in London

ABOVE Marines on duty at the US Embassy in London, February, 1942. Here, three privates first class are shown during a drill with a stirrup pump used for extinguishing incendiary bombs. The men, left to right, are Will H. Willmom of Tuscaloosa, Alabama, Adam W. Elkins of Guyton, Georgia, and James R. Eikel of Elfers, Florida. (USMC)

LEFT The photo appearing in the *Smyrna Times*, February 5, 1942. (LoC)

By Sergeant Robert T. Davis

Londonderry, Northern Ireland, June 1943 – Chief Torpedoman Floyd Moon, US Navy, of Toronto, Kansas, is an assistant to the combined Marine Corps–Navy Shore Patrol office here.

Chief Torpedoman Moon, who was on shore patrol duty in Boston for over four months before coming here, assists Shore Patrol Officer, a Marine Corps Captain, in the supervision of the 25 Marines and 25 Sailors permanently attached to the Shore Patrol.

Stationed at the Shore Patrol Office in Londonderry he and the Captain make hourly inspections during the evening of the patrols, each composed of one sailor and one Marine, which are stationed on the busiest streets in town and at the dance halls and American Red Cross Club.

Distinguished only by a brassard, Chief Torpedoman Moon, who is over six feet in height, has won the respect of the service men here, and usually can correct one with a word or two. When this cannot be done, the offender, whether he be Marines, sailor, or soldier, is taken in the Shore Patrol station wagon back to his camp for the night. Only rarely is one taken into custody, for as Chief Torpedoman Moon explains it, "our job is to see that they don't do anything that we'll have to arrest them for."

TOP "Heads of Navy–Marine Shore Patrol in Northern Ireland look over their records on the latest prisoners. First Lieutenant Michael Hines, Jr., USMC, of Kewanna, and Logansport, Indiana, former Notre Dame football star (left), and Chief Torpedoman Floyd E. Moon, USN (right), of Toronto, Kansas, can handle anything in the form of trouble." Photo dated May 29, 1943. (USMC, photo by SSgt James R. Kilpatrick)

CENTER "Marine and Navy members of the Shore Patrol in Northern Ireland look in on a dance to make sure no Americans need escorting home. Naval counterparts of the Army's Military Police, members of the Shore Patrol act as big brothers and 'Dutch Uncles' as well as policemen." Photo dated May 29, 1943. (USMC, photo by SSgt James R. Kilpatrick)

BOTTOM "United States Marines of the Embassy Detachment in London were recruited for shore patrol duty when sailors and Marines from US fleet units were on leave in England. The leave party was on hand to celebrate Navy Day with a dance in London." Photo dated October 25, 1943. (USMC, photo by SSgt James R. Kilpatrick)

RIGHT Original memo ordering a small detachment of US Marines to attend the new Royal Marines Commando training course in England. Two officers and 20 enlisted men were planned to be sent for two months, to arrive on April 1, 1942. (MCHD)

UNCLASSIFIED

_{Cominch File}
FF1/ P11-1/(0062) **UNITED STATES FLEET**
Office of the Commander in Chief
Serial (0062)   NAVY DEPARTMENT, WASHINGTON, D C

S E C R E T   February 5, 1942

From: The Commander-in-Chief, U. S. Fleet.
To: The Chief of Naval Operations.
          The Commandant, U. S. Marine Corps.

Subject: Commando Training of U. S. Marine Corps
          personnel in England.

Reference: (a) Spenavo London Secret despatch Ø213Ø1
               of February, 1942.
           (b) OpNav Secret Despatch 191737 of January,
               1942.

    1.   The Commander-in-Chief approves the arrange-
ments proposed in reference (a) for a detachment of two (2)
officers and twenty (20) enlisted men to proceed to England
for a two-month period of Commando training beginning April
1, 1942.

    2.   The Chief of Naval Operations is requested to
make the necessary administrative arrangements, and to notify
the Commandant, U. S. Marine Corps, of the date on which it
is desired that this detachment report to the Chief of Naval
Operations. Arrival of the detachment in England at least
one week prior to April 1, 1942 is desired.

    3.   The Commandant, U. S. Marine Corps, is requested
to form and equip this detachment and to issue the necessary
orders in conformity with the instructions of the Chief of
Naval Operations.

                            GEORGE C. DYER,
                            Flag Secretary.

E. J. KING.   12311

                          RECEIVED
                          FEB 6 1942
                          WAR PLANS SECTION
                          MARINE CORPS

                          FILE

LEFT Praise from the Royal Marine school on the US Marines' performance during the Commando course. (MCHD)

REPORT ON UNITED STATES MARINE CORPS.

Length of Course - 8th June 1942 to 29th June 1942.

Programme of Work - Already submitted.

GENERAL REPORT.

The whole of the detachment were a credit to the United States Marine Corps, from the start they were all keen and entered into an arduous training with enthusiasm and cheerfulness.

They have undergone an arduous Commando training with an exceptionally unconquerable spirit which never wavered during the course.

I am sure that they have very much benefited by the course and are fit to take their place in a Commando.

Captain Roy J. Batterton proved himself to be a fearless and efficient leader of his men. He would make an excellent Troop Leader in a Commando.

Staff Sergeant George V Clarke,   Sergeant Way Holland, Sergeant George J. Huddock and Sergeant Curtis A Tatum proved themselves excellent N.C.Os. and possess exceptionally fine leadership qualities and could control their men under very difficult conditions.

It was a pleasure to be associated with such an excellent detachment.

/s/ L.E. Vaughan,
Lieut.-Colonel,
Commandant,
Commando Depot.

Achnacarry,
Spean Bridge,
Inverness-shire.
29th June, 1942.

ELSEWHERE **IN 1941**

JANUARY 27: The Chief of Naval Operations orders the 3rd Marine Defense Battalion to Midway and directs the 6th Marine Defense Battalion to Pearl Harbor

FEBRUARY 3: Marine Corps Air Station Ewa in Hawaii is established

MARCH 18: The 7th Marine Defense Battalion arrives in Samoa

APRIL 6: Germany invades Greece and Yugoslavia

MAY 29: The Joint Board approves a plan for the occupation of the Azores. More than 28,000 troops are committed with half being Marines. The force is to be led by US Marine Maj. Gen. Holland M. Smith

JUNE 22: Hitler stuns the world by attacking the USSR

JULY 24: The 1st Marine Defense Battalion is established at Johnston Atoll

AUGUST 19: An advance party from the 1st Defense Battalion arrives on Wake Island

SEPTEMBER 11: The 6th Marine Defense Battalion relieves the 3rd Defense Battalion at Midway

NOVEMBER 27: The US withdraws Marine detachments in China: Peiping, Tientsin, and Shanghai

DECEMBER 7: Japanese forces attack Pearl Harbor and Wake Island

DECEMBER 11: Germany and Italy declare war on the United States

TOP From left to right is Marine Major Peter D. Lambrecht, RAF Wing Commander L. N. Hayes, and Major Homer J. Hutchinson at RAF Station Ford in Sussex, May 1943. The Marine aviators were temporarily assigned to the Marine Detachment in London with instructions on observing and learning from RAF Night Fighter Squadron 256. Their training pipeline with the RAF saw them take part in nighttime combat missions against the Germans. (MCHD)

BOTTOM LEFT Major Homer J. Hutchinson stands in front of his Bristol Beaufighter in which he flew combat missions with RAF Night Fighter Squadron 256 from Sussex air station. (MCHD)

BOTTOM RIGHT Major Peter D. Lambrecht and his Bristol Beaufighter in which he flew combat missions with RAF Night Fighter Squadron 256 from Sussex air station. (MCHD)

TOP LEFT US Marine Major C. E. Smith (center, hands crossed), of Augusta, Georgia, and several other American pilots attended a lecture on night-flying tactics at the Royal Air Force Empire Central Flying School in Britain in early 1943. Smith is flanked by US Navy pilots on both sides. The three are surrounded by RAF pilots. Smith's knowledge learned from the RAF during the Battle of Britain would go on to help create and expand the Marine Corps' night-fighting squadrons in the Pacific. (piemags/ww2archive/Alamy)

TOP RIGHT Led by a guard of Marines, the bodies of American officials killed in a plane crash are escorted to their graves near London, September 10, 1043. Commodore James A. Logan, former Commandant of NOB Northern Ireland, Captain Loren Lee Miles, USAAF, and David Grimes, official of the Philco Corporation, were killed in an airplane accident in Northern Ireland. (USMC, photo by SSgt James R. Kilpatrick)

BOTTOM In London on Memorial Day 1943, American Marines, sailors, and soldiers formed the guard of honor when wreaths were laid on the Cenotaph, Britain's memorial to its dead in World War I. Here, an Army bugler sounds "Taps," while British officials and American servicemen pay their respects to the dead. (USMC, photo by SSgt Keating)

Four Marines, who recently completed a course of instruction at the US Army Officer Candidate School at Shrivenham, England, pose with the commanding officer of the Marine Detachment at the US Embassy, London, before returning to their duties at NOB Londonderry. From left to right: Platoon Sergeant Henry J. Kelly, Jr., of Waltham, Massachusetts; Sergeant Marvin Thysse, of Kalamazoo, Michigan; First Lieutenant Alan C. Doubleday, of Millburn, New Jersey; Platoon Sergeant Charles S. Lucas, of Oakmont, Pennsylvania; and Platoon Sergeant Graham H. Cockefair, of Bloomfield, New Jersey. (USMC, photo by SSgt James R. Kilpatrick)

By Technical Sergeant Richard T. Wright

London, England, December 11, 1943 (Delayed) – After scouring Army personnel records for several days, Marine Sergeant Major Clement F. Betko of East Vandergrift, Pennsylvania, located his two younger brothers, who are serving with the Eighth Army Air Force in Southern England, and the three Pennsylvanians enjoyed a happy reunion recently.

The 33-year-old Leatherneck's youngest brother, Private John C. Licko, 20, has served with the Army Air Corps in England for three months, while 22-year-old Steve V. Licko has been here for 17 months. Sergeant Major Betko has served with the Marine Detachment in Londonderry, Northern Ireland for the last 19 months, making him the "long timer" in the family as far as overseas duty goes.

"It's really swell seeing my brothers again," he stated. "We had a tough time making our furloughs jibe so that we could all be here together, but we made it."

Sergeant Major Betko has been in the Marine Corps since 1930. Shortly after he enlisted, he served under the late Marine Major General Smedley Butler, at Quantico Virginia.

The Marine Sergeant Major remembers well "Those blue-white parades... General Butler used to have us parade in starched white trousers with the regulation dress blue coat, and I mean we really had to shine, or else. I also used to get a kick out of watching the General cheering for the Quantico Marines football team. He was a mighty rabid rooter."

The husky Marine Sergeant Major served with the present Commandant of the Marine Corps, Lieutenant General Alexander A. Vandergrift, at the American Legation Guard, in Peking, China for three and one half years. He saw duty aboard a light cruiser, and served at various Navy yards through the East Coast.

Sergeant Major Betko is the son of Mr. and Mrs. Julius Licko, of 247 Vandergrift Land, East Vandergrift, Pennsylvania. His wife, Pearl Betko, lives at 13461 Justine Street, Detroit, Michigan.

He has a son, Paul, who is 28 months old.

"Private John C. Licko, US Army Air Corps, points out a part of Dean's Yard, where the Dean of Westminster Abbey resides, as his two brothers, Sergeant Major Clement F. Betko, US Marines, and Sergeant Steve V. Licko, US Army Air Corps, look on intently. The three brothers enjoyed a happy reunion in London recently. They are from East Vandergrift, Pennsylvania." (USMC, photo by SSgt James R. Kilpatrick)

By First Lieutenant Herbert L. Merillat

Oxford, England – "Soldier-sailor" turned scholar for a week when Marine Staff Sergeant Harry R. Gasker, of 837 East 150th Street, Cleveland, Ohio, on duty with the Marines at the US Naval Operating Base, Londonderry, Northern Ireland, decided to spend his leave among the "dreaming spires of Oxford" where a seven-day course for officers and men of the United Nations armed forces is provided by Oxford University.

More than a thousand officers and men from the United Nations forces stationed in the British Isles have attended the course. The United States, Great Britain, Australia, Canada, New Zealand, South Africa, Belgium, Costa Rica, Czechoslovakia, Norway, Poland, and Venezuela all have been represented at one time or another.

Staff Sergeant Gasker, like many men in the United States forces in Great Britain, found the courses a pleasant and interesting way to spend his leave. A graduate of Collinwood High School in Cleveland, the sergeant attended Western Reserve University in Cleveland, one and a half years, and Ashland College, in Ashland, Ohio, two and half years before the war interrupted his education. He hopes to finish college after the war.

Staff Sergeant Gasker joined the Marines a month after Pearl Harbor and after finishing his "boot" training was sent to Londonderry, where he was among the first Marines to arrive. He has been serving there nineteen months.

Each man attending the seven-day course arrives at Oxford on a Monday, reports to Balliol College, where all students live, and begins a crowded program of lectures, entertainments, discussions, and tours. The course formally ends on Saturday, but members may stay on in Oxford over the weekend.

The course includes lectures on the history of England and the British Empire, English literature, English legal system, philosophy, and local government, with comparisons of American and British institutions.

The week begins with a dinner at Balliol College on Monday, followed by a welcome from Dr. A. D. Lindsay, Master of Balliol and former Vice-Chancellor of the University. Lectures begin the following day, and that night a dance is given at Rhodes House, long a center of hospitality for overseas students at Oxford. During the remainder of the week, in addition to the lectures, the program provides for a tour of Oxford colleges and historic monuments, an evening at the Oxford Playhouse where a repertory company produces a different play each week, a musical, and finally, on the last night, a "Brains Trust" meeting.

Modelled on American quiz programs, the "Brains Trust" panel consists of a distinguished visitor, an Oxford "don," two American and two British members of the school who answer questions submitted by other members of the course and lead the discussion. At various times Crown Prince Olaf of Norway, United States Ambassador John Winant, and Dr. Frank Aydelotte, American secretary of the Rhodes foundation, have been visiting experts on the Brains Trust program.

A typical schedule of lectures includes the following: English and American Character, Oxford, The Making of the British State, Shakespeare and the State, The Law Counts, Decision and Action, and Local Government. Each lecture is followed by a discussion period which usually proves lively and lasts well beyond the allotted time.

The course was first organized in April 1942, for the benefit of Canadians stationed in the United Kingdom. Dr. A. L. Goodhart, KC, Professor of Jurisprudence at Oxford, was a moving spirit in starting the school and still serves as one of the regular lecturers. Mr. Douglas LePan, of Toronto, Ontario, a former Oxonian himself, also played a large part in getting the school off to a good start.

For a year and a half the school for Canadian and British forces was held only during vacations when the Oxford undergraduates were not in college, and the members of the course were scattered among the twenty-odd Oxford colleges. Beginning in August 1943 the course was enlarged to permit attendance by Americans and other fighting men of the United Nations and all students were placed together in Balliol College, one of the three Oxford colleges which claim to be the oldest in the University. All three were chartered in the thirteenth century.

There the members of the course live in regular undergraduates' rooms, dine in the college hall, use the college lecture halls, and gather in the common rooms for tea and talk.

The Oxford dons who lecture the members of the course find them alert, intelligent, and eager for discussion. Mr. Idris Deane Jones, history don at Merton College, who helps train RAF cadets in addition to his teaching duties, remarked that "these people are right on their toes. There is always a barrage of questions when I finish my lectures and they aren't always easy to answer."

The members of the course, for their part, find that an amazing amount of learning is crammed into the short week at Oxford. All find that the seven days spent in the famous English University are packed full of instruction, fun, and new acquaintances.

A highlight of Staff Sergeant Gasker's visit was meeting with Sir William Beveridge, British economist whose "Beveridge Plan" for post-war social security has caused much discussion on both sides of the Atlantic. The sergeant visited University colleges, where Sir William Beveridge is master of the college, with Philip Goodhart, son of the Professor of Jurisprudence. There he was introduced to the famous economist.

Staff Sergeant Gasker's parents, Mr. and Mrs. H. J. Gasker, live at 837 East 150th Street, Cleveland, Ohio.

TOP "Marine Staff Sergeant Harry R. Gasker looks over his lecture notes while seated under an old tree in Balliol College quadrangle, Oxford, England. The musette bag at his side has travelled far. It was carried throughout the Guadalcanal campaign and lent for the Oxford visit by a Marine officer serving in Great Britain." (USMC, photo by SSgt James R. Kilpatrick)

BOTTOM "Following a lecture on the history of the British States, Idris D. Jones, center, history don of Merton College, continues the discussion with some of the students. Smoking is permitted during lectures, causing the haze in the background. Mr. Jones finds his service students alert, intelligent, and argumentative. Staff Sergeant Gasker stands at right." (USMC, photo by SSgt James R. Kilpatrick)

RIGHT "Gasker stops to discuss a point between classes with three Army Air Forces staff sergeants. Left to right: SSgt Joseph E. Fodor, Uniontown, PA; SSgt Don J. Sheff, Hamburg, NY; SSgt Isadore E. Friedman, Baltimore, MD; and SSgt Gasker of Cleveland, OH. At the right of the picture, a British officer chats with an American officer." Photo dated November 17, 1943. (USMC, photo by SSgt James R. Kilpatrick)

By Technical Sergeant Richard T. Wright

London, England, January 11, 1944 – Marine Corporal Louis Reese Grall, the son of Marine Sergeant and Mrs. Henry J. Grall, of Route 2, Anderson, South Carolina, is bruised but happy after being knocked down three times, by everything from an automobile and a bomb explosion during his tour of duty in the British Islands.

While walking along the streets of London during a blackout a short time after he arrived here in July 1942, Corporal Grall was hit by a taxicab when he stepped off a curb. The 21-year-old Marine was knocked down but was uninjured.

Two weeks later he was struck by a jeep which was driven by another Marine. The Leatherneck suffered a bruised hip, but otherwise was uninjured.

Five months later he was flattened when a bomb exploded outside of a friend's house, where he was visiting at a small town in southern England. This time he was knocked down and out, but Corporal Grall was "in the pink" within an hour afterwards.

"I suppose the next time I get knocked down it will be by a truck falling on me. I guess I had better start watching my step," he stated.

Corporal Grall's father, Sergeant Henry Grall, served with the Marines in World War I, and at present is on duty at Headquarters, Marine Corps, Washington DC.

Corporal Grall was one of three personal orderlies to Admiral Harold R. Stark, USN, at one time, and is now serving as a driver with the Marine unit here.

On duty as a driver, Corporal Louis Reese Grall ponders over a road map near the outskirts of London, January 16, 1943. (USMC, photo by SSgt James R. Kilpatrick)

By Technical Sergeant Richard T. Wright

London, England, January 11, 1944 (Delayed) – Marine Private First Class Robert G. Wilfong, the son of Mr. and Mrs. O. C. Wilfong, of Box 1141, Lakemore, Ohio, is serving with the Marine unit here as an official guard at the American Embassy.

Private First Class Wilfong has been on duty in the British Isles for the last 18 months, and previous to his coming here, he served with a Marine unit in Scotland. The 24-year-old Marine has also been on temporary duty with the Leatherneck unit in Londonderry, Northern Ireland.

The Ohio Marine has served as an orderly to high ranking Naval officers, and also as a driver.

According to Private First Class Wilfong, he has led a rather dull life since arriving at this base. "I've made quite a few interesting trips, but other than that things have been rather boring. I haven't been close to any bombs when they exploded; I haven't been knocked down by a cab in the blackout – in fact, I can't even get lost around here anymore."

Private First Class Wilfong was given a try out with one of the Cleveland Indians' baseball teams in 1941. The husky Marine pitched for his high school team for four years, and also played football.

He enlisted in the Marine Corps in January 1942. He has one brother, Corporal Ralph Mill, who is with the Army Air Corps.

"Marine Private First Class Robert G. Wilfong, of Lakemore, Ohio, checks his .45-caliber service pistol before going on guard at the US Embassy. Wilfong has been on duty with the Marine unit for the past 18 months." (USMC, photo by SSgt James R. Kilpatrick)

Story #19 by Technical Sergeant Richard T. Wright

London, England – Robert Harris, an 18-year-old American living here, is going down in history as the first United States Marine to be recruited in England.

Harris was sworn in as a Marine private by First Lieutenant Alan C. Doubleday, of a Marine unit in Great Britain. A check of records both in London and Washington reveal that, so far as is known, Harris was the first Marine who enlisted in this country.

"I always wanted to be a Marine," he said.

Private Harris will be sent to the United States, where he will undergo recruit training at the Marine base at Parris Island, South Carolina.

The husky youth came to this country with his parents, Mr. and Mrs. John E. Harris, of Milford Lodge, Milford, Near Stafford, England, from their home in Lynnfield, Mass., in September 1938. At that time, Private Harris was 13 years old.

All members of the Harris family are American citizens. His father is a consultant on shoes for the US Army and is employed in a large department store in London.

Harris was educated in England at Downside School, Stratton-on-the-Fosse, which is the equivalent of an American High School. The tall, dark-haired Marine, speaking with a pleasant English accent, explained:

"I always had a great deal of admiration of the Marines. My brother is in the Army Air Corps and I thought it was a good idea to have a Marine in the family."

Private Harris has two brothers and three sisters. One of his brothers, 20-year-old John Edward Harris, became a pilot with the RAF and later transferred to the US Army Air Corps.

"Private Robert Harris, of Milford Lodge, Milford, near Stafford, England, is being sworn in as a US Marine by First Lieutenant Alan C. Doubleday, of Millburn, New Jersey, The 18-year-old American, who came to England when he was 13, was the first Marine to be recruited in England during World War II. Private Harris formerly lived in Lynnfield, Massachusetts." (USMC, photo by SSgt James R. Kilpatrick)

By Technical Sergeant Richard T. Wright

London, England, February 7, 1944 – London fogs have proven baffling to Marine Sergeant Gilbert Cotton Jr. during his two years of service with Marine units in the United Kingdom.

The 22-year-old Leatherneck remembers one occasion distinctly.

"I spent half my time getting lost in the fog when I first came over here," he relates, "but one particular laundry run to a place called Putney was the worst. I started out and drove for five minutes. The fog got so bad I could only see five feet ahead of my motorcycle. It took me exactly three and one half hours to go three miles, and that is strictly a waste of time."

Sergeant Cotton has served as a police sergeant with a Marine unit in Scotland, and during his trip across the Atlantic, the ship that he was on was strafed by a German plane.

The Marine Sergeant found his first few months in England very amusing.

"Nobody knew our uniforms at first, and on many occasions enlisted men saluted us thinking we were officers," he said.

"One time in a town in southern England," he continued, "about 300 Canadians came out of their barracks to go on liberty as I was walking down the main throughfare. My arm got so tired from saluting that I went into a tea shop and waited until most of them had gone by," he concluded.

Sergeant Cotton is the son of Mr. and Mrs. Gilbert G. Cotton of 606 North Lincoln Street, Rockport, Indiana. He enlisted in the Marine Corps on September 12, 1940, at Cincinnati, Ohio. Sergeant Cotton is married to an English girl and is the father of a baby girl.

"Marine Sergeant Gilbert Gillian Cotton, Jr., gives a Marine dispatch rider orders for a run, at the motor transport office of the Marine unit here. The 22-year-old Leatherneck is from Rockport, Indiana, and has served in this area for the past two years. The origin of the moose head is unknown." (USMC, photo by SSgt James R. Kilpatrick)

TOP "A London 'Bobbie' gives directions to Marine Corporal John. B. Flowers at the gates of Buckingham Palace, where the 24-year-old Leatherneck has official business. Corporal Flowers, of Holliday, Tennessee, has served with Leatherneck units here for the past two years." Photo dated February 2, 1944. (USMC, photo by SSgt James R. Kilpatrick)

RIGHT "The wedding cake has been cut by the bride and groom. Sergeant Delbert O. Wilkins, of Lyons, New York, and guest prepare to taste this Anglo-American offering at a reception for the newlyweds who were married in London recently. The bride and best man look on." Photo dated January 16, 1944. (USMC, photo by SSgt James R. Kilpatrick)

TOP LEFT "'Here's the way we throw a forward pass,' says Marine Private First Class William C. Parsons to a group of English boys who watch intently. The 20-year-old Leatherneck from Revere, Massachusetts, was an All-State end with the Revere High School football team in 1942." Photo dated March 20, 1944. (USMC, photo by SSgt James R. Kilpatrick)

TOP RIGHT Admiral Sir Bertram Ramsay, Royal Navy, speaks with Captain L. A. Thackrey, Assistant Chief of Staff, US Navy, during the planning for D-Day. Colonel Robert O. Bare can be seen in the background. (piemags/Alamy)

RIGHT Marine Private First Class Robert F. Daigle of Newport, Vermont, during troop inspection in London, March 20, 1944. (USMC, photo by SSgt James R. Kilpatrick)

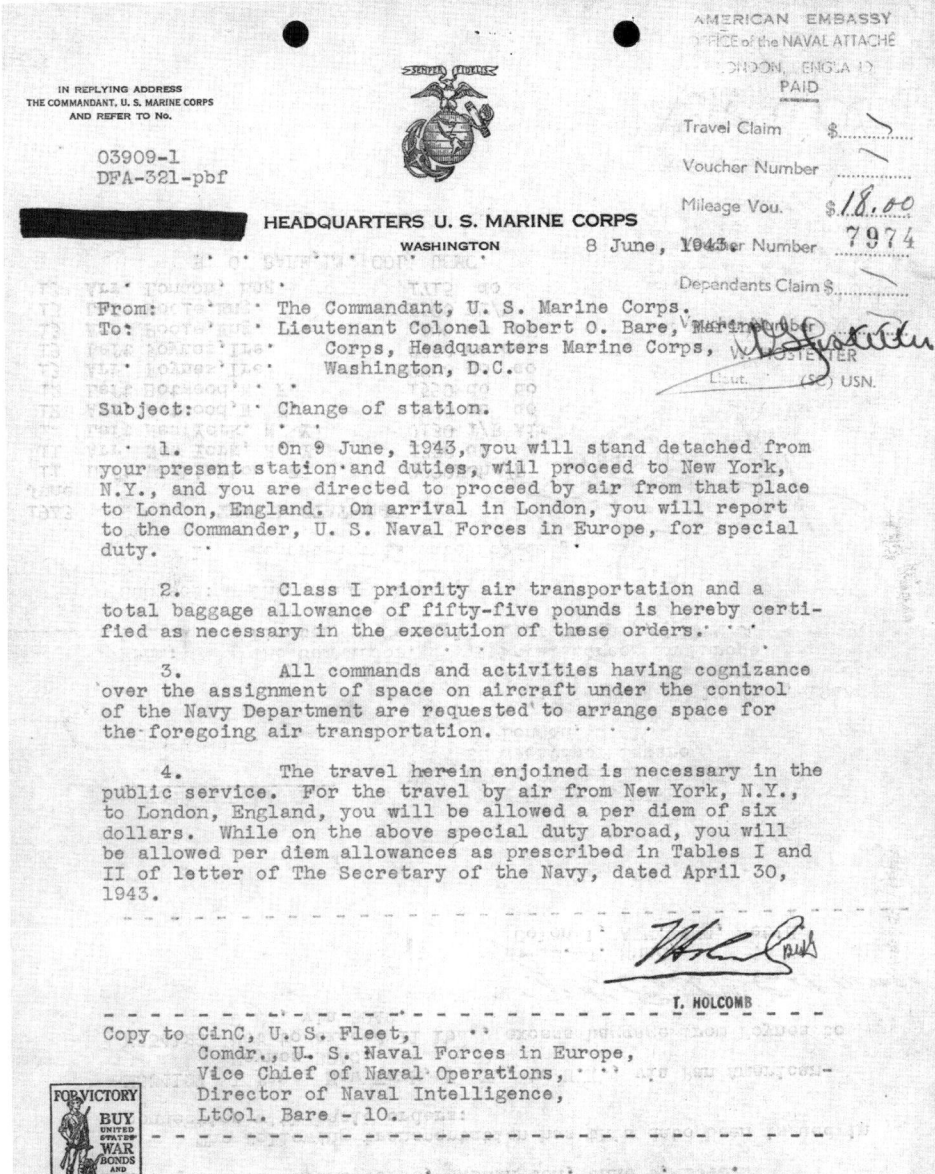

IN REPLYING ADDRESS
THE COMMANDANT, U. S. MARINE CORPS
AND REFER TO No.

03909-1
DFA-321-pbf

AMERICAN EMBASSY
OFFICE of the NAVAL ATTACHÉ
LONDON, ENGLAND
PAID

Travel Claim $

Voucher Number

Mileage Vou. $18.00

HEADQUARTERS U. S. MARINE CORPS

WASHINGTON   8 June, 1943   Number 7974

Dependants Claim $

From: The Commandant, U. S. Marine Corps.
To: Lieutenant Colonel Robert O. Bare, Marine
         Corps, Headquarters Marine Corps,
         Washington, D.C.

Subject: Change of station.

1.   On 9 June, 1943, you will stand detached from
your present station and duties, will proceed to New York,
N.Y., and you are directed to proceed by air from that place
to London, England. On arrival in London, you will report
to the Commander, U. S. Naval Forces in Europe, for special
duty.

2.   Class I priority air transportation and a
total baggage allowance of fifty-five pounds is hereby certified as necessary in the execution of these orders.

3.   All commands and activities having cognizance
over the assignment of space on aircraft under the control
of the Navy Department are requested to arrange space for
the foregoing air transportation.

4.   The travel herein enjoined is necessary in the
public service. For the travel by air from New York, N.Y.,
to London, England, you will be allowed a per diem of six
dollars. While on the above special duty abroad, you will
be allowed per diem allowances as prescribed in Tables I and
II of letter of The Secretary of the Navy, dated April 30,
1943.

T. HOLCOMB

Copy to CinC, U. S. Fleet,
         Comdr., U. S. Naval Forces in Europe,
         Vice Chief of Naval Operations,
         Director of Naval Intelligence,
         LtCol. Bare - 10.

FOR VICTORY
BUY
UNITED STATES
WAR
BONDS
AND
STAMPS

Colonel Robert O. Bare's original orders from the 1st Amphibious Corps
to the US Naval Forces, Europe. (MCHD)

A Royal Marine Base in England

By Technical Sergeant Richard T. Wright, February 15, 1944

Whether the Marines are British "Jollies" or American "Leathernecks," it is obvious after watching the recruits at this depot in their training phase, that the men of the two Corps really get "the works" during their initial course of instruction.

Here a Royal Marine drill instructor addresses a backward recruit in this manner: "I say, you bloomin' clown, you better learn your right foot from your left!"

A United States Marine drill instructor puts it this way: "All right Mac, snap out of it, you haven't got two left feet!"

No matter how different the two methods of training Marines are, the results are usually the same, as evidenced by the records of the brother Corps during the past 200 years.

According to Regimental Sergeant Major R. Keeble, of the Royal Marines: "The purpose of our Corps is to train Marines to serve aboard His Majesty's Ships, and to be able to undertake special landing operations. Basically, our Marines and your American Marines have the same function."

In the present war Royal Marines have already played an outstanding part in the Norwegian campaign, Suda Bay, Crete, Burma, Ceylon, and Madagascar. They also participated in the initial landings at Sicily and Salerno.

This recruit training base is situated in the moors of Devonshire, reputedly one of the few really sunny spots in England. The rolling hills, dense forests, and thick underbrush are ideal for military training tactics.

Shortly after arriving at this camp, Staff Sergeant James R. Kilpatrick, a Marine combat photographer, and I were greatly impressed by the rigid discipline which is a requisite of all Royal Marines.

I watched a private walk up to a sergeant at the main gate yesterday. The private snapped to attention, clicked his heels, and awaited the order "stand easy." It is pounded into these recruits that proper discipline is the foundation of all military successes.

This British "boot camp" is similar to our American marines camps at Parris Island, South Carolina, and San Diego, California. Not unlike these camps, physical examinations, haircuts, the issuing of clothes and rifles are the main features of the initial indoctrination course.

Royal Marines lay a great deal of emphasis on physical conditioning in order that the recruits can shoot straight when they fire the range with their caliber .30-3 rifles. American Marines call their rifle "A Marines' best friend," and the Jollies evidently have the same ideal.

We witnessed close order drill, bayonet and hand-to-hand fighting classes, and the firing of small arms. These recruits complete their training in six weeks, and then "pass out" to another center, where the business of getting set to whip the Nazis begins in real earnest.

The drill instructors at this base are composed largely of pensioners – men who were called back with the Royal Marines when the war started.

A tour of duty in the United States Marines is four years. In the Royal Marines it takes twelve years to complete a cruise, so it was not uncommon for us to encounter some salty old British Leathernecks who have sailed around the world as many as ten times. Some of them had made the acquaintance of American Marines everywhere from Shanghai, China to Norfolk, Virginia.

Staff Sergeant Kilpatrick asked one Sergeant whether or not he had any brothers in the service.

"I've four in the Marines," the sergeant replied.

"Holy mackerel!" said Staff Sergeant Kilpatrick, "that's almost a record."

"Not quite, laddie," a wizened old Company Sergeant Major chimed in, "I have five brothers

in the Corps and my father served with the Royal Marines in the first World War. We have 177 years of continuous service with the Marines." As the American Marines put it, Staff Sergeant Kilpatrick was "snowed."

The Royal Marine recruits are quartered in Quonset huts, while the non-commissioned officers live in rooms called "cubicles," each with a small stove which burns coal.

Recruits must run cross country races, box with six-ounce gloves, and participate in all athletic contests which are run on an intramural basis.

The camp is brightened considerably by an array of femininity in blue in the persons of the girls serving with the English Women's Royal Naval Service. These girls do most of the office work.

The training of these Royal Marine recruits is hard and rigorous, but as one officer explained it to me: "We train our men down to a fine edge, but with it we make gentlemen out of them."

A sergeant major showed me an excerpt from a piece which Rudyard Kipling wrote some time ago. It very accurately describes the British Royal Marines: "But they're camped and fed, and they're up and fed, before our bugle's blew, Ho! They ain't no limpin' procrastitutes, soldier and sailor too!"

Author note
This story is more than likely written about training at Royal Marines Barracks Chivenor, a Royal Marines training center from 1940 to 1995.

TOP Staff Sergeant James R. Kilpatrick and a Royal Marine recruit take up rifle positions on the school range at the Royal Marine camp in southern England, February 15, 1944. (USMC, photo by TSgt Richard T. Wright)

BOTTOM Technical Sergeant Richard T. Wright of Arlington, Virginia, inspects a platoon of Royal Marine recruits at a base in southern England, as a British drill instructor looks on, February 15, 1944. (USMC, photo by SSgt James R. Kilpatrick)

A British Royal Marine takes his life in his hands while letting a Leatherneck shave him. This "tonsorial treatment" took place during maneuvers somewhere in Wales, March 1943. (USMC, photo by SSgt Weldon L. Keating)

MARINES IN SCOTLAND

The Marine barracks in Scotland was short-lived, lasting only four months beginning in late 1942. However, the Marines had been visiting Scotland for quite some time already. In 1940, Major John C. McQueen was sent to the United Kingdom to observe the training of the Royal Marines and study the landing craft the British possessed. In the summer of 1941, Captain Edward C. Dyer and Brigadier General Ross E. Rowell visited RAF Coastal Command Headquarters in Scotland. In September 1942, 27 Marines from Londonderry and 16 Marines from London were sent to Rosneath to establish a three-week course on small arms weapons use for US Navy boat crewmen who would be taking part in the upcoming Operation *Torch*. At the end of the training, ten Marines were sent back to their respective units while the rest were given orders to take part in the operation in North Africa. In October 1942, the London barracks was deactivated, and the Marines transferred to NOB Rosneath, Scotland. However, on January 21, 1943, the Marines were transferred back to London to reactivate the Marine barracks there.

LEFT "Clad in a British Army 'zoot suit,' Corporal Joseph Leitch, of Douglas, Arizona, is shown repairing a bayonet practice dummy. These rugged Leathernecks knock them down as fast as they are putting them up. Because of a shortage of dungarees, British Army battledress has been issued to this detachment for use as work clothes." Photo dated September 10, 1943. (USMC, photo by SSgt Weldon L. Keating)

RIGHT "American Leathernecks talk it over with Britain's Royal Marines after Royal Marine Commandos staged a battle exercise on Scottish hills and beaches for the Marine detachments from USS *Alabama*. The Americans are, from left to right, Major Harold S. Roise, of Moscow, Idaho, and First Lieutenant Natt K. Hammer, of Decatur, Illinois. The demonstration was followed by training films on scouting and handling anti-personnel mines." Photo dated July 1943. (USMC, photo by SSgt Weldon L. Keating)

TOP Lieutenant Fenton H. Mae, USMC, and Captain Griffith, Royal Marines, discuss plans during a joint training exercise, March 1943. (USMC, photo by SSgt Weldon L. Keating)

BOTTOM LEFT "Major Harold S. Roise, of Moscow, Idaho, with officers and non-commissioned officers of his shipboard command, recently witnessed battle techniques used by the Royal Marines in taking strong points. Here, Roise discusses details of the demonstration with two officers of the Royal Marines, clad in battledress and wearing Britain's unchanged version of the trench helmets of the last war." Photo dated July 1943. (USMC, photo by SSgt Weldon L. Keating)

BOTTOM RIGHT "First Lieutenant George H. Bantley chats with a kilted officer of a Scottish regiment 'somewhere in Scotland.' First Lieutenant Bantley said he had heard plenty about the kilted 'ladies from hell,' as the Germans call them, but had never seen one before and had plenty of questions to ask. Leathernecks in background include First Lieutenant Weldon James (smoking pipe) and, to the right, Major Harold S. Roise." (USMC, photo by SSgt Weldon L. Keating)

TOP "Sergeant James L. Lowery, center, foreground, watches combat tactics displayed by British Royal Marines in northern Great Britain. Sergeant Lowery, 23, of Gadsden, AL, is serving with an Anglo-American task force searching for the German fleet. He attended Gadsden High School, and was a professional boxer in the south before enlisting in the Marine Corps. He and other American Marines and British Royal Marines shown in the picture find that they talk the same anti-Nazi language nowadays." Photo dated July 1943. (USMC, photo by SSgt Weldon L. Keating)

BOTTOM "A Royal Marine demonstrates a new weapon to Platoon Sergeant Dorsey N. Simms, Jr. of New Orleans, LA (right), and two other American Marines at a US Marine training base in Scotland. They are all members of the task force that has been searching for the German fleet for several months near the North Pole right on down to warmer European waters. As a change from their frigid search, they hope eventually for a warmer assignment in the South Pacific, after the Germans crack." Photo dated July 1943. (USMC, photo by SSgt Weldon L. Keating)

MARINES IN NORTHERN IRELAND

With the United States' entrance into World War II following the attack on Pearl Harbor, the US Navy established a base on the European side of the Atlantic in February 1942.

Londonderry, Northern Ireland, was strategically selected as the new post. The port of Derry provided a home port for escort ships and a waypoint for cargo ships. A makeshift battalion was formed and, in May 1942, the 400-man unit left the US for the newly created NOB Northern Ireland. A month later, another 152 Marines were sent to bolster the ranks and another 200 Marines were sent in October 1942.

The unit was designated the Marine Barracks, Naval Operating Base Londonderry and was divided into four companies: a Headquarters and Service Company, and A, B, and C Companies. As well as helping to operate the shooting ranges in Bangor, the Marines were in charge of protecting:

- The US naval ammunition supply depot at Fincairn Glen
- Several US Navy radio stations around the city of Londonderry
- Navy supply depots at Lisahally
- The US Naval Field Hospital at Creevagh
- US ships docked in the ports of Derry and Belfast

The large Marine unit was necessary to guard the facilities, which were under constant fear of being raided by small German units that could be landed by submarines to carry out sabotage operations. Additionally, the embassies of Japan and Germany were bustling with activity in Ireland because it was feared the Axis powers would align with the Irish Republican Army and carry out sabotage operations.

Alongside their guard duties, the Marines played a key role in supporting the Royal Ulster Constabulary by assisting with shore patrol operations, ensuring law and order when US servicemen and women came off ship. The Marines also participated in various defensive field exercises designed to repel a potential German amphibious invasion. These exercises involved Marines assembling and moving to coastal positions, where they would integrate with British forces to bolster the region's defenses. Other

OPPOSITE British Marines explain the operation of their Bren gun to American Leathernecks: looking on are First Lieutenant George H. Bantley (with pipe), of Windber, Pennsylvania, and (right) First Sergeant James Wilson, Jr., of Philadelphia, Pennsylvania. The US Marines, members of a Marine Detachment aboard a ship, went ashore in Scotland to see Royal Marine Commandos stage a demonstration of their skill in attacking "enemy" strong points. (USMC, photo by SSgt Weldon L. Keating)

LEFT The patch with a clover leaf under the Eagle, Globe and Anchor is often mistaken as an official patch and shown in countless history books as an official unit emblem. However, no photos exist of a Marine wearing it during World War II. Additionally, the patch was not authorized by the Commandant of the Marine Corps. The June 22, 1944 edition of the *Marine Corps Chevron*, base newspaper of Marine Corps Recruit Depot San Diego, states definitively the patch was unauthorized by the Commandant of the Marine Corps. (Author's collection)

Irish City Keeps Shore Patrol Busy

By Staff Sergeant M. H. Dunlap, Combat Correspondent
Marine Corps Chevron, **August 21, 1943**

Londonderry, Northern Ireland, July 7 (delayed) – It's an old saying that sailors no sooner get their land legs than they start losing them.

But American sailors and Marines in this British port are kept out of serious mischief by an American Shore Patrol which has the difficult task of enforcing strict rules of behavior in a foreign port.

Londonderry is a Shore Patrol problem. In addition to American sailors and Marines, sailors of other United Nations fill the place and Irish civilians also enjoy excitement.

At Shore Patrol headquarters in the city, where prisoners are booked, a "flying squad" is always ready to dash to trouble spots. Another squad, the "roving patrol," makes regular rounds of the town. Both squads use Marine-driven station weapons. Nine pairs of patrols, one sailor and one Marine in each, stroll through the streets.

Test Londonderry Defenses

Detroit Evening Times, **November 2, 1942**

London – large scale antiinvasion exercises to test the defenses of the great Londonderry naval base gave American marines and other United States units a stiff Sunday workout, it was revealed today.

The *Wilmington Morning Star*, October 4, 1944. (LoC)

———V———
Woman From Irish Free State Is Naturalized

A woman marine from the Irish Free State was naturalized in Superior court yesterday, the first time that a woman member of the armed forces has ever received her American citizenship in Wilmington, Jennings Otts, immigration inspector and naturalization officer, announced yesterday.

She is Florence Elizabeth McConnell of Dublin, Eire, and is now stationed at Camp Lejeune. Two other marines, William Totten, of Belfast, Northern Ireland, and John Aitkin Guy, Jr., of Scotland received their naturalization papers along with Miss McConnell.

Totten is stationed at Camp Lejeune and Guy is stationed at the Cherry Point Marine Base.

training scenarios included counterattacks from inland positions to the coastline, as well as reinforcing Allied units during counterattack drills. These activities not only enhanced the Marines' preparedness but also demonstrated their vital role in strengthening the Allied defense efforts across the British Isles during the early years of the war.

The Marine barracks in Londonderry would often provide men for additional collateral duties or assignments throughout the European Theater of Operations. As such, these Marines' regular training regimen saw them practice amphibious operations, hand-to-hand combat, close-quarter battle drills, land navigation, and patrolling. As the war dragged on, some of the Marines at Londonderry would be sent to take part in major events such as Operation *Torch*, or to stand up a Marine barracks in Oran. Some would be killed in the line of duty taking part in these events. In all, around 1,500 Marines were assigned to Londonderry at the peak of the war in Europe.

TOP American Marines spray the heather with machine-gun fire as they prepare for action against more warlike enemies, May 12, 1943. (USMC, photo by SSgt Keating)

CENTER Marine Corps officers at Waterside Railway Station in Londonderry after having arrived from Belfast, May 19, 1942. From left to right are Major Louis Shoemaker, Major John Bathum, Captain Frank Martincheck, and Lieutenant Colonel James J. Dugan. (MCHD)

BOTTOM His Majesty King George VI inspects the newly arrived Marines in Northern Ireland, June 26, 1942. (piemags/ww2archive/Alamy)

Newspaper clipping from the *Wilmington Morning Star*, July 2, 1942. (LoC)

NAVY COMPLETES BIG IRISH BASE

Built To Guard The Western Approaches Of England In Atlantic

UNITED STATES NAVAL BASE LONDONDERRY, Northern Ireland, Thursday, July 2—(P)— T h e U. S. Navy has completed a giant operating base here guarding the western approaches of Britain in the critical battle of the Atlantic.

Londonderry in this war has become the counterpart of Queenstown (Cobh), now in neutral Eire, which during the first World War was base for as many as 92 United States warships at one time.

The Londonderry base is designed to refit, repair and supply destroyers and other light craft on Atlantic convoy duty. It was commissioned Feb. 5, but is just now receiving its finishing touches— a job virtually completed seven months after U. S. entry into the war.

"It already has lifted a great burden off the convoy problem," said Commodore Ross Stewart, commander of the adjoining British naval establishment.

Actual construction of the big base was started last year with lend-lease funds and more than 3,000 Irish and American laborers, under direction of American civil engineers headed by Commander Henry P. Needham.

Now hundreds of United States marines and bluejackets operate machine shops, supply bases, drydocks, control rooms, a hospital, movies and barber shops. All this is spread over hundreds of acres.

Wartime security prevents relating details of the intricate mechanism of the establishment, but it is ready to repair or rebuild anything from a typewriter to the biggest American destroyer.

"Eveything in the base down to the last pork chop or nut and bolt has been brought from t h e United States," Capt. William Larson of Annapolis and Chicago explained. "It's a bit of the United States transplanted."

The hundreds of men required to operate the base are housed in deluxe "Quionset huts," prefabricated at home and put together here. Scores of warehouses are stuffed with supplies of everything from shoe polish to new propeller shafts.

In blacked-out buildings skilled Navy men operate millions of dollars worth of precision machinery, 24 hours a day if necessary.

Sleek new American destroyers glide up the river to the docks side by side with Royal Canadian corvettes which also use the base.

While the American base operates as a separate unit, jobs are done jointly with the nearby British yard as occasion demands.

In a 200-bed Quionset hut hospital, which is capable of doubling its capacity overnight, British sailors occupy beds alongside Americans.

"In fact, 80 per cent of o u r patients at the moment are British," said Capt. B. P. Davis of San Francisco, senior Navy medical officer.

RIGHT TOP The first major group of Marines exits the docking area in Londonderry to be bused to the newly built huts for them at the NOB, May 19, 1942. (MCHD)

RIGHT BOTTOM Two US Marines from Company A perform a change of the guard at Lisahally, Northern Ireland, June 1942. US Navy destroyers can be seen in the background. (SuperStock/Alamy)

But ofcourse there are a few places a Marine sentry
has to stop at in between

TOP A cartoon done by Captain Bruce Bairnsfather, creator of "Old Bill," while on a visit to Marine Barracks Londonderry. Photo dated January 3, 1943. (USMC, photo by Cpl William R. Gibbon)

BOTTOM American Marines on maneuvers in Northern Ireland. "The Leathernecks wend their way through heather, gorse, and broom, wondering what the terrain of the second-front-to-come will be like." Photo dated May 1943. (USMC, photo by SSgt Weldon Keating)

The Duke of Abercorn, Governor of Northern Ireland (center right with black hat), inspects US Marines during the celebration of the anniversary of their landing at Londonderry, May 12, 1943. Marine officers in party, from left to right, include Major John M. Bathum, of Chicago, Illinois; Colonel Lucian W. Burnham, of Needham, Massachusetts; and Lieutenant Colonel James J. Dugan, of Quincy, Massachusetts. (USMC, photo by SSgt Weldon Keating)

TOP "Thousands of Irish and British civilians perched atop the famous walls that withstood the 17th-century Siege of Derry look on as Marines march into Guildhall Square to celebrate the anniversary of their landing in Northern Ireland. Leading the Leathernecks is Captain John Hudson, Post Adjutant, of Washington DC." Photo dated May 12, 1943. (USMC, photo by SSgt Weldon Keating)

BOTTOM The Duke of Abercorn, Governor of Northern Ireland, and General Edmund Hill, commanding officer of the US Forces in Northern Ireland, were among the reviewing party. (USMC, photo by Cpl William R. Gibbon)

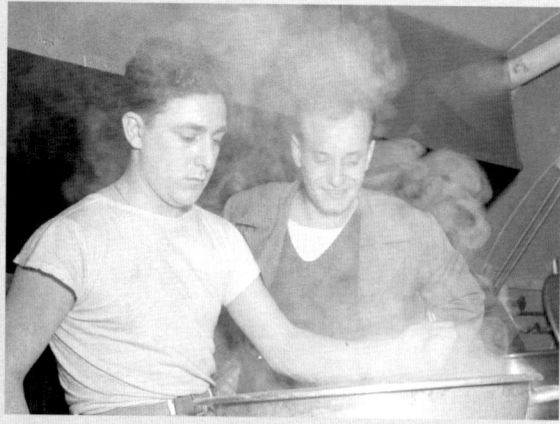

TOP LEFT The ceremonies included a parade through the streets of Londonderry and an inspection in Guildhall Square. Marines wore battledress for the occasion. (USMC, photo by Cpl William R. Gibbon)

TOP RIGHT Marines in front of Londonderry Guildhall. The Guildhall served as a site for many of the town's social functions, including Marine Corps dances, boxing matches, and, on the afternoon of the anniversary, a tea. (USMC, photo by Cpl William R. Gibbon)

CENTER "Sergeant Francis Fabyanic, of Turtle Creek, Pennsylvania, gives an okay to Corporal Phillip Soloneto, left, of Philadelphia, Pennsylvania, who just finished a batch of hot chocolate in Londonderry." Photo dated February 10, 1943. (USMC, photo by SSgt Weldon Keating)

BOTTOM "These birds traveled thousands of miles before coming to rest in a US Marine mess. Field Cook William Fedorka, of Cleveland, Ohio, and Assistant Cook Robert Clement, of Flint, Michigan, prepare the turkeys for dinner. These Leathernecks were trained to whip up a meal in an elaborate kitchen or on the field under fire." Photo dated February 10, 1943. (USMC, photo by SSgt Weldon Keating)

By Sergeant Robert Davis

Londonderry, Northern Ireland, June 1943 – Bringing with him an Irish brogue that can't be cut with a bayonet, an infectious smile, and a determination to get along, John Joseph Hargadon, 17, son of Mrs. Rose Hargadon, Box 126, Ithan, Pennsylvania, has joined the United States Marines.

To every Marine at this base, he's the "Irish recruit" but Hargadon is just as much an American citizen as any of them, having been born and brought up in the United States in Philadelphia before coming to Ireland at the age of seven to live with his grandmother.

But ten years in Ireland have left their mark on him, and even the Marine slang he has picked up in his first week as a Marine is marked with his brogue.

Reaching the age of 17, Private Hargadon turned down chances to enlist in the British forces to try to join some American service. Through the cooperation of Lieutenant Colonel James J. Dugan of Quincy, Massachusetts, the executive officer, his enlistment consent was obtained from his mother in Pennsylvania, and early in June, Private Hargadon's enlistment was completed.

It's an old Marine Corps saying that every Marine has either Parris Island or San Diego sun in his blood, but Private Hargadon will break that saying, for he'll have his recruit training at this base. To make it complete, like any other new recruit, he won't have liberty for over a month. His drilling is being given him by non-commissioned officers, and every Marine in his Quonset hut is out to see that he becomes a real Marine as soon as possible.

He's not finding the Marine Corps life too strange, however, for after finishing several years at St. Joseph's Academy, Termonbacca, Londonderry, he worked in the Navy Yard here for several months for the United States Navy and met many Marines.

One thing is troubling him, however, that is that he will be unable to visit his grandmother in Creeslough, Erie, for that is a neutral country, and as a United States Marine he cannot enter the country.

But right now he's too busy with his "drill instructors", who drill him individually each morning and afternoon. He completed the Junior Technical Course at St. Joseph's, before his enlistment and hopes to get into the Marine Air Corps.

So far as Marines here know, he's the first Marine in the history of this war to earn the right to wear the European Theater of Operations ribbon on the day of his enlistment.

TOP "Private John J. Hargadon (right) waves goodbye to fellow students at St. Joseph's Academy before joining the United States Marines. Leaving with Private Hargadon is Sergeant Jack F. Burns, of Upper Darby, Pennsylvania, stationed at Londonderry." (USMC, photo by Cpl William R. Gibbon)

BOTTOM "A welcome to a new Marine is extended by Lieutenant Colonel James J. Dugan, of Quincy, Massachusetts to Private John J. Hargadon, just after the latter was sworn into the Marine Corps. Center is Captain John S. Hudson, of Washington DC, adjutant at the Londonderry base. Lieutenant Colonel Dugan arranged for Private Hargadon's enlistment by obtaining consent papers from the recruit's mother in the United States." Photos dated June 11, 1943. (USMC, photo by Cpl William R. Gibbon)

TOP Corporal William R. Gibbon, of Columbus, Ohio, a combat photographer, during field maneuvers at Londonderry, May 12, 1943. (USMC, photo by Cpl Robert Brathumn)

BOTTOM Sergeant Robert Davis, combat correspondent, during field maneuvers in Northern Ireland, May 12, 1943. Davis was eventually transferred to the Pacific in 1944 and took part in the battle of Iwo Jima and continued writing stories of Marines on ship detachments. (USMC, photo by Cpl William R. Gibbon)

While a Navy crew prepares their landing craft in the background, Marines prepare to start a rehearsal of a landing maneuver on a river near Londonderry, July 12, 1943. (USMC, photo by Cpl William R. Gibbon)

Standing in the landing craft as it heads for the beach are First Lieutenants Samuel S. Smith, Jr., Missouri, and James P. Metzler, Kansas City, Missouri. They are giving a unit of Marines a last-minute word before the Marines "hit the beach" in the practice landing maneuver, July 12, 1943. (USMC, photo by Cpl William R. Gibbon)

Even the backs of these US Marines express excitement as the ramp of their landing barge goes down and the men in the bow prepare to "hit the beach." (USMC, photo by Cpl William R. Gibbon)

Marines spread out along the beach as they leap from their landing barge. Ahead of them through the trees can be seen the smokescreen that will cover their advance across the field beyond the shore. (USMC, photo by Cpl William R. Gibbon)

TOP Just a few feet from the shore, Marines meet a high stone wall as their first objective. (USMC, photo by Cpl William R. Gibbon)

RIGHT A Marine machine-gun team on an Irish hillside during battle exercises, July 1943. The Marine on the right is 20-year-old Private First Class Lynn F. Kirk, of Rensselaer, New York. (USMC, photo by SSgt Weldon Keating)

Marines in Northern Ireland practice disembarking from their "ship" using cargo nets, September 1943. "With the help of a mock-up and constant practice, the Leathernecks have learned to save precious seconds on the time down to their landing craft." (USMC, photos by SSgt Weldon L. Keating)

TOP "Against a typical Irish background, these Marines pause at the roadside for a ten-minute break. Constant drill in combat exercises keeps them in peak fighting condition." Photo dated September 1943. (USMC, photo by SSgt Weldon L. Keating)

RIGHT "Through the mists and smoke of artificial battle in peaceful Northern Ireland, a lone Leatherneck charges toward the 'enemy.'" This photo was taken in September 1943 during exercises in which Marines demonstrated their landing skills and approved techniques for assaulting enemy strong points. (USMC, photo by SSgt Weldon L. Keating)

"From the looks on their faces, these Marines would more than welcome going to the front. They posed for their company picture at the end of recent battle exercises in the Irish hills. That sailor on the left, they say, is just a figment of your imagination. Commanding officer of the company is Captain George O. Ludoke, Jr., of Minneapolis, Minnesota, a former University of Minnesota boxer, wrestler, and footballer, seen in the center of the front row holding one of the company's mongrel mascots." Photo dated May 1943. (USMC, photo by SSgt Weldon Keating)

TOP "The finest shooting in the world isn't any good if your weapon isn't in condition, and at the Marine Corps camp, Private First Class Clifton Walker of Bullock, North Carolina, checks on the mechanism of an air-cooled .30-caliber machine gun as part of his duties as armorer for the Marines at Londonderry." Photo dated July 10, 1943. (USMC, photo by Cpl William R. Gibbon)

CENTER "First Sergeant James G. Oliver, left, of Selma, South Carolina, and Private First Class William H. Ryall, of Ansonia, Connecticut, show off a newly made flag of the United States Marine Corps detachment at Londonderry, where they are both stationed." Photo dated August 15, 1943. (USMC, photo by Cpl William R. Gibbon)

BOTTOM "Sergeant David L. Watson, of Tenafly, New Jersey, is the driver for Colonel Shaler Ladd, commanding officer, Marine Barracks, Londonderry, Northern Ireland." Photo dated October 15, 1943. (USMC, photo by Cpl William R. Gibbon)

TOP Sergeant John E. French, of Sterling, Connecticut, mail clerk at Marine Barracks, Londonderry, January 12, 1944. (USMC, photo by Cpl William R. Gibbon)

CENTER Mail driver Private First Class Charles Owen, of San Diego, California. Photo dated October 15, 1943. (USMC, photo by Cpl William R. Gibbon)

BOTTOM "Knowledge of the rifle, which may at times mean the winning of a battle, is also a source of amusement for US Marines, November 10, 1943. During a field day, Marines engage in a rifle assembling and disassembling contest while blindfolded. The winner of this event took his Garand M1 rifle apart and put it back together again in two minutes and 35 seconds." (USMC, photo by Cpl William R. Gibbon)

TOP A US Marine shore patrolman, Private First Class William L. Strong, Jr. of Toledo, Ohio, talks shop with members of the Royal Ulster Constabulary. Marine and Naval shore patrolmen patroled the streets of Londonderry to maintain order among servicemen, while members of the Constabulary acted as civilian police. Photo dated August 21, 1943. (USMC, photo by Cpl William R. Gibbon)

RIGHT This Christmas tree was a feature of USMC Christmas dance, parties, and other events. Photo dated December 23, 1943. (USMC, photo by Cpl William R. Gibbon)

LEFT Executive officer Lieutenant Colonel James J. Dugan, Marine Barracks, Londonderry, uses a walkie-talkie near the camp, November 6, 1943. (USMC, photo by SSgt James R. Kilpatrick)

RIGHT Beside a fireplace in the Lion and Eagle Club in Londonderry, a Marine and British Wren get together over a cigarette, November 2, 1943. (USMC, photo by SSgt James R. Kilpatrick)

"Turkey in the straw" is the objective of these Marines near the base of
Londonderry, November 1, 1943. (USMC, photo by SSgt James R. Kilpatrick)

"In case the quartermaster gets mixed up and forgets to send turkeys for Christmas, Marines can obtain some fine ones at nearby farms. Tender turkeys from the United States were on hand for Thanksgiving, but these live ones look a lot more like home." Photo dated November 1, 1943. (USMC, photo by SSgt James R. Kilpatrick)

Triple Drowning Near Derry – Three US Marines in Combat Exercise

Belfast Telegraph, **September 24, 1943**

In a triple drowning accident near Londonderry on Thursday afternoon three members of the United States Marine Corps lost their lives. The victims were Sergt. Fred I. Brevik (29), Pfc. Hughes W. Gobble, and Private James T. M'Gowan.

The tragedy took place while the men were engaged in combat exercises near their camp at Londonderry. The three men were drowned while the unit was fording a stream, and the bodies were recovered shortly afterwards. Every attempt was made at resuscitation, but without success.

Sacrificed Own Life

Details of the accident reveal that Sergt. Brevik, who had successfully crossed the river returned to the water and sacrificed his own life in an attempt to help his men.

Corporal Richard. A Hickland of 95 Buckingham St., Springfield, Mass., who with Sergt. Brevik had successfully crossed the river, said the sergeant dived into the water when he saw that his men were in trouble, but sank himself almost immediately. Corporal Hickland immediately removed his own pack and ammunition belt so that he could swim more freely, but by the time he had divested himself of his heavy gear all three had vanished.

Pfc. Harry E. Davis, of Weatherly, Penn., who had also crossed the stream attempted to warn those behind him that the water was deeper than had at first thought but by that time the others were in trouble. Reaching the bank Pfc. Davis held his rifle out to Sergt. Brevik, who had just reached the surface following his dive but the sergeant sank without grasping it. Five other Marines who had crossed the stream immediately began diving for the bodies, and sent a messenger for 1st Lieut. Wm. E. Skye, of Alexandria, Louisiana who was in charge of the detail of men engaged in the exercise. Lieut. Skye organized a search upon his arrival on the scene.

Also aiding in the search for the bodies were Royal Naval personnel stationed near the scene of the tragedy and American sailors from the Naval Base.

Sergeant Fred I. Brevik

By Commandant, Naval Operating Base Londonderry, Northern Ireland
November 13, 1943

CITATION:

The President of the United States of America takes pride in presenting the Navy and Marine Corps Medal (Posthumously) to Sergeant Fred I. Brevik (MCSN: 360164), United States Marine Corps, for heroism while engaged in leading a group of men across the Faughan River during a combat problem. Sergeant Brevik, after having safely made the crossing himself, noticed that several of his men were having difficulty in crossing the river. With utter disregard for his own safety, he assisted one man to climb up the bank of the river and then jumped back into the river and swam to the aid of two other men. His heroics were without avail, however, as during the ensuing struggle the lives of all three men were lost.

By Sergeant Robert Davis

Londonderry, Northern Ireland, September 27, 1943 – Funeral services for Sergeant Fred I. Brevik, USMC, son of Mrs. Jacob Brevik, 704 Second Street, SE, Watertown, South Dakota, were held here September 27.

Sergeant Brevik drowned when, after successfully crossing a stream near his camp here, he turned into the stream to attempt to rescue two of his men who were in trouble. All three drowned. At the time, the unit was on a combat training exercise.

Full military honors were rendered Sergeant Brevik and the other two Marines, Private First Class Hughes W. Gobble, son of Mrs. Mary A. Gobble, RFD 5, 101 Johnson City, Tenn. and Private James T. McGowan, son of Mrs. Rose McGowan, 27 Minot Street, Lynn, Mass.

Lieutenant (jg) Puall Hann, US Navy Chaplain Corps, of Winterset, Iowa, officiated at the services for Sergeant Brevik. The remains are to be interred at Brookwood Cemetery, an American military cemetery near London.

Detachments of United States Marines and sailors under Captain John Curley, USMC, of Glen Head, Long Island, NY acted as funeral escort. The temporary chapel used for the services on the base was crowded with Sergeant Brevik's fellow Marines.

Bearers were Corporals Frank L. Edwards, of Erie, PA, Philip N. Dzavison, of Chevy Chase, MD, Linwood J. Rathbone, of Charlestown, RI, William H. Maneely, of Philadelphia, PA, Harold Fogarty, of Detroit, Mich., James W. Ker, of Jordan, NY, Walter L. Hudson, of Atlanta, GA, and Richard A. Hickland, of Springfield, Mass.

US Marines and sailors assigned to NOB Londonderry hold funeral services for Sergeant Fred I. Brevik, Private First Class Hughes W. Gobble, and Private James T. McGowan. Photo dated September 27, 1943. (USMC, photos by Cpl William R. Gibbon)

The officer-in-charge and three members of the first USMC bagpipe band talk things over between rehearsals. From left to right are Private John A. Chartowich, of Bound Brook, New Jersey, First Lieutenant Doyle R. Walker, of Claude, Texas, Private William E. Meirs, of Kendall, New York, and Private First Class George E. Master, of Valley View, Kentucky. Photo dated April 1943. (USMC, photo by SSgt Weldon Keating)

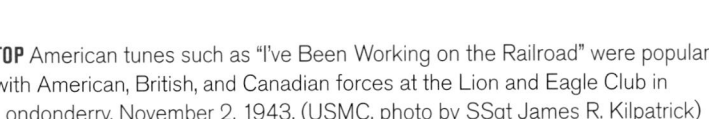

TOP American tunes such as "I've Been Working on the Railroad" were popular with American, British, and Canadian forces at the Lion and Eagle Club in Londonderry, November 2, 1943. (USMC, photo by SSgt James R. Kilpatrick)

LEFT Colonel Shaler Ladd, commanding officer, Marine Barracks, Londonderry, receives the colors during the 168th Marine Corps Birthday Ball, November 10, 1943. The ceremonies marked the 168th anniversary of the founding of the Marine Corps. (USMC, photo by Cpl William R. Gibbon)

RIGHT Private First Class John H. Kimbro, of Charlotte, North Carolina, stands a lonely vigil at the edge of his camp, November 4, 1943. (USMC, photo by SSgt James R. Kilpatrick)

ELSEWHERE **IN 1942**

JANUARY 23: The 7th Defense Battalion is reinforced by the 2nd Marine Brigade on Samoa

FEBRUARY 15: The British Garrison at Singapore surrenders to the Japanese

FEBRUARY 23: An oil refinery near Santa Barbara, California, is shelled by a Japanese submarine

FEBRUARY 27: US, UK, Dutch, and Australian naval forces are defeated at the battle of the Java Sea

MARCH 10: 132,000 acres are purchased in Santa Margarita Ranch, north of San Diego, and is named Camp Joseph H. Pendleton 11 days later

APRIL 9: Japanese artillery begins bombardment of Corregidor

MAY: Battle of the Coral Sea begins

MAY 5: Marines with 1st Battalion, 4th Marine Regiment engage Japanese forces landing on Corregidor

JUNE 3: Japanese forces strike Dutch Harbor, Alaska

JUNE 4: Japanese forces attack Midway Island

JUNE 5: US declares war on Bulgaria, Hungary, and Romania

JUNE 12–21: The Japanese occupy Attu and Kiska Islands in Alaska

By Sergeant Robert Davis

Londonderry, Northern Ireland, October 5, 1943 – Private Donald G. Trimby, USMC, who joined the United States Marines here a month ago, isn't quite sure just where they will hang out a service star in his honor.

It could be Carlisle, England, where he has lived for the past several years; in Hillsboro, Ill., where he was born and lived to the age of 8; in Perry, Iowa, where he spent the last war while his father was in charge of music for the YMCA at Camp Dodge; in Davenport, Iowa, where he lived from 1918 to 1920; or in Defiance, Ohio, where he lived between 1920 and 1923.

In 1923 he came with his parents, Mr. and Mrs. George Trimby to the British Isles, living first in Belfast, Northern Ireland, and later in Carlisle, England, where he was employed by a tailoring firm before joining the Marines.

His wife, a native of Belfast, Northern Ireland, has moved to Londonderry, where Private Trimby is stationed, as have his parents.

During his first month in the Marine Corps, Private Trimby received individual recruit instruction by a Marine non-commissioned officer. Now he is ready to start regular guard duty.

"Individual recruit training is being given to Private Donald G. Trimby, a native of Carlisle, England, who has joined the United States Marine Corps at Londonderry, September 20, 1943. Born in Hillsboro, Illinois, in 1909, Private Trimby lived there until 1917, when he moved, with his family, Mr. and Mrs. George Trimby, to Perry, Iowa. Later he lived in Davenport, Iowa, and Defiance, Ohio, before coming to the British Isles in 1924. His wife, a native of Belfast, Northern Ireland, is living in Londonderry, a few miles from the Marine camp, at present. In this picture with Private Trimby is Corporal Norman LeBel." (USMC, photo by Cpl William R. Gibbon)

FILE NO.
SERIAL:

U. S. NAVAL OPERATING BASE
LONDONDERRY, NORTHERN IRELAND

C-O-N-F-I-D-E-N-T-I-A-L W-A-R D-I-A-R-Y

17 July 1944:

Work continued on the USS DONNELL, USS DAVIS and USS NELSON by the Repair Force. US LST 289 slipped from Berth #19 at 1105 this date and proceeded to sea.

Stores and provisions were issued to USS BATES, USS BULL, USS NELSON, USS HURST, US LST 289, USS DAVIS, USS RICKETTS and S/S HILLSBORO INLET (W.S.A. #5).

The Commanding Officer, Marine Barracks, U.S. Naval Operating Base, Londonderry requested that the Marine Guards at Talbot House (Communication Center) and Marine Guards at Lisahally Tank Farm be secured in view of the British Civic Guard assuming responsibility this date. Permission was granted by the Commandant at 0930 this date to secure both Marine Guard Details at Talbot House and Lisahally Tank Farm.

18 July 1944:

Work continued on the USS DONNELL, USS DAVIS and USS NELSON by the Repair Force.

Stores and provisions were issued to USS NELSON and USS DONNELL.

19 July 1944:

Work continued on the USS DONNELL, USS DAVIS and USS NELSON by the Repair Force.

Stores were issued to the USS NELSON.

A fire broke out in the Springtown Camp Brig at 2210 this date due to overheating of the stove pipe which in turn ignited the insulation within the bulkhead. Fire was completely extinguished at 2235. No casualties were reported. Damage resulting from fire consisted of five (5) frames of the hut which require replacement.

20 July 1944:

Work continued on the USS DONNELL, USS DAVIS and USS NELSON. USS NELSON slipped from Drydock and tied up to Berth #19 at the Repair Yard at 2230.

- 8 -

THIS AND SUBSEQUENT PAGES Document detailing the removal of the Marine guards from Talbot House and Lisahally Tank Farm, July 1944. (US Navy)

FILE NO.
SERIAL:

U. S. NAVAL OPERATING BASE
LONDONDERRY, NORTHERN IRELAND

C-O-N-F-I-D-E-N-T-I-A-L W-A-R D-I-A-R-Y

26 July 1944: (continued)

PATRICK at 1610, USS PETERSON at 1625, and USS GANDY at 1645.

The decommissioning records of the U. S. Naval Hospital No. ONE were shipped

to the Medical Officer in Command, Medical Supply Depot, New York.

27 July 1944:

Work completed on the USS NELSON.

29 July 1944:

The following ships arrived at Lisahally at times indicated: USS LAWRENCE

at 1315, USS HOPPING at 1455, USS SIMS at 1345, USS GRIFFIN at 1615, and USS

REEVES at 1815.

A draft of 160 men and 2 officers from the 97th Naval Construction Battalion

departed for Exeter, England.

31 July 1944.

Three motor launches slipped from berth #19, Repair Yard, at 0800 and pro-

ceeded to Belfast, Northern Ireland. These launches were transferred to the

Naval Port Officer at that port as part of the decommissioning program of this

base.

Personnel on board as of this date. Enlisted personnel; ship's company-

1382; for further transfer - 92; 97th Construction Battalion 895; U.S. Marines

406. Officer Personnel: Ships Company - 56; 97th Construction Battalion - 18;

U.S. Marines - 19.

12

CHAPTER 2

MARINES HELP BEFORE US INVOLVEMENT IN WORLD WAR II

OCCUPATION OF ICELAND

At the outbreak of World War II, Iceland was of keen interest to the Germans. It could provide an excellent staging area and base from which to further harass the British. After several failed diplomatic attempts to persuade the Danish government to join the side of the Allies, Churchill sent an invasion force on May 10, 1940, one month after Germany invaded Denmark, of which Iceland was a part. The initial invasion force of 700 Royal Marines was followed up by soldiers from the British Army and then replaced by Canadian troops. By the summer of 1941, the British would have 25,000 troops on Iceland. Throughout the war, Iceland's government would remain officially neutral but would cooperate with the Allies.

While insignificant from a US military planner perspective, the island of Iceland was of major strategic value to the British. The island's location provided intermediate naval and air facilities, and more importantly, the stationing of US troops in Iceland freed up British troops to be redeployed to defend Great Britain's interests. On June 5, 1941, Roosevelt directed the Chief of Naval Operations, Admiral Harold R. Stark, to have a Marine brigade ready to sail for Iceland within 15 days. The news could not have reached Churchill at a better time. British forces had completed the famous withdrawal from Dunkirk, France, exactly one year prior and were in the midst of rebuilding and rearming their forces. The freeing of thousands of troops from Iceland to bring back to the UK was welcome news for the British.

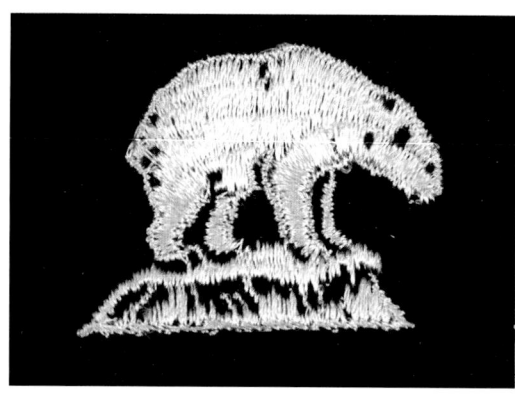

Patch of the British 49th Infantry Division that was bestowed upon the Marines stationed in Iceland. (NARA)

On June 16, 1941, the 1st Provisional Marine Brigade was formed with Brigadier General John Marston in command. Marston's instructions from Stark were simple. "In cooperation with British garrison, defend Iceland against hostile attack." The 4,100-strong Marine brigade departed Charleston, South Carolina, on June 22, 1941. Upon leaving Charleston Harbor, the transports were met by their escorts: USS *New York* (B-34), USS *Arkansas* (BB-33), USS *Nashville* (CL-43), and USS *Brooklyn* (CL-40), all of which carried their own Marine detachments. In all, close to 4,600 Marines were now on their way to Iceland.

After some initial conversations about command relationships, it was decided the Marines would be placed under British control as they had the most senior ranking officer and had more forces on the island. Major General Henry O. Curtis, commander of the British Army's 49th Division, suggested to Marston that the Marines should wear the patch of the 49th Division as a show of solidarity. On September 10, 1941, Marston received approval from the Commandant of the Marine Corps, Lieutenant General Thomas Holcomb, for the Marines to wear the patches on both shoulders of their uniform. However, the order also stated that once the Marines left Iceland, the shoulder patches had to be removed. Although limited, this was the first approved shoulder patch worn by Marines in World War II.

During their time in Iceland, the Marines practiced defense of the island, played sports with their British cousins, and made friends with the locals, with some even being invited into Icelandic family homes for Christmas dinner. Christmas was particularly merry. The Marines received a proper Christmas dinner complete with baked ham, turkey, and the accustomed side dishes. Most importantly, the beer and cigars were free that night. The week prior, the Navy was able to provide a small number of Christmas trees for the mess halls and the first heavy snow of the season fell, providing a real white Christmas. While the news of the December 7 attack was grim, it did not change their stance as they had been on an alert status upon their arrival.

In January 1942, US Army units began arriving in Iceland to take over defense missions, and the Marines received orders to return to the United States. By March 31, 1942, a majority of the Marines had returned stateside, save a few small elements. Many of the Marines who returned would go on to participate in battles at Guadalcanal and Tulagi six months later, fighting the Japanese in the Pacific, after taking part against the Germans in the Battle of the Atlantic. A company of Marines was left in Iceland for the duration of the war to guard the Navy fleet air base at Reykjavik. The company would be disbanded and sent back stateside in October 1945.

LEFT The *Daily Alaska Empire*, July 7, 1941. (LoC)

RIGHT *Imperial Valley Press*, July 7, 1941. (LoC)

Seen from the quarterdeck of USS *New York* (BB-34), Atlantic Fleet ships steam out of Reykjavik Harbor at the time of the initial US occupation in early July 1941. The next ship astern is USS *Arkansas* (BB-33), followed by USS *Brooklyn* (CL-40) and USS *Nashville* (CL-43). (US Navy)

INSET The *Evening Star*, Washington DC, September 6, 1941. (LoC)

Britain and U. S. Make Iceland Their Gibraltar of the North

American Marines, in Position Alongside English, Occupy an Important Place

(Drew Middleton of the London Associated Press Bureau, who covered the B. E. F. in France and reported subsequent war developments in Britain, has arrived in Iceland. He tells in this dispatch of military activities on the North Atlantic island.)

By DREW MIDDLETON,
Associated Press War Correspondent.

REYKJAVIK, Iceland, Sept. 6.— Within a few short months this Atlantic island ocean has been turned into a United States-British Gibraltar of the North.

Iceland bristles today with guns, airfields dot the countryside and warships of America and Britain comb surrounding waters in ever-watchful patrols.

Newly-arrived observers are impressed at once with the defenses of this keystone in a communications arch over which arms and materials pass from America to Great Britain. Gibraltar itself and Malta in the Mediterranean are scarcely more strongly-held than this barren land, which is half again the size of Ireland.

Marines Have Important Place.

Censorship, of course, will not permit disclosure of the number of men or the amount of equipment here, but it can be said that the American, British and Norwegian forces on the island exceed the number of trained troops Britain had to repel invasion in the summer of 1940.

United States marines in olive-green uniforms occupy an important place in Iceland's defense plans. Their guns and tanks have taken up positions alongside the British.

The British appear to have great respect for the marines, who settled on the island as though it were the most natural place in the world to be.

In planning the defenses of Iceland no possibility has been overlooked.

Within Planes' Range.

The island is within range of troop-carrying planes based on the European continent, and the long nights would afford protection for a hostile flotilla creeping down past Greenland to effect a landing in the north.

American and British officers have studied these problems and have made their plans accordingly.

So well have these forces done their work that submarine sinkings in this part of the Atlantic have dropped to a new low. One report has it that not a single merchant ship has gone down along the northern route from the United States to Great Britain in the past seven weeks.

TOP An LCP takes fully equipped Marines to a landing inside the breakwater at Reykjavik Harbor, July 1941. (US Navy)

BOTTOM LEFT Uniforms reminiscent of World War I characterize this detachment of Marines in the city of Reykjavik, 1941. (USMC)

BOTTOM RIGHT Private Robert C. Fowler is welcomed by British gunner Harold Ricardi, as the Marines arrive at a British base in Iceland, July 1941. (US Navy)

PRIME MINISTER CHURCHILL VISITS ICELAND

Accompanied by a U. S. Marine officer (left), British Prime Minister Winston Churchill (knee-length coat) and Ensign Franklin D. Roosevelt, Jr., (center) salute the United States flag as they inspected U. S. Marines during a recent visit to Iceland on Churchill's return trip to England from his meeting with President Roosevelt.

TOP LEFT The *Nome Nugget*, September 10, 1941. (LoC)

OTHER IMAGES Prime Minister Churchill's visit to Iceland, August 16, 1941. On the return journey from his meeting with President Roosevelt, Churchill stopped in Iceland to inspect the Marines. (piemags/ww2archive/Alamy)

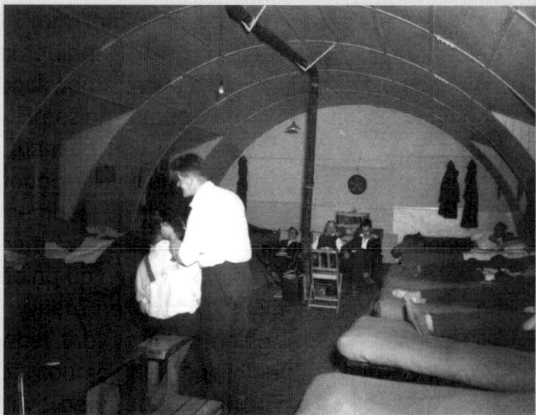

TOP Marines practice movement and trench-clearing procedures, 1941. (USMC)

BOTTOM RIGHT Living quarters for Marines in Iceland. Photo dated October 23, 1941. (USMC)

BOTTOM LEFT Among the many types of weapons brought to Iceland by Marines in 1941 and 1942 was the small but deadly 37mm gun. A Marine gun crew, wearing the British polar bear insignia on their caps, prepares its piece for action in maneuvers. (USMC)

TOP LEFT Marine sentry on duty, October 13, 1941. (USMC)

TOP RIGHT Marines on liberty in Iceland, October 1941. (USMC)

BOTTOM "To walk my post in a military manner." A Marine sentinel walks his post along the shore of one of Iceland's many lakes. Photo dated March 23, 1942. (USMC)

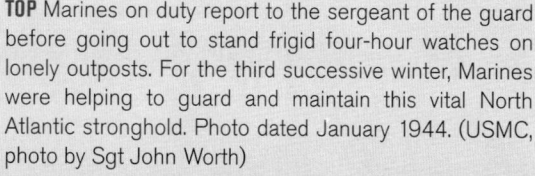

TOP Marines on duty report to the sergeant of the guard before going out to stand frigid four-hour watches on lonely outposts. For the third successive winter, Marines were helping to guard and maintain this vital North Atlantic stronghold. Photo dated January 1944. (USMC, photo by Sgt John Worth)

BOTTOM LEFT A US Marine reports to his superiors over a walkie-talkie. Photo dated 1942. (USMC)

BOTTOM RIGHT "These Marines in fur-collared cold-weather gear stand on the chilly 'Main Street' of their wooden-fronted and coke-and-coal-stove-heated Nissen hut encampment." Photo dated January 1944. (USMC)

TOP Five sergeants on the corner of the company street running through their camp, January 1944. Note the street sign. The streets were named after Marine camps in the United States. (USMC)

BOTTOM "From the sunny climes of Dixie to the bleak Icelandic shore, these Southern lads have come to serve at one of the most northern outposts ever maintained by the Marine Corps." Photo dated October 28, 1943. (USMC)

Marine ship detachment patch, approved by the Commandant of the Marine Corps for Marines serving aboard ships. (Author's collection)

MARINE SHIP DETACHMENTS

Since the founding of the United States, Marines had traditionally served aboard Navy ships, primarily in a security role, while also providing short-term ship-to-shore landing support and raiding parties when necessary. By 1940, Marine detachments were assigned to all large capital warships of the US Navy, including carriers, battleships, heavy and light cruisers. These detachments varied in size depending on the ship; battleships typically carried the largest Marine contingents, with two to three officers and over 100 enlisted personnel, while carriers and heavy cruisers might have one or two officers and approximately 80 enlisted Marines. Light cruisers, on the other hand, generally carried one officer and 45 enlisted personnel. Occasionally, destroyers would have a small group of Marines aboard, usually if a high-ranking official, such as a general or an admiral, was being transported. Some escort carriers might also carry Marines, depending on the availability of personnel for sea duty.

In the years leading up to World War II, the US Navy often deployed ships on diplomatic and goodwill missions to strengthen relations with other nations. During these missions, it was common to see Marines participate in local parades or engage in other public-facing activities to enhance diplomatic ties.

However, by 1942, the bulk of Marine detachments aboard Navy ships was concentrated in the Pacific. This shift was driven by the Navy's increased need for vessels in the Pacific due to the vast distances between islands and the limited ability of European nations such as France and the United Kingdom to provide naval support so far from home. As the fighting in Europe and North Africa moved inland, the need for naval gunfire support in those theaters diminished, allowing many ships to be reassigned to the Pacific. A few ships, however, would be transferred back from the Pacific to the Atlantic to continue supporting convoy operations.

Marine duties aboard ship included:

- Running the ship's brig
- Limiting access to sensitive areas of the ship such as the bridge and engine room
- Acting as a training element for the ship's landing parties, which comprised both Marines and sailors
- Providing personnel for ceremonial occasions
- Serving as orderlies and drivers for sea-based flag officers and ships' captains

- Operating secondary ship gun batteries such as the 5-inch, 40mm, and 20mm guns.

MARINE DETACHMENTS ON SHIPS

Carriers

USS *Ranger* (CV-4) – Notable participation: Operation *Torch*, Operation *Leader*. Transferred from the Atlantic to Pacific July 1944

USS *Wasp* (CV-7) – Notable participation: Convoy escort duty, Operation *Bowery*, Operation *Calendar*. Transferred from the Atlantic to Pacific May 1942

USS *Santee* (CVE-29) – Notable participation: Convoy escort duty, South Atlantic antisubmarine patrols, Operation *Torch*. Transferred to the Pacific February 1944

USS *Chenango* (CVE-28) – Notable participation: Operation *Torch*, antisubmarine patrols. Transferred to the Pacific December 1942

USS *Suwannee* (CVE-27) – Notable participation: Operation *Torch*, antisubmarine patrols. Transferred to the Pacific December 1942

USS *Sangamon* (CVE-26) – Notable participation: Operation *Torch*, antisubmarine patrols. Transferred to the Pacific December 1942

Battleships

USS *Arkansas* (BB-33) – Notable participation: Convoy escort duty, Operation *Overlord*, Operation *Dragoon*. Transferred to the Pacific November 1944

USS *New York* (BB-34) – Notable participation: Convoy escort duty, Operation *Torch*. Transferred to the Pacific November 1944

USS *Texas* (BB-35) – Notable participation: Convoy escort duty, Operation *Torch*, Operation *Overlord*, Operation *Dragoon*. Transferred to the Pacific September 1944

USS *Nevada* (BB-36) – Notable participation: Operation *Overlord*, Operation *Dragoon*. Transferred from the Pacific to the Atlantic summer 1943

USS *Washington* (BB-56) – Notable participation: Convoy escort duty. Transferred to the Pacific August 1942

USS *South Dakota* (BB-57) – Notable participation: Convoy escort duty, Operation *Husky*. Transferred from the Pacific to the Atlantic February 1943 and back to the Pacific August 1944

Heavy Cruisers

USS *Augusta* (CA-31) – Notable participation: Convoy escort duty, Operation *Torch*, Operation *Overlord*, Operation *Dragoon*

USS *Tuscaloosa* (CA-37) – Notable participation: Operation *Torch*, Operation *Leader*, Operation *Overlord*, Operation *Dragoon*. Transferred to the Pacific September 1944

USS *Wichita* (CA-45) – Notable participation: Convoy escort duty, Operation *Torch*. Transferred to the Pacific January 1943

USS *Quincy* (CA-71) – Notable participation: VIP escort duty, Operation *Overlord*. Transferred to the Pacific March 1945

Light Cruisers

USS *Omaha* (CL-4) – Notable participation: South Atlantic antisubmarine patrols, convoy escort duty, Operation *Dragoon*

USS *Milwaukee* (CL-5) – Notable participation: South Atlantic antisubmarine patrols, convoy escort duty

USS *Cincinnati* (CL-6) – Notable participation: South Atlantic antisubmarine patrols, convoy escort duty

USS *Marblehead* (CL-12) – Notable participation: South Atlantic antisubmarine patrols, convoy escort duty, Operation *Dragoon*. Transferred from the Pacific to the Atlantic winter 1942

USS *Memphis* (CL-13) – Notable participation: South Atlantic antisubmarine patrols, convoy escort duty, VIP escort duty

USS *Brooklyn* (CL-40) – Notable participation: Convoy escort duty, Operation *Torch*, Operation *Husky*, Operation *Shingle*, Operation *Dragoon*

USS *Philadelphia* (CL-41) – Notable participation: Convoy escort duty, Operation *Torch*, Operation *Husky*, Operation *Avalanche*, Operation *Dragoon*

USS *Savannah* (CL-42) – Notable participation: South Atlantic antisubmarine patrols, convoy escort duty, Operation *Torch*, Operation *Husky*, Operation *Avalanche*

USS *Boise* (CL-47) – Notable participation: Operation *Husky*, Operation *Avalanche*

US Ambassador to France Admiral William D. Leahy is welcomed aboard USS *Tuscaloosa* (CA-37) on December 17, 1940 by the Marine Detachment. The *Tuscaloosa* departed Norfolk and transported Leahy and his wife, Louise, to France. It was hoped Leahy could open lines of communication with Philippe Pétain, the Chief of the French State, also known as Vichy France. This was a government allowed to remain in place for a short while by Nazi Germany due to French leaders adopting a policy of collaboration with the Germans after the 1940 armistice. (US Navy)

Marines assigned to USS *Ranger* (CV-4) take part in short-range target practice with the ship's 5-inch/.25-caliber antiaircraft deck guns, August 1942. This was a heavy antiaircraft gun for the US born from the constraints and requirements of the Washington Naval Treaty prior to the start of World War II. It would be replaced by the 5-inch/.38-caliber as the war went on. Photos are taken near Norfolk, Virginia, after the ship had just returned from North Africa delivering Army P-40 Warhawks in time for the Second Battle of El Alamein. (US Navy)

TOP Ship's Marine Detachment on the flight deck of USS *Wasp* (CV-7) during an inspection, June 1942, at San Diego. (USMC)

BOTTOM LEFT Captain Forrest P. Sherman, commanding officer of USS *Wasp*, inspects the Marine Detachment. The *Wasp* and its crew had been taking part in defending Allied convoy escort duties in the Atlantic just one month prior. *Wasp* saw action in both the Atlantic and Pacific. (USMC)

BOTTOM RIGHT Taken during an inspection aboard USS *Wasp* at San Diego, California, in June 1942. Note that these two sergeants have Navy "gun pointer first class" and "E" with "hash mark" insignia on their right sleeves. These Marines would be some of the few to see action in both the Atlantic and Pacific. (USMC)

TOP In August 1942, Marines aboard USS *Ranger* man a CXAM-1 radar and Mk 33 gun director apparatus atop the ship's superstructure during gunnery practice offshore near Norfolk, Virginia. Note the "MD" on the back of the jackets denoting Marine Detachment. (USMC)

BOTTOM The Marine Detachment aboard USS *South Dakota* (BB-57) salute during an inspection on May 22, 1943 at Scapa, Scotland. (piemags/ ww2archive/Alamy)

ABOVE His Majesty King George VI inspects the Marine Detachment aboard USS *Washington* (BB-56) on June 7, 1942. During his visit, the King toured several ships assigned to the Home Fleet near Scapa. (piemags/ww2archive/Alamy)

INSET Marines salute President Harry Truman and his aide Captain James K. Vardaman coming aboard the USS *Augusta* (CA-31) for the return voyage from Potsdam Conference, August 6, 1945. (US Navy)

TOP Secretary of the Navy Frank Knox inspects the Marine Detachment aboard USS *Augusta*, September 1943. (piemags/ww2archive/Alamy)

BOTTOM Marine Detachment aboard USS *Tuscaloosa* goes through a fitness drill with weapons, April 6, 1943. (US Navy)

General Dwight D. Eisenhower inspects USS *Quincy* (CA-71) at Belfast Lough, Northern Ireland, on May 18, 1944, shortly before the Normandy invasion. Rear Admiral Alan G. Kirk is following immediately behind. Note the Fleet Marine Force seahorse shoulder patch worn by the Marine at right. (US Navy)

"A veteran of the Solomon Islands campaign, Gunnery Sergeant Ernest Roessner, aboard the USS *Alabama* (BB-60), of Burke, South Dakota, can now claim the distinction of having served in all theaters of this war. As the ship's score painted in the background indicates, their fighting ability is well established in the South Pacific. Now ships, sailors, and Marines are in the North Atlantic with hopes of testing their fighting ability against the Nazis." Photo dated July 1943. (USMC, photo by SSgt Weldon Keating)

Marine Captain Francis R. Schlesinger, of Franklin, New Hampshire, salutes King George VI during an inspection of USS *Augusta* following the Normandy invasion. The King talked with Captain Schlesinger for several minutes, asking his age, length of service aboard the *Augusta*, and how he liked the US Marine Corps. (USMC)

Illinois Marine on Battleship

By First Lieutenant Weldon James, US Marine Corps Public Relations Officer
August 29, 1943

USS *Alabama* – Look for the typical young American aboard one of the great ships of the "new Navy," and you wouldn't go far wrong in picking out Marine First Lieutenant Natt Kemper Hammer, of Decatur, Illinois.

Today, Hammer, like all his shipmates, is primarily concerned with striking as hefty a blow as can be struck against whatever part of the German navy or air force that dares show itself.

Husky, pink-cheeked, possessed of an infectious grin and a no-less-evident impatience to get on with the war, Hammer is a fighting man well trained for his job. He has qualified as an expert with the bayonet, the automatic rifle, and the machine gun, and as a sharpshooter with the rifle. By training, and now by experience, he knows his business as controlling officer of an anti-aircraft battery of this dreadnought, knows how to discharge all the duties required of him as an officer of the ship's Marine Detachment.

None of these things were true a scant 30-odd months ago.

Back in the spring of 1941 young Hammer was what he believes as green a civilian as ever attended James Millikin University. He was pretty remote from the war, even in thought, in those days; he was busy holding down the job of president of Sigma Alpha Epsilon and of Alpha Beta (business), of getting ready for graduation, of pleasantly worrying over when would be the best time for him to marry his best girl (he's done that, too since, along with becoming a Marine), of debating just what his first post-graduation job in the business world ought to be.

He had gained vacation-time experience earlier as a salesman for the American Tobacco Company – "the Lucky Strike man, I was," he recalls – and decided in favor of more.

But in the summer after his graduation young Natt Hammer, like many another Americans, decided that war was not only coming, but soon. He wrapped up all his peace-time plans, except those for his girl, and in July he enlisted in the Marine Corps.

Ten months after his enlistment Private First Class Hammer, having completed the officer-candidates training at Quantico, Virginia, pridefully accepted his commission as a second lieutenant in the Marine Corps. He had reason to be doubly proud. He knew in advance that the program was tough, that the instructors regularly flunked out 30-percent of the hand-picked candidates. He knew, too that only a handful of those qualifying for commissions were chosen as regular (and not reserve) officers of the Marine Corps – but on April 3, 1942, he found that Natt Kemper Hammer, the green young business man of the summer before, was one of the handful of regulars in his class.

From that time on, he recalls, time ceased dragging. "I used to think it was even going backwards, in candidates' class," he said.

Breezing through more months of training in Quantico and at Portsmouth, the transformed young Illinoisan found himself eventually a member of the Marine Detachment of this battlewagon, found himself, too, last January, going up a notch in rank.

Where he and his shipmates have been and what they've been doing in recent months is, of course, not public information. But they have been sticking their necks out in various parts of the world, including a spot too near the top of it, they will tell you, and among their prized possessions is the blue-nose certificate awarded to all seafaring men who have crossed the Arctic Circle.

Most of the millions of young Americans in uniform, of course, have not yet come to close grips with the enemy. In this, Hammer, again like his shipmates, thinks his typicalness is grievous, unfair.

In the midst of this potential deadliness to which they are constantly exposed, Hammer and his shipmates in what they ironically term their spare time make this dreadnought a floating university. The new Navy and the expanding Marine Corps want every man-jack and officer in the service to qualify himself for the next two and three and four notches above his current job and this entails an endless amount of schooling at sea as well as at the training bases ashore. Like other officers in the naval service, Hammer not only bones up on textbook, lectures, and correspondence schooling himself, but instructs classes of enlistment men in subjects designed to earn them higher rating and improve their usefulness in war.

He is eagerly ambitious to go up in the service, and he wants his men to be as well. Besides, as he explains, it makes even the dullest of routine days at sea fly by, and he is all for that.

Talk with him some night on the mid watch, as a driving wind from the north sends shivers through the vigilant members of his gun crew, and you'll get the rest of the picture.

First Lieutenant Hammer is not troubled by any complicated or conflicting attitudes toward the war. He believes quite simply that both the Germans and Japanese richly deserve the beating they are going to get, and he is impatiently eager to speed that beating, as he put it, by lending a very personal hand.

He speculates a great deal, with his men and his brother officers, on what the shape of peace is likely to be. But it doesn't worry him much; he is convinced that it will be a confounded sight better than the war, and of one thing he is quite happily certain: it will enable him to be much more with his young wife.

And that, of course, is pretty much the crux of the matter. Lend an ear for a moment, and Hammer, like a million other young husbands overseas, will cease to be a tough, professional fighting man; he will show you not only the picture of his wife, but all the snapshots as well, and happily will tell you about how lovely and charming a girl she is.

You will sense that he cannot think about the war, or any aspect of it, except in terms of his wife and his home. That his normal, efficiently motivating hatred for the enemy is doubled every day by the pursuit of the enemy that keeps him from her side.

"I guess I'm like a lot of you guys," Hammer muses. "I guess she is my war aim and my peace aim."

She lives in Chicago, Illinois.

"First Lieutenant Nate Kemper Hammer of Decatur, Illinois, is pictured here at his battle station on USS *Alabama* in the North Atlantic in July 1943. Born August 30, 1919, in Indianapolis, Indiana, he attended the public schools in Decatur, and graduated from James Millikin University in 1941 after serving as president of the local chapters of Sigma Alpha Epsilon (social) and Alpha Beta (business) fraternities and engaging in intramural athletics. Formerly a salesman of the American Tobacco Company, he enlisted in the Marine Corps Reserve in July 1941, ten months later won a commission as a regular officer, and in January 1943 was appointed a first lieutenant." (UMSC, photo by SSgt Weldon Keating)

Indiana Marine on Battleship

By First Lieutenant Weldon James, US Marine Corps Public Relations Officer, and Staff Sergeant M. H. Dunlap, US Marine Corps Combat Correspondent, August 12, 1943

USS *Alabama* – Sergeant Donald R. Zinn is one Marine who can tell the boys in the South Pacific what the other side of the world is like, from the North Pole right down to the warmer waters off the European coast.

Sergeant Zinn, a 21-year-old from Alma, Michigan, is a member of the Marine detachment aboard this great battlewagon. These Leatherneck guardsmen and ack-ack gunners, with their naval shipmates, have for months past been engaged in a deadly game of hide-and-seek with the German naval forces.

The details of their frigid search and the composition of the Anglo-American task force with which they have been serving must remain military secrets. But it is permissible to say that in their long months away from America these sailors and Marines have seen much of the "far off norther lands," that they crossed the

Arctic Circle and were issued their blue-nose certificates, and that at one time they were within a scant 800 miles of the North Pole itself.

For Sergeant Zinn it's been much colder weather than he ever dreamed of when he enlisted in the Marine Corps back in Detroit in November 1940. From there he went to Parris Island, South Carolina, for recruit training, then to Quantico, Virginia, and to Sea School at Portsmouth, Virginia, prior to joining the battleship.

Born Sept 4, 1922, he attended high school in Alma, where he played baseball and was cartoonist on the school paper, before enlisting.

Like other "arctic veterans," Sergeant Zinn wants to crack the Germans first, hopes then for "a warmer assignment with the Japs in the South Pacific."

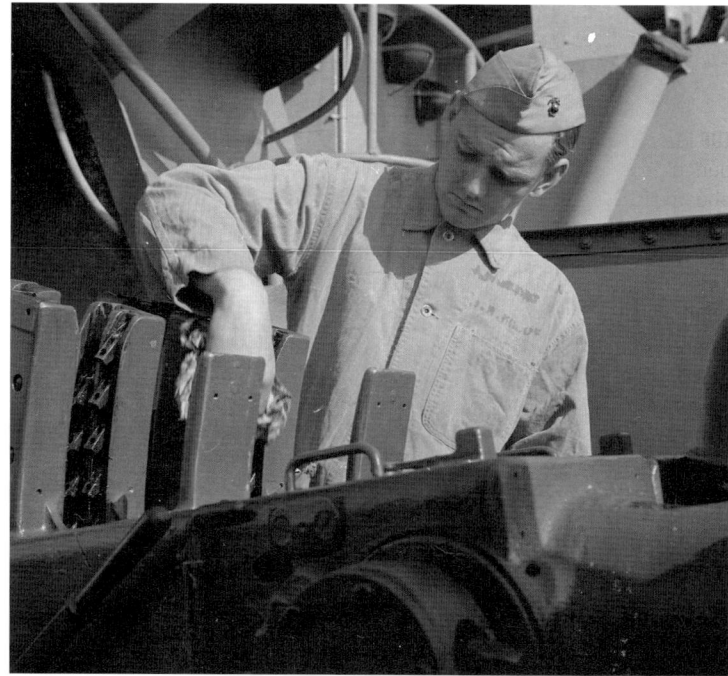

"Private First Class James R. McCoy aboard USS *Alabama* can tell the men in the South Pacific what the weather is like near the North Pole. He's been about everywhere the Arctic winds blow, he says. The 22-year-old son of Mrs. Cloe McCoy, of Churubusco, Indiana, Pfc McCoy attended Churubusco High School and was active in a rifle club before enlisting in the Marine Corps in November 1941." Photo dated July 1943. (USMC, photo by SSgt Weldon Keating)

TOP Major Harold S. Roise during general quarters drill aboard USS *Alabama*, July 1943. (USMC, photo by Cpl William R. Gibbon)

RIGHT Privates First Class Charles Makiunis and John L. Yan practice firing at a sleeve target in the North Atlantic aboard USS *Alabama*, July 1943. "While on search for the hidden German fleet, they constantly try out their antiaircraft guns and other powerful new weapons now carried by new US battleships." (USMC, photo by SSgt Weldon Keating)

THE ATLANTIC CHARTER

The Atlantic Charter was a pivotal document released on August 14, 1941, following a meeting between President Franklin D. Roosevelt and British Prime Minister Winston Churchill aboard the USS *Augusta* (CA-31) in Placentia Bay, Newfoundland. The Charter outlined the shared objectives of the United States and the United Kingdom in their fight against the Axis powers and set the tone for the postwar world order. Although the United States had already supported Britain with the Lend-Lease Act in March 1941, the British were facing significant challenges on multiple fronts. German forces had inflicted severe defeats on British Empire troops in Greece and North Africa. There was also the threat of Axis forces cutting off British access to India by sealing the Suez Canal. India had become an economic, military, and strategic cornerstone of the British Empire, providing vital resources, manpower, and a base for operations across Asia. Its loss would have meant the collapse of Britain's global influence, making its defense a top priority during World War II. So influential was India to the British that it was often referred to as the "jewel in the crown" of the Empire. Meanwhile, in the Pacific, Britain feared that Japan might seize the opportunity of Britain's weakened position to take control of British, French, and Dutch territories in Southeast Asia.

The signing of the Atlantic Charter had mixed results. While both Roosevelt and Churchill hoped it would rally American public support for entering World War II, it did not achieve that immediate goal. However, the Charter did serve a vital purpose in publicly solidifying the strong

Sailors and Marines from both the United Kingdom and the United States at church services aboard the Royal Navy battleship HMS *Prince of Wales* during the Atlantic Charter, August 10, 1941. Note the three US Marines in dress blues. The original caption for this photo states the US ship in the background is the USS *Augusta* (CA-31). However, this is incorrect as the ship is too small and the *Augusta*'s main turrets had three barrels each whereas the above has two. The ship is more than likely USS *McDougal* (DD-358), one of five US destroyers at the conference. Other photos exist of the *McDougal* tied up alongside the *Prince of Wales* for the event. (NARA)

partnership between the US and Britain in their common struggle against the Axis powers. This alignment was significant in demonstrating to the world the resolve of the two nations, even as the United States remained officially neutral in the conflict. The principles laid out in the Atlantic Charter would later serve as a foundation for many postwar agreements and the creation of international institutions like the United Nations.

As was customary during the time, Marines provided security details for the President on ship and were present during the activities of the historical event.

TOP Informal group photograph including President Franklin D. Roosevelt and Prime Minister Winston S. Churchill on the deck of HMS *Prince of Wales* following church services during the Atlantic Charter. Shown behind Roosevelt and Churchill are Admiral Ernest J. King and General George C. Marshall. A US Marine can be seen in the background, center. (NARA)

BOTTOM *Evening Star*, August 15, 1941. The US Marine from the group photo can also be seen in the newspaper. (LoC)

CHAPTER 3

TAKING THE FIGHT TO THE GERMANS

Of the nearly half a million men and women who served in the US Marine Corps during World War II, only several hundred can claim the distinction of directly engaging with German forces. These engagements ranged from a sole US Marine among hundreds of US Army troops to hundreds of Marines.

OPERATION *JUBILEE*

In early 1942, American and British planners were deep in discussions on where and how to strike Hitler next. Following the evacuation at Dunkirk and the successful defense of the British homeland during the Battle of Britain in 1940, Fighter Command of the Royal Air Force found itself with fewer immediate threats to confront. To keep their pilots active and their skills sharp, British leadership began tasking them with small-scale "hit-and-run" raids against German airfields, supply depots, and defensive positions along the French coast. For a short while, RAF pilots enjoyed near-total air superiority, wreaking havoc on German trucks, aircraft, fuel depots, and ammunition stockpiles. However, this dominance was challenged in the spring of 1941 when the Luftwaffe introduced the formidable Focke-Wulf Fw 190 fighter, which quickly tipped the balance in the skies.

Unwilling to cede control of the skies to the Germans, British planners decided to launch an amphibious raid along the French coast to provoke a German response. It was anticipated that the Luftwaffe would react

OPPOSITE *Imperial Valley Press*, August 19, 1942. (LoC)

aggressively, sending a large force of fighters into battle. The hope was that a massive air engagement would unfold over western France, allowing the RAF to draw out and destroy a significant portion of the German fighter force.

Dieppe was selected as the site for the Allied raid, involving 5,000 Canadian troops, 1,000 British Commandos, 50 US Army Rangers, and three US Marines: Captain Roy Batterton, Sergeant Robert R. Ryan, and Corporal Paul E. Cramer. Originally scheduled for July 3, 1942, the plan called for seizing and holding the town of Dieppe for a single day. The objectives were to destroy German supplies, capture prisoners, gather intelligence, and test German coastal defenses. The operation also served as a critical opportunity for the Allies to trial tactics, techniques, and procedures for landing troops and equipment on a defended shoreline.

ELSEWHERE **IN 1942**

JULY 11: The last elements of the 1st Marine Division arrive in Wellington, New Zealand

AUGUST 7: The 1st Marine Division lands on Guadalcanal; the 1st Raider Battalion lands on Tulagi Island and the 1st Parachute Battalion lands on Gavutu Island

AUGUST 24: The US Army assumes command of the Amphibious Corps, Atlantic Fleet, from the Marine Corps

SEPTEMBER 16: The 3rd Marine Division is activated

SEPTEMBER 19: MCAS Eagle Mountain Lake, in Fort Worth, Texas, is organized to function as a glider training base for glider assault Marines. The unit would never leave the experimental phase

OCTOBER 2: The 5th Marine Defense Battalion occupies Funafuti, Tuvalu

OCTOBER 14: A Japanese night bombing attack on Henderson Field on Guadalcanal causes heavy casualties and damages 42 of the 90 aircraft

NOVEMBER 7: The organization of the Marine Corps Women's Reserve is approved

NOVEMBER 29: Military planners approve the US Army's 25th Division to relieve the 1st Marine Division on Guadalcanal

DECEMBER 17: The 35th Infantry Regiment of the Army's 25th Division arrives on Guadalcanal

Lieutenant General
Franklin Hart service
photo, 1950. (MCHD)

In 1942, Marine Colonel Franklin Hart was assigned to the staff of Naval Forces, Europe, based in London. He was joined by Marine Lieutenant Colonel Harold Campbell. Together, Hart and Campbell served as liaison officers to the Commander of Combined Operations, Royal Navy, Vice Admiral Lord Louis Mountbatten. Their positions embedded them within the planning process for major Allied operations, including Operation *Jubilee*. Campbell, leveraging his background as a Marine aviator, played a particularly significant role in planning the air operations for the raid, ensuring coordination between naval, air, and ground elements.

The raid was postponed twice due to poor weather conditions before being rescheduled for August. Hart and Campbell remained assigned to the operation and observed the raid from aboard HMS *Fernie*, a Royal Navy destroyer. However, following the second delay, the three Marines initially assigned to participate were removed from the operation and redirected to continue Commando training in England with the Royal Marines.

After Dieppe, Hart was reassigned to the Pacific Theater, where he went on to command the 24th Marine Regiment during the campaigns in the Marshall Islands, Saipan, and Tinian, and later fought at Iwo Jima. He was succeeded in London by Colonel William T. Clement, who would play a key role in the planning of Operation *Overlord*, the Allied invasion of Normandy.

Operation *Jubilee* ultimately proved to be a costly failure, particularly for the Canadians, who suffered heavy casualties with no strategic gain.

OPERATION *TORCH*

The attack on Pearl Harbor ignited the wave of patriotism and public support that President Roosevelt had long needed to formally bring the United States into the war. With a declaration of war swiftly made, America turned its full attention to mobilizing its industrial might and expanding the ranks of its armed forces. A massive buildup of manpower and materiel would be essential before the nation could undertake large-scale offensive operations.

In early 1942, military leaders and planners from the United States and United Kingdom held a series of meetings to determine the next steps of the war. The Rainbow 5 war plan had provided the US a solid foundational plan to begin mobilizing, but events were moving faster than anticipated. Japanese forces were advancing rapidly across the

Pacific, there were growing fears that the Soviet Union might collapse under the weight of the German onslaught since Hitler had surprisingly turned on Joseph Stalin, and British forces were in no position to launch a major ground offensive in Europe. American leadership agreed that US forces needed to engage German troops on a limited scale first – to work out logistical challenges, refine air support tactics, and most importantly, gain real world combat experience.

It was decided to strike German forces at the periphery of Hitler's empire: North Africa, where British forces were already locked in a back-and-forth struggle against German Panzer divisions. Attacking in North Africa would reopen the Mediterranean to Allied shipping, defeat the German Afrika Korps, reinforce the British Eighth Army defending Egypt, and relieve pressure on the Soviets by forcing Hitler to divert forces away from the Eastern Front. Just as important, it would pit American troops initially against the weaker Vichy French forces – allowing the US military to gain real world battlefield experience before facing the full strength of the German and Italian armies.

Dubbed Operation *Torch*, the invasion marked the beginning of Allied efforts to reclaim Axis-controlled North Africa. The landings took place at multiple locations across French-controlled Morocco and Algeria. The Western Task Force, led by Admiral Henry Hewitt, relied extensively on established Marine Corps operating procedures to plan a successful amphibious assault. Within the Western Task Force's land component, two Marines played crucial roles: Lieutenant Colonel Homer L. Litzenberg, assistant operations officer, and Major Francis Millet Rogers, an intelligence officer. Rogers worked directly under Hewitt, while Litzenberg was attached to Major General George Patton's headquarters. The Marine Corps' experience from FLEX proved invaluable during the landings, despite not having resolved every challenge. In keeping with late-1930s Marine Corps amphibious doctrine, it was decided that once the Task Force set sail, Army and Navy forces would fall under naval command. Hewitt would maintain command until Patton could land and assume control. Due to the Army's lack of an amphibious doctrine to guide their planning, many of the tactics and techniques developed by the Marine Corps through years of exercises in Puerto Rico were adopted by the Army for the assault.

Enormous political considerations were at play as well. The Vichy French troops stationed in North Africa had agreed to collaborate with the Germans following France's surrender, complicating any Allied action in the region. Moreover, these French forces were known to be hostile toward the British, creating a delicate political situation. However, the

MARINE LANDING SITES DURING OPERATION *TORCH*

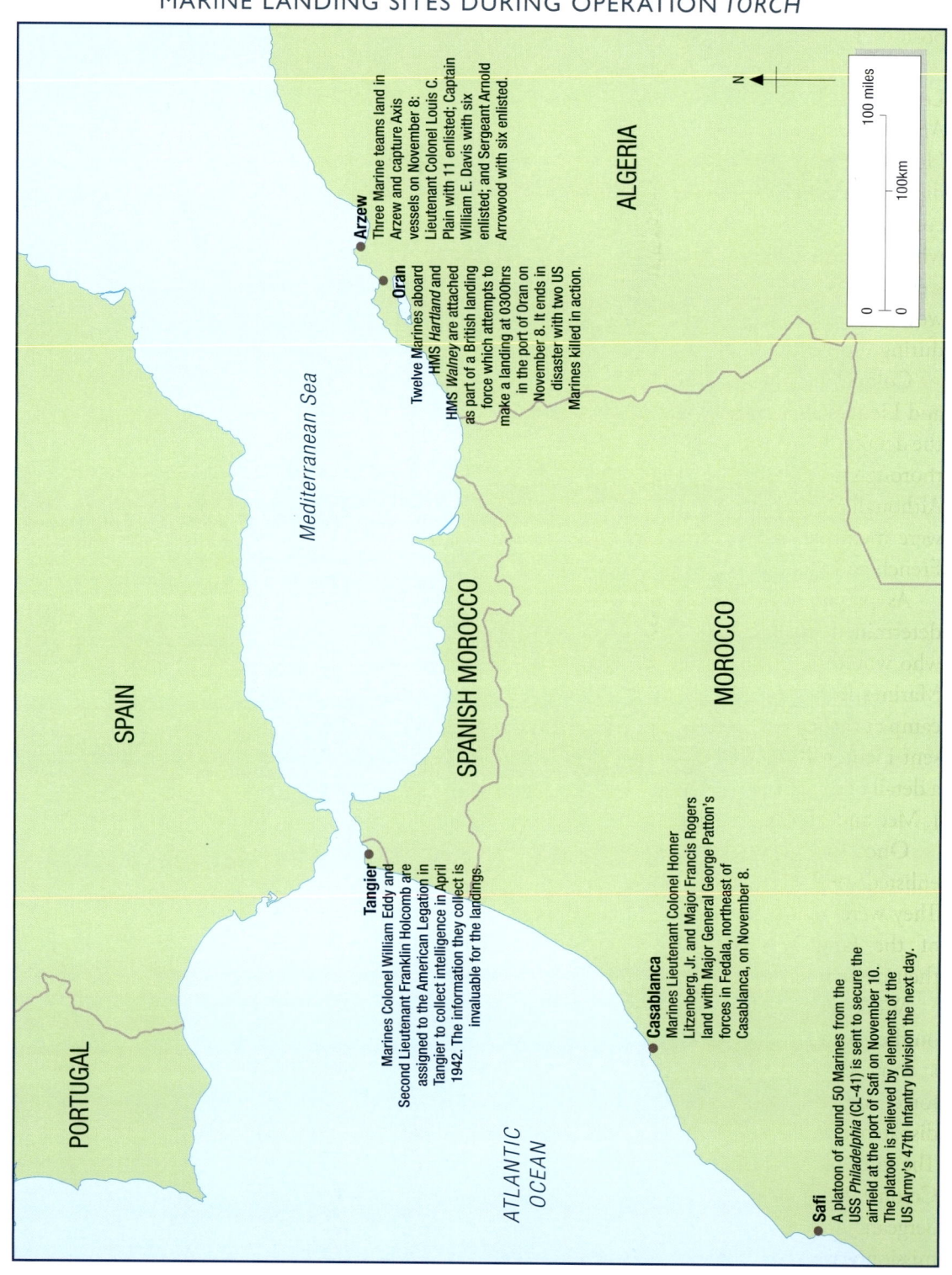

Arzew
Three Marine teams land in Arzew and capture Axis vessels on November 8: Lieutenant Colonel Louis C. Plain with 11 enlisted; Captain William E. Davis with six enlisted; and Sergeant Arnold Arrowood with six enlisted.

Oran
Twelve Marines aboard HMS *Hartland* and HMS *Walney* are attached as part of a British landing force which attempts to make a landing at 0300hrs in the port of Oran on November 8. It ends in disaster with two US Marines killed in action.

Tangier
Marines Colonel William Eddy and Second Lieutenant Franklin Holcomb are assigned to the American Legation in Tangier to collect intelligence in April 1942. The information they collect is invaluable for the landings.

Casablanca
Marines Lieutenant Colonel Homer Litzenberg, Jr. and Major Francis Rogers land with Major General George Patton's forces in Fedala, northeast of Casablanca, on November 8.

Safi
A platoon of around 50 Marines from the USS *Philadelphia* (CL-41) is sent to secure the airfield at the port of Safi on November 10. The platoon is relieved by elements of the US Army's 47th Infantry Division the next day.

ALGERIA

MOROCCO

SPANISH MOROCCO

SPAIN

PORTUGAL

Mediterranean Sea

ATLANTIC OCEAN

N

100 miles
100km

Marine Corps already had a presence in North Africa prior to the landings, positioning them to play a key role in the operation.

Marine Colonel William A. Eddy was assigned to the American Legation in Tangier, Algeria, as one of several assistant naval attachés in April 1942. He was assisted by Marine Second Lieutenant Franklin Holcomb, who quickly embraced his role as a uniformed officer in a diplomatic capacity. While stationed there, Holcomb made valuable connections both locally and abroad. These connections proved essential when he managed to smuggle out two boatmen from Casablanca, who were well versed in the region's complex hydrography. These boatmen would later play a crucial role, guiding portions of the landing force during Operation *Torch*.

Colonel Eddy was called from Morocco to brief President Roosevelt and Lieutenant General Dwight D. Eisenhower, along with his staff, on the details of the upcoming operation. Eisenhower, impressed with Eddy's thorough work, promoted him to senior military attaché for Africa. Although officially assigned as assistants on staff, both Eddy and Holcomb were members of the OSS, tasked with gathering intelligence on both French and German forces in the region.

As preparations were well under way for Operation *Torch*, it was determined small arms training was required for US Navy boat crews who would be involved in the Eastern Task Force. In September 1942, Marines from Londonderry and London created a three-week training camp at the naval base in Rosneath, Scotland. The Londonderry barracks sent Lieutenant Colonel Louis C. Plain, Captain William E. Davis, and a detail of 25 enlisted Marines. Joining them was First Lieutenant Fenton J. Mee and 15 enlisted Marines from the London detachment.

Once the training was completed, the three officers and 30 of the enlisted were selected to take part in landings during Operation *Torch*. They were divided into six teams and assigned to different ships as part of the landing force. The remaining Marines were sent back to their detachments.

While the main landings of Operation *Torch* took place around 0800hrs on the morning of November 8, 1942, the Marines had already been hard at work for several hours. In the early hours of November 8, a pre-landing force composed of US Marines, US Army Rangers, and others was dispatched to secure parts of the harbor at Arzew, east of Oran, at 0100hrs. The force of 26 Marines was divided into three smaller teams: Lieutenant Colonel Plain led 11 enlisted Marines, Captain Davis commanded six, and Sergeant Arnold Arrowood took charge of the remaining Marines. Their mission was to secure the French Vichy ships in the harbor. Upon arrival, they found a greater number of ships than expected, and each Marine, assisted by the Vichy French crews who had decided to switch sides, took control of a ship. Despite some sporadic sniper fire, no Marines were injured or killed during this part of the operation.

The situation was much grimmer for the Marines involved in the mission to open the port of Oran. At 0300hrs, HMS *Hartland* was detected by searchlights at the port's entrance and came under gunfire from French ships and coastal batteries. Marine Corporal Norman Boike was wounded by machine-gun fire during the attack, and Privates First Class Robert F. Horr and James E. Earheart were killed. Earheart was posthumously awarded the Silver Star for his heroic actions in attempting to save wounded Allied troops.

The survivors from the vessels, both American and British, were captured by Axis forces but were later released after the Vichy French signed an armistice.

Later in the morning on November 8, Patton's troops landed at Fedala (modern-day Mohammedia), a port city in Morocco, where Rogers joined the assault. Litzenberg landed with Patton's headquarters element and remained ashore for several days. Initially, Litzenberg went ashore to assist in securing and setting up the headquarters for Admiral Hewitt and his staff. However, Rogers soon found himself acting as an interpreter during peace negotiations with the Vichy French.

Two days later, on November 10, the Marine Corps' birthday, a landing party of approximately 50 Marines from USS *Philadelphia* arrived at the port of Safi to take control of the airfield. They were relieved the following day by soldiers from the 47th Infantry Regiment.

In total, around 100 Marines landed in North Africa during Operation *Torch*. Additionally, about 600 Marines were aboard ships during the operation, where they assisted in operating secondary gun batteries and antiaircraft batteries, vigilantly watching for enemy aircraft, sea mines, and submarines.

- - -

Marines In Africa On 167th Birthday

The marines, sea-soldiers of the United States who celebrate their 167th birthday November 10, again are in action in Africa now as they were in the United States military operation against that continent in the early 1800's.

In 1803 United States marines accompanied U. S. naval forces to Tripoli to enforce a blockade of the regency, whose pirates were harassing American shipping in the Mediterranean. Again in 1815 they were in the squadron which Stephen Decatur led to Tripoli to eliminate attacks on our commerce.

"To the shores of Tripoli" is a phrase known throughout the world because of its inclusion in the marine hymn.

The *Daily Republican*, November 9, 1942. (LoC)

Marines man the CXAM-1 radar and Mk 33 gun director apparatus aboard the USS *Ranger* during an amphibious landing during Operation *Torch*, November 1942. The "MD" on the back of their jackets denotes Marine Detachment. (US Navy)

A Grumman F4F-4 Wildcat fighter taking off from USS *Ranger* to attack targets ashore during the invasion of Morocco, November 1942. The radar director apparatus the Marines are manning can be seen on the ship's superstructure. (US Navy)

TOP USS *Wichita* (CA-45) is straddled by three shells from French battleship *Jean Bart* during the naval battle of Casablanca, November 1942. (US Navy)

BOTTOM Rear Admiral J. L. Hall, Jr. checks a communique aboard USS *Augusta* during Operation *Torch*. A Marine serves as his orderly to the right. (US Navy)

Major General George S. Patton, Jr., US Army, Commanding General, Western Task Force (left), and Rear Admiral Henry Kent Hewitt, Commander, Western Naval Task Force (center), share a light moment aboard USS *Augusta*, off Morocco during the Operation *Torch* landings, November 9, 1942. Note the two Marines on the right of the photo. (US Navy)

Marines aboard USS *Philadelphia* go ashore at the port of Safi, Morocco, during Operation *Torch*, November 10, 1942. The Marines were utilized by the US Army's 47th Infantry Regiment, 9th Infantry Division, as a forward element to secure the Safi airport and guard it until relieved by the soldiers the next day. (USMC, photos by Pfc Donald Passoth)

Marines and sailors manning the gun batteries aboard USS *Augusta* look on as shells from Vichy French ships and shore batteries impact around their ship. (US Navy)

TOP Navy SBD Dauntless dive bombers at Safi airport on November 10, 1942. In the background stand Marines from USS *Philadelphia*. (USMC, photo by Pfc Donald Passoth)

BOTTOM Marines aboard the USS *Ranger* at the ready after general quarters was sounded after a submarine spotting during Operation *Torch*. (US Navy)

SECRET   17 November 1942.

From: Lieutenant Commander G.D. Dickey, U.S. Navy,
            Commanding Officer, U.S. Naval Detachment
            Reservist Party.

To: U.S. Naval Flag Officer in Charge, Oran, Algeria.

Subject: Report of the conduct of personnel during
            the attack on Oran by Reservist Party.

    1.   The following named officers and men formed part
of the boarding party aboard the H.M.S. HARTLAND. The mission
was to board and hold the merchant ships in the harbor of Oran
until the town was captured by American Landing Forces.

DICKEY, G.D.	Lt. Comdr.	USN
GILL, J.M.	Lt.(jg)	USNR
FOX, V.C.	Ensign	USN
OBELKEVICH, E.	Gunner	USN

ADKINS, William E.	100 21 72	CMM(PA)	USFR
ALDRIDGE, James A.	644 24 26	F2c	USNR
CONNORS, Francis X.	650 44 85	PhM2c	USNR
DARDEN, William R.	658 32 19	Sea2c	USNR
DORAN, James E.	403 02 65	F2c	USNR
HEDGES, Paul L.	266 39 66	F2c	USN
HINTON, Charles E.	214 93 67	MM1c	USN
HOLT, John R. Jr.	658 19 64	MM2c	USNR
KLINE, Stanley F.	243 22 66	EM1c	USNR
LUMBY, Russell (n)	321 24 13	MM2c	USN
MAGEE, Howard F. Jr.	265 78 17	EM3c	USN
MOORE, William B.	406 73 89	Sea2c	USNR
O'CONNOR, John B.	311 76 21	F3c	USN
POULSEN, Theone L.	368 65 08	F3c	USN
RANDALL, Frank L.	316 01 47	F2c	USNR
ROWE, Carl E.	316 57 17	Sea1c	USNR
SHELEY, George H.	299 39 48	BM1c	USNR
STANFIELD, William J.	616 16 77	Sea1c	USNR
TROTT, Martin	256 26 95	CWT(AA)	USN
WADE, George W. Jr.	265 76 65	WT2c	USN
WATERS, Charles A.	274 02 72	CWT(PA)	USN
WILKINSON, Charles V.	550 00 25	F1c	USNR

BOIKE, N.H.	Corp.	USMC
DICKINSON, W.T.	Pvt.	USMC
EARHEART, J.E. Jr.	Pfc.	USMC
HORR, R.F.	Pvt.	USMC
SPENCER, R.K.	Pfc.	USMC
WHITTAKER, F.P.	Sgt.	USMC

1 259 7/c

-1-

THIS AND SUBSEQUENT PAGES Scans of a report of the conduct of US Marines and sailors who took part in direct action against Axis forces during the initial landings. (NARA)

SECRET

Subject: Report of the conduct of personnel during
             the attack on Oran by Reservist Party.
- -

2.   All of the U.S. Navy group of 28 men and four
officers with the exception of the U.S. Navy officers in
charge had action stations in the Captain's cabin in the
after part of the ship. The Officer in Charge's station
was on the bridge.

3.   During the engagement the ship was repeatedly
holed by 3" and 4.7" shells. This caused the compartment
in which the men were stationed to be filled with smoke
and later by fire. It was reported to me that during this
period of the action no single man showed sign of panic
or made any attempt to leave his station. Also during this
period several men were killed in these close quarters and
the smoke made conditions practically intolerable. Upon
abandoning ship these officers and men again showed the
highest kind o leadership and spirit in helping to save the
lives of many U.S. soldiers who were unfamiliar with the
ship and the use of the life jackets. Also in addition upon
arriving at the wharf they continued to help b pulling many
men out of the water although physically exhausted themselves.
The heroism and spirit displayed by the officers and men of
this detachment was exceptional and from all observation it
can be said that no one did less than the maximum that could
be expected of him.

4.   The following men were killed:

EARHEART, J.E. Jr.	Pfc.	USMC
HORR, R.F.	Pvt.	USMC
HINTON, Charles E.	MM1c	USN
KLINE, Stanley F.	EM1c	USNR
POULSEN, Theone L.	F.3c	USN

The following officers and men were wounded:

DICKEY, G.D.	Lt-Comdr.,	USN
FOX, V.C.	Ensign	USN
ADKINS, William E.	CMM(PA)	USFR
HOLT, John R. Jr.,	MM2c	USNR
DARDEN, William R.	Sea.2c	USNR
SHELEY, George H.	BM1c	USNR
BOIKE, N.H.	Corp.	USMC

5.   It is recommended that each man be advanced
to the next higher rating and that whatever commendation
that is considered adequate be given to the three junior
officers.

                         G.D. DICKEY.   77
             -2-

SECRET

S-E-C-R-E-T   26 November, 1942.

Subject: Operation of U.S. Naval Detachment, Reservist
            Party, Operation TORCH, in Assault of Oran,
            8 November, 1942.
- -

EARHEART, James E. Jr., Pfc., U.S.M.C.

        When the order to abandon ship was given aboard H.M.S.
HARTLAND, a line was thrown from the HARTLAND to a French harbor
tug nearby, and was secured by a seaman who had swam to the tug.
This line was being used by wounded and men unable to swim as a
means of getting ashore. When the crew aboard the tug started to
move the boat away from the mole, and it was evident the lives
of the men on the line would be jeopardized when the rope parted,
Earheart volunteered to swim to the tug and halt it. While leaving
the HARTLAND, he came under heavy machine gun fire and was instantly
killed.

        This act beyond the normal course of duty was only another
example of initiative and of his courageous behavior under heavy
fire.

                        JOHN M. GILL, Jr.
                        Lieutenant (jg), U.S.N.R.

The report includes a summary of the action taken by Private First Class James E. Earheart, Jr. It concludes, "This act beyond the normal course of duty was only another example of initiative and of his courageous behavior under heavy fire." He was posthumously awarded the Silver Star. (NARA)

19 November 1942

Subject: Operations of U.S. Naval Advance Party,
            Port of Arzeu, Algiers, 8 November 1942.

            Enclosure (A).

- -

Lt-Colonel L.C. Plain, U.S.M.C.
Lt-Commander C.B. Munson, U.S.N.
Ensign F. Olender, U.S.N.

Bowen, G.A.	Corp.	USMC.
Damato, A.P.	Pfc.	USMC.
Elias, E.	Pfc.	USMC.
Hager, R.D.	Pvt.	USMC.
Jones, S.O.	Sgt.	USMC.
Marsh, R.W.	Pfc.	USMC.
Orlando, D.	Sgt.	USMC.
Pledger, L.L., Jr.	Corp.	USMC.
Skelly, T.F.	Pfc.	USMC.
Smith, K.A.	Pfc.	USMC.
Trail, H.W.	Pfc.	USMC.

25   ENCL (E)   88

Major Francis M. Rogers

CITATION:

The President of the United States of America takes pleasure in presenting the Silver Star to Major Francis M. Rogers, United States Marine Corps, for gallantry in action while attached to the staff of Admiral H. K. Hewitt, United States Navy, on the afternoon of 8 November 1942. On that date, he drove a commandeered automobile for the Chief of Staff, Western Task Force, from Fedala through the enemy lines to Headquarters French Military District in Casablanca, thence to Headquarters French Naval District, thence returning to Red Beach 2, at Fedala. Although fired upon several times by small arms fire and in spite of the fact that the French Naval-Military District at the time of the visit to Headquarters, that District was under severe bombardment from American bombers, Major Rogers drove boldly forward with utter disregard to his own safety. His calmness, courage and boldness contributed materially to the successful completion of the trip.

Vice Admiral Henry K. Hewitt presents the Silver Star to Major F. M. Rogers for actions above and beyond the call of duty during Operation *Torch*, awarded on February 23, 1943. Rogers was attached to the headquarters element, Western Task Force. (US Navy)

Private First Class James E. Earheart, Jr.

CITATION:

The President of the United States of America takes pride in presenting the Silver Star (Posthumously) to Private First Class James E. Earheart, Jr., United States Marine Corps, for conspicuous gallantry and intrepidity as a member of a United States Navy anti-sabotage party aboard HMS HARTLAND during entry into the port of Oran, Algeria, on 8 November 1942. After crashing boom defenses and facing heavy gunfire from hostile shore emplacements and anchored warships, the Hartland secured a throw line to a harbor tug to provide escape for wounded personnel and non-swimmers during abandonment of the damaged vessel. When the tug began to move and the lives of the men on the line were jeopardized by an imminent break, Private First Class Earheart, with utter disregard for his own personal safety, volunteered to swim out and halt the boat. Unhesitatingly leaving the ship while it was still under vigorous shelling, he exposed himself to a riddling blast of machine-gun fire and was instantly killed. His heroic conduct was in keeping with the highest traditions of the United States Naval Service.

Corporal Anthony P. Damato

February 20, 1944
CITATION:

For conspicuous gallantry and intrepidity at the risk of his life above and beyond the call of duty while serving with an assault company in action against enemy Japanese forces on Engebi Island, Eniwetok Atoll, Marshall Islands, on the night of 19–20 February 1944. Highly vulnerable to sudden attack by small, fanatical groups of Japanese still at large despite the efficient and determined efforts of our forces to clear the area, Corporal Damato lay with two comrades in a large foxhole in his company's perimeter which had been dangerously thinned by the forced withdrawal of nearly half of the available men. When one of the enemy approached the foxhole undetected and threw in a hand grenade, Corporal Damato desperately groped for it in the darkness. Realizing the imminent peril to all three and fully aware of the consequences of his act, he unhesitatingly flung himself on the grenade and, although instantly killed as his body absorbed the explosion, saved the lives of his two companions. Corporal Damato's splendid initiative, fearless conduct and valiant sacrifice reflect great credit upon himself and the United States Naval Service. He gallantly gave his life for his comrades.

TOP Private First Class Damato's last letter home to his mother before leaving to help teach Allied sailors how to operate small arms weapons in Scotland. Damato would go on to take part in Operation *Torch* in North Africa. (MCHD)

BOTTOM AND INSET Corporal Anthony P. Damato was one of the Marines who landed at Arzew on November 8, 1942. Previously, Damato was stationed at Londonderry and was one of the few to be selected to help train Navy personnel in smalls arms weaponry in Scotland. From there he was sent to take part in the landings in Operation *Torch*. Later on, Damato was transferred to the 22nd Marine Regiment and was killed on February 19, 1944, in the Marshall Islands fighting the Japanese. When an undetected enemy approached his foxhole and threw in a grenade, Damato covered it with his body and absorbed the blast, sacrificing himself while saving his comrades. He would be awarded the Medal of Honor posthumously. Today, he is memorialized on Marine Corps Base Quantico with a street named after him. (US Navy; Author's collection)

TOP "A Marine who lost his life in the landing in North Africa last November has been honored at Londonderry with the naming of a road at the Marine Corps camp there. He was stationed at Londonderry when assigned to the invasion. He was Private First Class James E. Earheart, Jr. Standing by the sign is Private First Class Earl Peterson, of Penn Yan, New York." Photo dated June 27, 1943. (USMC, photo by Cpl William R. Gibbon)

BOTTOM "A Detroit Marine, Sergeant Norman H. Boike, received the Purple Heart when wounded during the landing operation in North Africa. He has been honored by the naming of a road at the Londonderry Marine Corps camp. Standing beside one of the signs on the road is Private Alexander J. Davis, of Washington DC." Photo dated June 1943. (USMC, photo by Cpl William R. Gibbon)

TOP Rear Admiral H. Kent Hewitt and his staff aboard USS *Augusta*, December 4, 1942. Marine Colonel Francis M. Rogers can be seen in the rear row near the center, while another unidentified Marine officer can be seen in the front row on the right. (US Navy)

BOTTOM "A New England Marine Corps private, Robert F. Horr, who is missing in action from the landing operations in North Africa last November, has been honored by the naming of a road in his memory at his home camp of Londonderry. Corporal Walter Suly, of Cleveland, Ohio, stands next to the new road sign." (USMC, photo by Cpl William R. Gibbon)

Marines aboard USS *Augusta* patrol the dock in the port of Morocco, November 1942. The Marines aboard the *Augusta*, like their Navy counterparts, took part in five different combat engagements during Operation *Torch* with their ship coming under fire numerous times from Axis ships and shore batteries. (US Navy)

OTHER MARINES IN NORTH AFRICA

Throughout the entirety of the war, North Africa would average about 20 Marines on the entire continent, except during Operation *Torch*. However, the Marines who did work there, and passed through, made contributions to the Allied war effort that are incalculable. Among the first US Marines to make their way through Africa in early 1941 were Colonels Roy S. Geiger and Christian F. Schilt. The two had been tasked to observe British military operations, particularly air operations. Geiger was temporarily assigned to HMS *Formidable*, a Royal Navy aircraft carrier, while it was performing escort duty in the Mediterranean Sea.

Colonel Eddy would continue to lead the OSS Marines in North Africa for the duration of the war. However, one Marine who served in Africa stands out from the rest: Peter Ortiz.

From serving in the French Foreign Legion in the 1930s to being captured behind enemy lines in 1945, Ortiz's involvement in the OSS is more akin to a James Bond novel than a military service record. Born in the US but raised in France by his American mother and French father, Ortiz grew up well educated but very bored with school. To bring excitement to his life, Ortiz joined the French Foreign Legion as a lowly private in 1932 at the age of 19. By the end of his enlistment in 1937, he had reached the rank of sergeant and was the non-commissioned officer in charge of an armored squadron and considered a model soldier. He was extremely proficient in desert warfare and parachute qualified. Wanting a change in pace, Ortiz returned to the US, attempting a career in Hollywood as a military technical advisor. When Germany invaded Poland in 1939, Ortiz attempted to make his way to France; however, the transport he was on was sunk by a German submarine. By October 1939, Ortiz was back in the uniform of a Legionnaire as a first lieutenant and fought in combat against the Germans in North Africa in 1940. Recognized for his leadership prowess, Ortiz was made the officer in charge of his regiment's motorcycle platoon. In this capacity, he personally led numerous hit-and-run raids and scouring missions.

Ortiz's regiment was eventually overwhelmed by German forces, and he was captured and made a prisoner of war. During Ortiz's regiment's final stand, while attempting to destroy a fuel dump, he was injured and briefly paralyzed from the waist down due to shrapnel in his spine. Over the course of the next 15 months, Ortiz recovered in various prisoner-of-war camps and through the efforts of German doctors. Throughout this time, Ortiz attempted to make several escape attempts. Finally, in October 1941, Ortiz was able to make a clean getaway and make it to neutral Portugal and arrived in the United States two months later.

Arriving a week after the Japanese attack on Pearl Harbor, Ortiz initially attempted to join the US Army. However, bureaucratic red tape dragged the process out and Ortiz was itching to get back to the war. Wanting to get back into the fight quickly, Ortiz decided to enlist in the Marine Corps. Upon completing recruit training, Ortiz put on his previously received awards and badges from the Legion, much to the shock of his drill instructors. Realizing Ortiz's experience could best be served better than in the rank and file, Ortiz was offered a commission. He accepted and became a second lieutenant on August 1, 1942. Shortly after accepting the commission, he was assigned to Company D, 1st Battalion, 23rd Marine Regiment at Camp Lejeune. Upon arrival he requested to train with the Marine Corps' new Parachute Battalion. While there, Operation *Torch* had already been completed and the Allies were requesting more personnel in the OSS due to the invaluable work done by its members collecting intelligence behind enemy lines. By December 3, 1942 he had been promoted to captain and was on a transport bound for Tangiers, Morocco – the Corps recognizing that his fluency in French, German, Arabic, and his aggressive war-fighting spirit could be utilized in special operations.

During January 1943, Ortiz spent much of the month studying Operation *Torch* and had attached himself to the Army's 509th Parachute Battalion the last part of the month. While there, he created a team that could blend into the local populace and operate deep behind enemy lines to gather intelligence. On the return of one such mission, Ortiz and his team were caught by US soldiers crossing back into American lines. Wearing his Marine Corps utilities under his local clothes, he was unable to convince the soldiers he was an American, much less a US Marine. As far as the soldiers were concerned, all the Marines were in the Pacific.

In the following months, Ortiz was attached to a variety of British, French, and American units partaking in various combat actions behind the lines, and at times, side by side with rank-and-file troops. On March 18, 1943, Ortiz received a Purple Heart when his patrol encountered German troops and he was shot in the hand while leading a nighttime reconnaissance patrol. He spent some time recovering in a hospital in Algiers before being ordered back to the US to recover in April 1943. Ortiz quickly made impressions at Headquarters Marine Corps, and he was sent back to Europe and was again administratively attached to the Marine Detachment in London.

Lieutenant General George S. Patton and Rear Admiral Alan G. Kirk (right), US Navy, tour American forces before the invasion of Sicily, July 30, 1943. A Marine guard can be seen behind Kirk, to the left. (US Navy)

OPERATION *HUSKY*

One of the often-overlooked chapters of World War II is the Allied campaign to liberate Italy. After hard-fought victories against German and Italian forces in North Africa, and now more proficient in amphibious operations, the Allies turned their attention to the European mainland, beginning with Italy.

As was typical in the European Theater, relatively few Marines participated in ground operations. However, Marines remained actively engaged by serving aboard Navy vessels, manning secondary gun batteries. Marine detachments aboard USS *Brooklyn* (CL-40), USS *Philadelphia* (CL-41), USS *Savannah* (CL-42), and USS *Boise* (CL-47) provided support during the invasion of Sicily. Additionally, around a dozen Marines landed ashore, serving in roles such as amphibious coordination staff and security for high-ranking fleet officers. Among them were Colonel Richard Hall Jeschke, Sergeant Charles W. Marker, and Sergeant Edward F. McKnew, Jr. Jeschke's contributions to the operation's planning were so impactful that he was later transferred to General Omar Bradley's First Army Staff to assist in planning Operation *Overlord*.

The success of Operation *Husky* opened new opportunities for Marine involvement in the region. Beginning on Christmas Eve 1943, First Lieutenant John Hamilton operated out of the port of Monopoli,

Rear Admiral Alan G. Kirk (center), US Navy Commander, Amphibious Force, Atlantic Fleet watches maneuvers from aboard USS *Ancon* (AGC-4) as Allied troops practice for Operation *Husky*, May 31, 1943. A Marine orderly can be seen behind to the left of Kirk. (US Navy)

Marines Who Landed in Sicily Last July

By Technical Sergeant Richard T. Wright, US Marine Corps Combat Correspondent December 5, 1943

London, England – Sergeant Charles W. Marker Jr., the son of Mr. and Mrs. Charles W. Marker, of 41 Beeson Street, Uniontown, Pennsylvania, has the unique distinction of being one of a handful of Marines to land with the invasion forces at Sicily last July.

Colonel Richard Hall Jeschke and Sergeant Edward F. McKnew Jr. were among the other Marines who took part in the landing on Sicily.

Sergeant Marker served as personal orderly to Rear Admiral Alan G. Kirk, USN, the commander of a Naval Task Force during the invasion. He joined Admiral Kirk's staff in May 1942 and has served as his orderly for the past year and a half.

The 22-year-old Sergeant went ashore with Admiral Kirk twice during the first few days of the landing. He was subjected to repeated Nazi dive bombing attacks during his stay on land.

According to Sergeant Marker, the most exciting incident that happened occurred on our ship out in the harbor. The German planes flew very low during their attack, and as a result, the gunners from Allied ships were forced to fire their shots very low.

"One morning a group of German Heinkels came buzzing over and the gunners started banging away at them. I heard a loud explosion in the fantail and by the time I got there they were carrying men down to the sick bay on stretchers. A shell from one of our ships had landed on the deck. A number of the men were wounded, but nobody was killed."

Marker enlisted in the Marine Corps February 14, 1939, in Maryland. Since that time he has served at numerous Marine bases. After recruit training at Parris Island, South Carolina, he went to the Marine sea school in Portsmouth, Virginia, and was then assigned to sea duty. He took part in the Pacific Fleet maneuvers in 1940, and served with the Second Marine Regiment, Second Marine Division.

At present, Sergeant Marker is serving with the Marine detachment here as Admiral Kirk's orderly.

"Sergeant Edward F. McKnew, Jr. looks on as Sergeant Charles W. Marker, Jr., USMC, of Uniontown, Pennsylvania, field strips the .45-caliber pistol that he carried during the invasion of Sicily last July." Photo dated December 6, 1943. (USMC, photo by SSgt Kilpatrick)

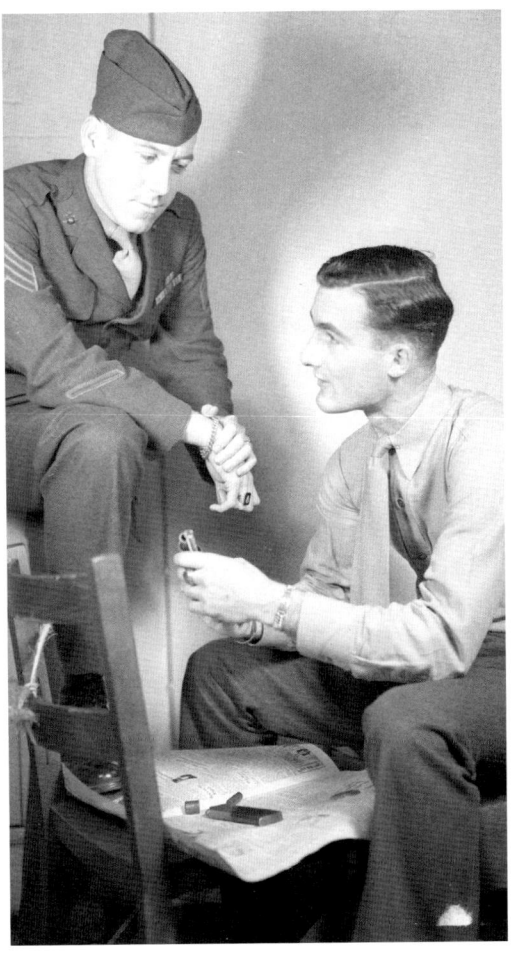

By Technical Sergeant Richard T. Wright

London, England – A handful of Marines landed with the Allied Forces at Sicily last July, and Sergeant Edward F. McKnew Jr., the son of E. F. McKnew, 1326 Jefferson Street, N.W., Washington DC, had the distinction of being one.

Along with Colonel Richard Hall Jeschke, and Sergeant Charles W. Marker Jr., Sergeant McKnew landed at Scoglitti, Sicily, on July 10, 1943. Sergeant McKnew served as Colonel Jeschke's orderly. Several other Marine officers were also present as observers.

The Marine sergeant went ashore three times at Sicily, and during his stay on the island was under constant dive-bombing attacks by Nazi planes. He was also on board a Navy ship in the harbor during intermittent bombing attacks.

The 24-year-old sergeant was most impressed by a group of German prisoners that he saw in Oran. "They were a very healthy-looking bunch of men," according to Sergeant McKnew. "Most of them were blond-headed, well-built, and it was clear to see, that as opponents, they were not to be underestimated."

Sergeant McKnew arrived at Sicily with Rear Admiral Alan G. Kirk's Naval Task Force, and as he put it, "my stay there was exciting, but brief."

The Washington DC Marine enlisted in the Marine Corps November 18, 1936 and saw duty at the Washington Navy Yard, Guantanamo Bay, Cuba, the Philadelphia Navy Yard, and at Marine Corps Base Quantico, Virginia.

His wife, Mrs. Gayle O. McKnew, lives at 2300 North Washington Boulevard, Arlington, Virginia. Sergeant McKnew is a graduate of Central High School in Washington.

At present, Sergeant McKnew is serving with the Marine detachment here as Colonel Jeschke's orderly.

Italy, until January 2, 1944, assisting Yugoslav resistance fighters across the Adriatic Sea. (Today, Yugoslavia's former territory is divided into Bosnia and Herzegovina, Croatia, Montenegro, North Macedonia, Serbia, and Slovenia.)

During this period, Hamilton, aided by Marine Gunnery Sergeant John Harnicker, commanded a fleet of 22 sailing vessels manned by 400 Yugoslav partisans. Their mission was to transport vital supplies to communist guerrilla fighters battling Nazi forces. Their efforts extended to the islands of Korčula, Hvar, Brač, and Vis. For his leadership and bravery, Hamilton was awarded the Silver Star.

Hamilton and Harnicker continued their operations throughout 1944, conducting Commando raids, coordinating additional supply missions, and fighting alongside partisans against the German 118th Jäger Division. That summer, the pair parachuted into Yugoslavia with a Navy operator to gather intelligence on German movements. They also assisted in rescuing downed Allied airmen and safely extracting them back to Italy. After completing these operations, Hamilton was reassigned to support OSS missions in France and Belgium under Lieutenant General Courtney H. Hodges's US First Army.

Captain John Hamilton

CITATION:
Captain John Hamilton (AKA: Sterling Hayden) United States Marine Corps, for gallantry in action while serving with the Office of Strategic Services in the Mediterranean Theater of Operations from 24 December 1943 to 2 January 1944. Captain Hamilton displayed great courage in making hazardous sea voyages in enemy infested waters and reconnaissance through enemy held areas. His conduct reflected great credit upon himself and the United States Armed Forces.

John Hamilton's birth name was Sterling Hayden. Not wanting to be recognized and treated differently due to his successful Hollywood career, he legally changed his name. (NARA)

Recommendation for Award of the Silver Star Medal to Captain John Hamilton, USMCR
28 February 1946
1. It is recommended that Captain John Hamilton, O-22085, USMCR, be awarded the Silver Star Medal for exceptional meritorious service and gallantry in action while assigned to a Strategic Services operational unit in MEDTO from December 1943 to February 1944, inclusive.

2. Captain John Hamilton (then a 1st Lieutenant) was assigned to the OSS, SO Shipping Operation based at Bari and Monopoli, Italy, in December 1943. This unit established the initial American contact with Marshal Tito's National Liberation Army in Yugoslavia by landing from small naval surface craft on the German-occupied coast of Dalmatia and penetrating through enemy lines to several of the most important headquarters of Tito's forces. After negotiations with Tito and his staff and after having obtained the necessary authority from the Allied Commander-in-Chief, the unit established shipping bases on the coast of Italy, collected a fleet of some 40 Yugoslav steamships and sailing vessels, procured cargoes of arms, ammunition, food and clothing as well as medical supplies, and organised a clandestine supply line across the Adriatic Sea, penetrating the German sea and air blockade along the Balkan coastline and landing in all some 7,000 tons of vitally needed war supplies for the National Liberation Army of Yugoslavia.

3. Owing to the timing as well as the local conditions in connection with the military situation in this particular area, the immediate results of this operation placed the German forces in Dalmatia at a great disadvantage and served to enhance the activates of Tito's forces in Dalmatia to a very considerable degree. The unit made 70 sailings altogether across the Adriatic, losing only four ships in spite of intensified enemy action on land, at sea and in the air along the clandestine supply line. Furthermore, the few American officers engaged in commanding and supervising the above-mentioned supply operations made more than a dozen armed reconnaissance penetrations deep into enemy territory in Yugoslavia and collected a substantial amount of original and at that time exceedingly valuable intelligence covering both German order of battle and the complete order of battle of Tito's Partisans in Yugoslavia.

4. On 24 December 1943, Captain John Hamilton (then 1st Lieutenant) was ordered to proceed by surface craft to the Islands of Korcula, Vis, Hvar and Brac, then reportedly under German attack. The object of his mission was to find out on the spot whether the islands in question had actually been occupied by German landing forces and to make contact with staff officers of Tito's Headquarters in

charge of the coastal area of Dalmatia, situated on the Island of Hvar.

Owing to exceedingly bad weather, Captain Hamilton's ship stranded and sank during the night of the 24th and 25th of December on the coast of Italy. However, Captain Hamilton managed to get ashore and returned to Bari, from where he proceeded on board another ship on the morning of the 25th.

After an extremely rough crossing, he landed on the Island of Korcula during the night of the 25th and 26th of December and made contact with units of Tito's forces. The island was under German attack. However, in order to acquaint himself with the situation, Captain Hamilton made a reconnaissance tour in a jeep accompanied by a Yugoslav staff officer and two Partisans. During the drive the car was ambushed, and the Yugoslav driver sitting next to Captain Hamilton was killed by enemy gunfire. However, Captain Hamilton and the remaining Partisans managed to shoot their way out of the ambush and escaped with the jeep.

After having ascertained the fact that the Island of Korcula was lost to the enemy, Captain Hamilton escaped with the remnants of the Partisan garrison during the night of the 26th and 27th of December, and after a hazardous sea voyage through waters patrolled by enemy E boats and landing craft, he arrived on the Island of Hvar on the morning of 27 December. He established contact with the Partisan Headquarters and had a six-hour conference with the Partisan staff officers, from whom he collected exact information as to the immediate military situation on the Dalmatian islands as well as on the mainland. The conference took place in the open outside the buildings of the said headquarters which were constantly subjected to enemy attacks from the air including Stuka dive-bombing.

Captain Hamilton remained on the Islands of Hvar and Brac until 30 December, taking an active part in the defense of the islands and the repulsion of a number of German attacks.

As the only American in the area, he gave a magnificent account of himself and received the unanimous admiration and respect of the fighting Yugoslavs.

In accordance with his orders which directed him to return to his base in Italy not later than 2400 hours, New Year's Eve, Captain Hamilton boarded a small local vessel on the night of the 30th and 31st of December, again sailed through waters patrolled by enemy naval craft and proceeded to Italy across the open Adriatic through a severe winter storm. Captain Hamilton returned with complete information concerning the situation in the Dalmatian coastal areas, on the basis of which immediate steps were taken to bring aid and relief to the threatened islands. Furthermore, Allied naval operations were initiated without delay and obtained extremely favorable results against German naval craft. Also, Allied air operations were at once undertaken against German occupation forces in Dalmatia, causing the German military operation to come to a temporary standstill.

5. While stationed in Italy at the OSS shipping bases, Captain Hamilton did outstanding work and was for a period of time in command of all operations out of the port of Monopoli, working day and night with his Partisan crews totaling some 400 men, organizing maintenance and repairs of ships, loading cargoes of guns, ammunition, mines, food, clothing and medical supplies, attending to the legion details in connection with the collection of cargoes, transportation, fueling, watering and clearing of the ships, as well as providing for housing and feeding his Yugoslav crews, all under a rigid system insuring the strictest security. Captain Hamilton conducted himself at all times in a manner which commanded the greatest respect from everyone who served with him and which reflected honor to the Allied military forces in the Middle East.

Hans V. Topte, Major, AUS. (formerly Chief OSS/SO Shipping Operations in the Adriatic)

OPERATION *LEADER*

Operation *Leader* was a US Navy air raid conducted in October 1943, targeting German shipping and port facilities near Bodø along the Norwegian coast. At the time, Norway was under Nazi occupation, and the primary objective of the operation was to disrupt German maritime supply lines that supported their garrison and operations in Scandinavia. The attack also aimed to weaken German control over vital resources, including the flow of Swedish iron ore critical to the Nazi war effort.

The carrier USS *Ranger*, supported by a screen of British and American warships, launched waves of Grumman TBF Avenger torpedo bombers, SBD Dauntless dive bombers, and F4F Wildcat fighters against enemy targets. In a carefully coordinated series of strikes, US aircraft successfully sank or severely damaged several German and Norwegian merchant vessels, tankers, and coastal installations. The raid caused significant disruption to German logistics in the region, and it was regarded as a sharp blow to Axis shipping at a time when German forces were already stretched thin across multiple fronts.

While Marine Corps aviators did not participate directly in the aerial attacks, hundreds of Marines were embarked aboard the *Ranger* and accompanying cruisers. Their role was critical: they manned antiaircraft batteries and provided internal ship security, protecting the fleet against potential German air assaults and reconnaissance threats. Their presence ensured the carrier and its escort vessels could operate with confidence in enemy-controlled waters.

Nazis Dared by Force Near Norwegian Coast

By First Lieutenant Weldon James, US Marine Corps Public Relations Officer

WITH AN ANGLO-AMERICAN TASK FORCE – The sailors and Marines of this great United States battleship got within 90 miles of Norway yesterday and dared the Germans to come out.

The great fleet of American and British warships steamed majestically through the northern seas to within 90 miles of the Norwegian coast – where, in other months, they might well expect hundreds of German torpedo planes and dive bombers to give battle – let the Blohm and Voss 138 take a good look, gave it plenty of time to radio back its findings.

Then they shot it down.

"We were robbed"

Two Seafires got it. Launched from a British carrier, they brought it down miles away from the fleet, robbing these sailors and Marines of the visual satisfaction of seeing Jerry zoom seaward in flames, but giving them all the other cause for celebration they could have asked.

After that, nothing happened. "Absolutely nothing," growled one Marine sergeant. "There weren't even any ants on this picnic."

No German warships, no German planes came out to harry the armada as the well-advertised fleet maneuvered in the northern seas, then steamed back whence it came.

Here in this quiet anchorage another group of American marines and sailors learned with relief that they had missed no action, then joined with the travelers in deriding the Germans for not giving battle.

Sign of weakness

Officers and men, in the inevitable and endless post-mortem of discussion aboard the various ships, agreed on one thing: the Germans might be too busy elsewhere, or they might be too fearful of the great firepower of such a fleet as this – but in any case their non-appearance was just one more indication of the weakness of a Germany whose days are numbered.

The Germans could answer other questions: Did Berlin panic with fear that a Norwegian invasion was on the way? How many German divisions were rushed northward? And which one of several of these "invasion feints" will finally be the real thing?

The sailors and Marines figured they were looking for the *Tirpitz*.

Add them to the list of those who failed to find her – but who, with their hard and vigilant campaign, played their part in "keeping the German Navy put."

They sailed the trackless northern seas for months. They moved from Point X to Point Y, from Point A to Point B and back again.

They pulled in here and slipped out there. They crossed the Arctic Circle and pocketed their blue-nose certificates with freezing satisfaction, and played about the top of the world, and manned their guns and kept their grim day-and-night watches in waters where there is no night. They pushed out tempting bait to lure the Germans out and lay in deadly wait.

They're only human, these sailors and Marines, drawn from every corner of America, and they're disappointed. They're like that great public of which they remain a part. Most of them, a few brief ages ago, were your peace-time drugstore cowboys, your soft jitterbugs, your truck-drivers, your schoolteachers, your lawyers, your mechanics and your soda jerkers. Once at war, they, like their greater public, were all for action.

They haven't found this action, and they're furious.

Their "gripe sessions" are unending, and they're probably the best – or the worst – in all the fleet. Their bitterness against the Germans increases in direct ratio to the number of days and weeks and months the Germans remain invisible. These sailors and Marines are contemptuously certain that the Japanese would be more accommodating; they can see a little German-sense, perhaps, in the TIRPITZ and the GNEISENAU and the SCHARNHORST and the rest of the German battle fleet hugging their harbors, but when this battleship and other British and American warships sweep within easy range of German land-based aircraft and no attack develops, they're puzzled. And, in their renewed disappointment, furious.

Cruise with this lively crew for awhile, listen to them talk, look at what they're talking about – and you'll have a fine idea of what America's "New Navy" is like.

You'd never surpass its confidence and enthusiasm, not on any of the fighting fronts.

The battlewagon itself is one of the newest, biggest and fastest in the world. It has what the reservists call "all the latest gadgets," and its men are willing to light any from any other ship who deny that it is the most powerful and deadly dreadnought afloat.

They are willing, it is evident, to try conclusions repeatedly with the crew of any other battleship in this fleet.

You'd believe them, too, if you could see them "in action" now against non-hostile targets, blasting away with terrifying accuracy – if you could see the enthusiasm with which they demonstrate their marvelous gadgets and their own know-how. It isn't just blind fighting pride that is responsible for their confidence. It's the magnificent ship itself, it's their training, their knowledge that their ship is new and deadly, their own admiration for the instruments and weapons they handle.

A ship like this, of course, is a collection of some experts who know everything about almost everything, other experts who know everything about one thing, and hundreds of guys who know everything about the particular job or possibly two jobs they've been trained to handle.

A lot of the men who man these guns and operate these instruments were trained in three- or four-months' time. For others it took six to eight months, for others, years. Now in line of battle for months, they represent all kinds, all types of Americans, every branch of general and specialized training.

Roughly two-thirds are wartime sailors, ex-civilians who a few months ago knew nothing about the jobs they now handle so efficiently. A salty third, officers and men, are the old-timers, the backbone of the new Navy. Between them and the highly-skilled ex-civilian experts of the reserves, they continue the Navy's unending program of education and training, making the great ship a floating university, a floating training base, so that the lowliest seaman or the greenest officer, as the months pass, acquires the training and skill for higher classifications, for handling two and three times the jobs he could handle when he first came aboard.

Then when the battleship touches home again, of course, it loses hundreds of these newly produced "old salts" to other new ships, takes on fresh hundreds of basically trained but green men, begins anew its seasoning process, in and out of battle. More than anything it will give, along with added knowledge and added training, the superb confidence and enthusiasm of the great new Navy.

Author note

It is likely Lieutenant Weldon was aboard one of the American ships when he wrote the article. The *Tuscaloosa* was a heavy cruiser with large 8-inch gun mounts that would make it appear like a battleship from a distance. The ship was one of seven US Navy ships to take part in Operation *Leader*, a planned attack on the Norwegian port of Bodø. On October 2, 1943, the American ships plus 12 Royal Navy vessels departed Scotland and made their way to Norway. Embarked aircraft from USS *Ranger* sank numerous German support

ELSEWHERE IN 1943

JANUARY 12: The 1st Marine Division arrives in Melbourne, Australia, for rehabilitation

JANUARY 29: Ruth C. Streeter is commissioned as major in the USMC Women's Reserve and becomes its first director

FEBRUARY 9: Major General Alexander Patch, US Army, announces the "total and complete defeat of Japanese forces on Guadalcanal"

MARCH 1: Australian and US forces engage the Japanese in what becomes known as the battle of the Bismarck Sea

MARCH 12: The F4U Corsair is employed in combat for the first time when VMF-123 arrives at Henderson Field

APRIL 1: Marine Aircraft Group 53 arrives at MCAS Cherry Point as the first Marine night fighter group

MAY 11: The battle to retake the island of Attu, Alaska, back from the Japanese begins with the US Army landing 12,500 soldiers

MAY 24: The Marine glider program is abandoned

JUNE 3: All Japanese resistance on Attu Island ceases

JUNE 21: The last Marine ground unit, the 3rd Marine Defense Battalion, is withdrawn from Bougainville

JUNE 30: The active-duty strength of the Marine Corps is 308,523 – 21,384 officers and 287,139 enlisted

vessels such as troop carriers and fuel transports, damaged port facilities, and dealt a crushing blow to the German navy and denying the German military complex of desperately needed iron ore for their war effort.

German air forces did attempt to locate the Allied fleet and launch counterattacks. However, these scout planes were intercepted by the *Ranger's* combat air patrols miles from the task force and was the sight Weldon and the other Marines likely saw. The Royal Navy task force contained no aircraft carriers, and the aircraft the British battleships HMS *Duke of York* and HMS *Anson* and cruisers HMS *Teazer* and

HMS *Belfast* carried were Supermarine Walrus single-engine amphibious biplanes designed for maritime patrol and scouting. Additionally, gun camera footage exists of American F4F Wildcats on combat air patrols shooting down German aircraft that were scouting for the Allied fleet.

The mission was deemed a strategic success. Operation *Leader* was the only carrier operation above the Arctic Circle during the war. Combined detachments from the *Ranger* and *Tuscaloosa* would equal around 150 Marines present for the operation.

Vice Admiral H. K. Hewitt inspects Marines aboard USS *Philadelphia* in Naples, Italy, May 16, 1944. Note the 1903 Springfield rifles. From February 14 to May 23, *Philadelphia* provided fire support for Allied troops near Anzio. Just four months later, on September 11, *Philadelphia* narrowly evaded being seriously damaged by a KG-100 "Fritz" anti-ship glide bomb. While bombarding targets off Aropoli, Italy, on September 15, the cruiser downed one of 12 attacking planes and assisted in driving off a second air attack the same day in the vicinity of Altavilla. It downed two more hostile aircraft on the 17th. (US Navy)

OPERATION *SHINGLE*

By the end of 1943, a stalemate had emerged in Italy after the Allies experienced initial success during the landings the previous year. However, relentless German resistance, coupled with heavy rains and the constant melting of snow, made it nearly impossible to break through the German lines. To overcome this deadlock, an amphibious landing at Anzio was authorized, codenamed Operation *Shingle*. The operation commenced in January 1944 and continued through June 4, 1944, with the liberation of Rome.

Initially, the landings were met with minimal resistance, as the Germans had concentrated most of their forces to the south, near Cassino, to halt the Allies' advance from that direction and were caught off guard by the Allied landings. However, within 24 hours, the Germans were able to quickly assemble elements from several divisions and halt the Allied push from the Anzio beaches after Allied leaders failed to seize on their good fortune to quickly move inland. This delay in progress gave the Germans time to reinforce their positions, bringing in additional troops from the Balkans, southern France, and northern Italy.

By mid-February, the Germans had made significant strides pushing the Allies back toward the beaches. An Allied offensive from the south at Cassino, aimed at linking up with the forces at Anzio, failed to achieve its objective. In response, the Germans launched heavy assaults to dislodge the Allies from Anzio. These attacks were met with fierce resistance, including devastating artillery barrages, with the US Navy providing vital support through artillery strikes from battleships and cruisers. Around 700 Marines took part in Operation *Shingle*, providing antiaircraft gunfire and ship-to-shore bombardment assistance.

THE EVROS MISSION

Based out of Cairo, Egypt, Gunnery Sergeant Thomas L. Curtis, a 29-year-old with 11 years of service in the Marine Corps, was a seasoned and skilled veteran. In March 1944, he was assigned as a demolition expert within the OSS. His team's primary objective was to disrupt the flow of vital materials – such as metals – being transported from Turkey to German weapons factories in Greece and Bulgaria. These shipments were essential to the Axis war effort, and the mission aimed to slow or halt their progress by destroying key infrastructure, particularly bridges.

The half-dozen-member team infiltrated Turkey, then split up to operate in Greece. Curtis, along with US Navy Radioman Third Class Michael Angelos, led a contingent of 50 Greek resistance fighters to demolish the strategically significant Alexandroupolis Bridge, a vital link for German supply lines.

For his contributions to the success of the Evros Mission, Curtis was awarded the Bronze Star for his bravery and service. His efforts were further recognized with a meritorious promotion to warrant officer, an acknowledgment of his exceptional abilities in executing complex and dangerous operations while leading others. Curtis's involvement in the mission was a significant achievement, underscoring his dedication to the success of Allied operations in the Mediterranean Theater and his critical role in disrupting Axis supply chains.

Gunnery Sergeant Thomas L. Curtis

By B. F. Giles Major General, US Army, for his work during the mission

CITATION:

For exceptionally meritorious conduct and heroic achievement in May 1944, in connection with military operations against the enemy in Greece. Gunnery Sergeant Curtis, serving in the capacity of liaison non-commissioned officer in the Evros district of Greece, was placed in command of a unit of fifty guerrillas and ordered to locate and destroy an important bridge, over which passed important raw materials for enemy industry. He traveled for a period of three days through a dangerous enemy-occupied area, carrying a great quantity of explosives, and although detected by the enemy, approached the bridge and was able to demolish it after capturing the guard. Through his courage, leadership and demonstrated ability, Gunnery Sergeant Curtis was mainly responsible for the successful completion of this mission.

OPERATION *UNION I*

By early 1944, preparations for the Allied invasion of Europe were well under way. In southern France, the mountainous region of Haute-Savoie had become home to several thousand French Resistance fighters, known as the Maquis. This region was of interest to both French General Charles de Gaulle and Allied planners, who saw its potential as a major base of operations to disrupt German forces prior to the upcoming invasion.

To assess and strengthen the Maquis, the OSS launched Operation *Union*. A small, elite team was formed, consisting of British SOE (Special Operations Executive) agent H. A. Thackwaite, French radio operator

Captain Pierre Fourcaud, and Marine Corps Captain Peter Ortiz. Their mission was twofold: to evaluate the strength and capabilities of the Resistance fighters, and to encourage a shift in focus from passive intelligence-gathering to more active guerrilla warfare against German forces.

The three-man team parachuted into Vercors, France, from an RAF Halifax bomber from No. 138 Squadron at Tempsford airfield north of London, in early January 1944. Codenamed "John 38," their mission was to insert near the Vercors Plateau, located in southeastern France.

Following the rules of war, the operatives wore their military uniforms; had they been captured in civilian clothes, they would have been classified and executed as spies. Ortiz, known for his boldness, proudly wore his Marine Corps uniform often with ribbons and insignia, even when venturing openly into towns, an act that won him the admiration and cheers of the French locals but quickly attracted German attention.

Despite the growing risks, *Union*'s operations flourished. The team coordinated the delivery of weapons, explosives, and supplies to the Maquis via aerial drops. They also organized extensive training sessions to enhance the fighters' guerrilla capabilities and even took part in direct raids on German military infrastructure. In addition to all of this, Ortiz volunteered to rescue four downed RAF crewmen and smuggled them through Spain, nearly 500km away.

While Thackwaite and Fourcaud generally remained concealed in the hills with the Resistance, Ortiz became something of a local legend for his daring exploits. On one famous occasion, Ortiz reportedly entered a café where he overheard German soldiers insulting American troops. According to legend, Ortiz dramatically threw open the overcoat his was wearing, revealing his Marine Corps uniform and .45-caliber pistols in each hand, and forced the German soldiers to toast to President Roosevelt and then toast to the United States Marine Corps.

The successes of Operation *Union* did not go unnoticed. By February 1944, the German command grew so alarmed by the Maquis' increasing strength and boldness that they dispatched three Panzer Grenadier battalions to Haute-Savoie to crush the uprising. Despite facing overwhelming odds, the Resistance, bolstered by *Union*'s leadership and training, held out for months. In May 1944, as Allied operations shifted focus toward the imminent D-Day invasion, the members of Operation *Union* were withdrawn. Due to his efforts and participation in Operation *Union*, Admiral Harold R. Stark awarded Ortiz his first Navy Cross.

Major Peter J. Ortiz

CITATION:

For extraordinary heroism in connection with military operations against an armed enemy, in enemy-occupied territory, from January 8, 1944 to May 20, 1944. During this period, Major Ortiz, together with two other officers of an inter-Allied Mission, after having been dropped from an airplane, reorganized existing Maquis groups and organized additional groups in the region of Rhone in a highly successful manner. By his tact, initiative, resourcefulness and leadership, he was largely instrumental in the acceptance of the mission by local Resistance leaders and in the effecting the organization of parachute operations from the delivery of arms, ammunition and equipment for the Maquis in his region. When four Royal Air Force officers were shot down in his region Major Ortiz, although his identity had become known to the Gestapo with the result increase in personal hazard, voluntarily conducted them to the Spanish border, after which he returned and fearlessly resumed his duties until he was directed to return to the British Isles.

Throughout the period of assignment, Major Ortiz repeatedly led successful raids against enemy forces greatly superior in number, inflicting heavy casualties with small losses to his own forces. His courageous leadership, and the astuteness with which these forays were planned and executed were an inspiration to his subordinates.

The actions of Major Ortiz throughout his dangerous mission reflect great credit upon himself and the United States Marine Corps.

The conditions of this awards are secret until the occupation of France is completed.

Harold R. Stark
Admiral, US Navy
Commander, US Naval Forces in Europe

OPERATION *OVERLORD*

"Why weren't the Marines at D-Day?" Let the record be straightened that at least seven Marines were confirmed to have landed in France on June 6, 1944. Additionally, at least another 600 Marines were present aboard Navy ships at sea as part of Marine detachments. These included: USS *Arkansas* (BB-33), USS *Texas* (BB-35), USS *Nevada* (BB-36), USS *Augusta* (CA-31), USS *Tuscaloosa* (CA-37), and USS *Quincy* (CA-71).

General Eisenhower even stated the usefulness of having the Marines on ships. The Marines would fire down upon mines in the water to clear the way to allow cruisers and destroyers better access to the beach areas to provide more accurate fire support.

Marines known to have taken part in Operation *Overlord*:

1. Colonel Robert O. Bare – Landed at Juno Beach as a joint staff observer for the Chief of Staff, Supreme Allied Commander, attached to 3rd Canadian Infantry Division (Assault Force J).
2. Colonel Richard Jeschke – Landed at Omaha Beach and was assigned to the Western Naval Task Force as the assistant planning

officer and joint operations officer, attached to US First Army HQ on D-Day.

3. Colonel James E. Kerr – Staff member assigned to Assault Force U, Western Naval Task Force. Kerr was sent ashore to assist with logistics deconfliction as reinforcements and supplies began landing. Kerr's leadership is credited with much of the logistics decongestion between Red and Green sectors of Utah Beach.

4. Captain Herbert L. Merillat – Public relations officer attached to 48 Commando Royal Marines in support of 3rd Canadian Infantry Division and the 2nd Canadian Armoured Brigade at Juno Beach.

5. First Lieutenant Weldon James – Public relations officer who landed with US sailors at Omaha Beach and helped provide targeting data for the USS *Texas*, allowing it to provide more accurate naval gunfire as Allied forces moved inland.

6. Staff Sergeant James R. Kilpatrick – Combat photographer attached to 48 Commando Royal Marines in support of 3rd Canadian Infantry Division and the 2nd Canadian Armoured Brigade at Juno Beach.

7. Technical Sergeant Richard T. Wright – Combat correspondent attached to 48 Commando Royal Marines in support of 3rd Canadian Infantry Division and the 2nd Canadian Armoured Brigade at Juno Beach. Wright manned a 20mm gun on his landing ship and exchanged fire with German forces ashore.

ELSEWHERE IN 1944

JANUARY 16: The withdrawal of the 3rd Marine Division from Bougainville is complete

FEBRUARY 4: Two planes from Marine Photographic Squadron 954 carry out the first photo reconnaissance of the Truk Atoll in the Marshall Islands

FEBRUARY 16: The 22nd Marine Regiment lands on beach White 1 and Blue 3 on Engebi Island, Eniwetok Atoll

MARCH 21: Marines with the 3rd Battalion, 22nd Marine Regiment, land on Ailinglaplap Island, in the Marshalls, and secure it

APRIL 1: The 9th Marine Aircraft Wing is activated at MCAS Cherry Point, North Carolina

APRIL 14: Marine Night Fighter Squadron 532 fly the Marine Corps' first successful interception by the F4U at night

MAY 10: James V. Forrestal is appointed Secretary of the Navy

JUNE 4: The US Fifth Army enters Rome

JUNE 15: The 2nd and 4th Marine Divisions assault Saipan

JUNE 17: The 105th Infantry Regiment of the Army's 27th Infantry Division lands on Saipan

JUNE 25: Japanese barges from Tinian carrying reinforcements to Saipan are intercepted by US Navy destroyers

JUNE 30: The active duty strength of the Marine Corps is 475,604 – 32,788 officers and 442,816 enlisted

US Marines train their 40mm antiaircraft gun on a Nazi aircraft, somewhere off the coast of France, June 6, 1944. These Marines were aboard USS *Texas*, which participated in initial action during the invasion. (USMC, photo by Cpl William R. Gibbon)

Marines aboard USS *Texas* man a 40mm antiaircraft gun at a position just off the coast of France, June 6, 1944. The Leathernecks are having a dull time due to the absence of the German Luftwaffe. (USMC, photo by Cpl William R. Gibbon)

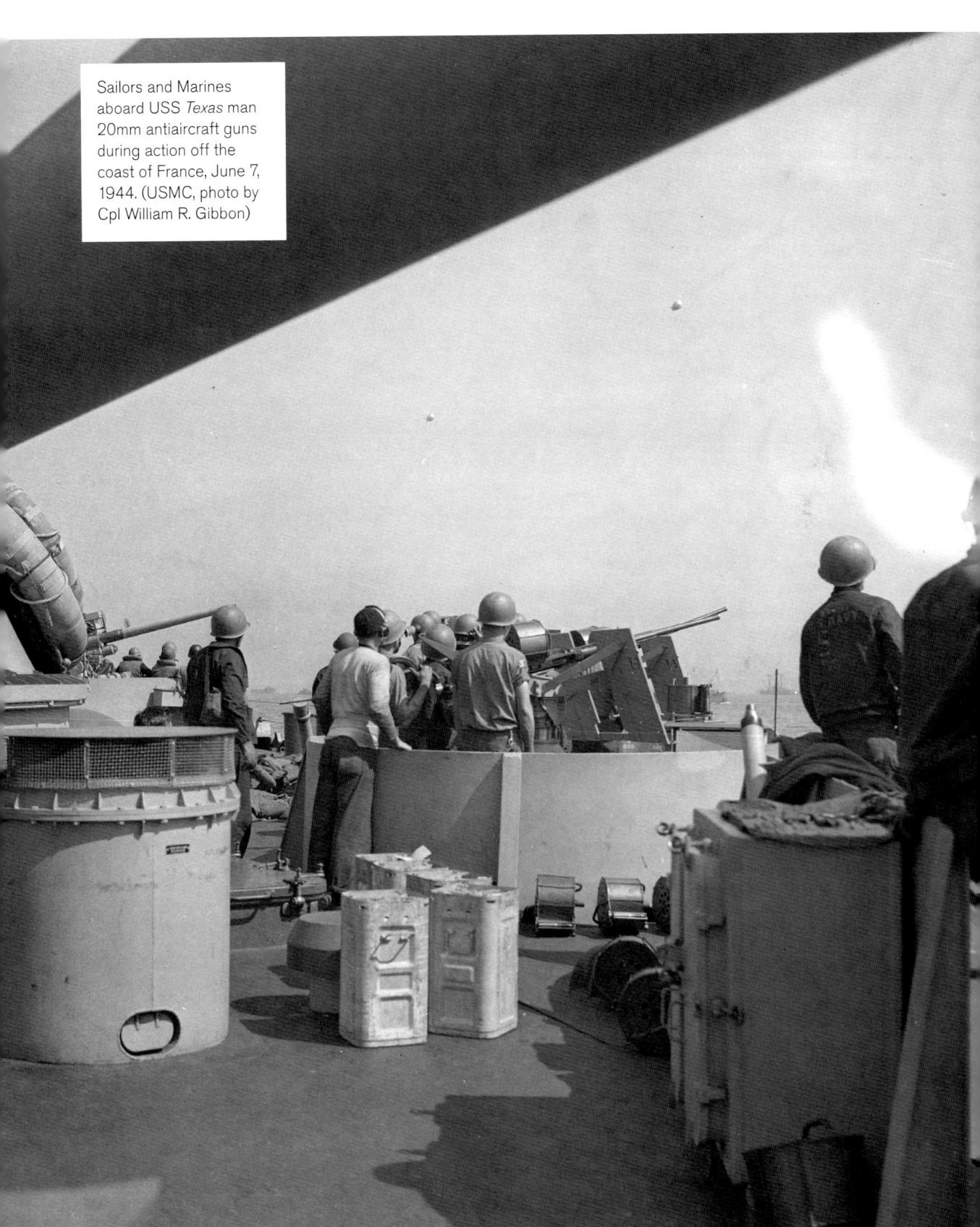

Sailors and Marines aboard USS *Texas* man 20mm antiaircraft guns during action off the coast of France, June 7, 1944. (USMC, photo by Cpl William R. Gibbon)

Marine guards aboard USS *Texas* take German prisoners of war into custody on June 7, 1944. (USMC, photos by Cpl William R. Gibbon)

Marine Sergeant Joseph S. Sivy, of Aliquippa, Pennsylvania, passes out cotton to German and Italian prisoners who were captured off the coast of France and brought aboard USS *Texas*, June 7, 1944. The cotton should protect their ear drums from the 14-inch batteries that are about to start firing. Sergeant Sivy, who also took part in the invasion of North Africa, enlisted in the Marine Corps in May 1942 and joined the *Texas* in September 1942. (USMC, photo by Cpl William R. Gibbon)

Wounded Army Rangers being brought aboard USS *Texas* from Omaha Beach. Marines assigned to the 40mm antiaircraft gun behind look on. (USMC, photo by Cpl William R. Gibbon)

THIS AND SUBSEQUENT SPREADS Sailors and Marines crowd the deck to see the wounded Rangers brought aboard. (USMC, photos by Cpl William R. Gibbon)

US Marines and British Royal Marines at D-Day

By Technical Sergeant Richard T. Wright, US Marine Corps Combat Correspondent June 6, 1944

Aboard a British Landing Craft, Guns, June 6, 1944 – The crew of Royal Marines and sailors on this courageous craft just finished the hottest 50-minute fight of their lives.

With guns belching death many times every minute, this "floating artillery" platform steamed to within 500 yards of German shore batteries today, as British Leathernecks blasted beach installations enabling the first wave of General Montgomery's Canadian troops to storm ashore in France.

At one stage in the assault this fighting ship was 400 yards ahead of the nearest supporting ship and drew most of the German fire from beach defenses. Her casualty list was very light in contrast to the hundreds of salvos which this landing craft guns smashed into the German-occupied village.

Forty-five minutes later I arrived on deck just in time to see a British battleship thunder the opening round in the invasion of this sector of the continent.

Low hanging clouds made the coast of France seem a long grey line off in the distance. I could see a large water tower and what appeared to be houses along the beach, as other warships began to pound away in an effort to blast everything that lived along the coast.

Hundreds of small landing craft, blue-grey transports, and many British men-of-war ploughed easily through heavy seas toward the sleepy-looking coastline.

Lieutenant Christopher D. Graham, Royal Navy, the skipper of this ship, spotted our particular target, which proved to be a battery of three-inch guns. Leaving the cruiser and destroyers behind, we moved out in front of the other assault units, and steamed full speed ahead toward our target.

Ten minutes later, at 0700, terrific blasts shook the beach while columns of dust and smoke rose high into the air. Although we could not see them because of the clouds, we knew that the American Army's Ninth Air Force was somewhere above.

Along with Royal Marine Corporal James Easton, of Glasgow, Scotland, I get set to man one of the 20mm twin Oerlikon guns on the port side of the bridge.

The first salvo from our guns landed somewhere to the left of our target. Shells from our warship whistled overhead while three-inch enemy shells cut the water around our ship. I strafed the houses along the shoreline with the Oerlikon, and then loaded for Corporal Easton who took great delight in, as he put it, "peppering the hell out of the Jerrys."

After firing four magazines of ammunition at German defenses on the coast, Corporal Easton and I were ordered off the gun to tend to two wounded Marines, who had been shot through the hand. We bandaged their hands as best we could and moved into their place on the larger gun.

The gun crew looked like seven dwarfs with their white-helmeted anti-flag gear and white gloves. They appeared glassy-eyed and the gun captain had blood streaming from a wound over his eye.

We fired salvo after salvo at the Germans as their three-inch shells continued to hit the ship.

Occasionally, I watched our skipper, who stands five feet six inches. He and the Royal Marine commander, Lieutenant Germa A. M. Ritson, were ducking three-inch shells on the bridge and barking orders. I began to understand how the traditions of the Royal Navy were made.

Finally, the order to cease firing came. I looked out over the water and saw hundreds of landing craft moving into the beach. Large tanks began to lumber up onto the sandy shore while the pop of machine gun fire, the blast of heavy cruiser shells bursting further in toward town, and occasionally a group of rocket shells bursting on the beach, heralded the initial landing of troops on French soil.

Royal Marines, who manned our gun, just lay and gasped for breath. Nobody said anything. They were too tired and dazed after firing their salvos at the Germans.

Five minutes later we saw two large explosions from the shore line, and were ordered to gun stations again. Two Landing Craft Tanks seemed to bend in the middle and turn over on their sides.

It was still unsafe to stand on the gun platform upright, as stray machine gun bullets and sniper fire were evident.

A small escort vessel came alongside, and one of our wounded was moved to the other craft where he was put in the care of a British doctor.

After 50 minutes of fighting, we took stock of our damage and found 15 three-inch shell holes in the hull of the ship, one in the bridge, and several on the gun platforms.

One shell had entered the mess deck and had chased a Royal Marine who was helping in the magazine room around the mess tables before it dropped to the deck, spent. He grabbed the shell, raced for a forward hatch, and tossed it into the sea.

"Harry," the galley chief, brought all hands a cup of hot tea, while the skipper cruised up and down the coast sector looking for trouble.

Battleships, cruisers, and destroyers continued to bombard the coast this afternoon as Allied air forces moved toward the front lines. At four o'clock we saw two Junker 88s being chased by two North American Mustangs.

With the aid of field glasses, we could see our infantry tanks, trucks, and an occasional jeep moving up the road to our right.

At four-thirty our tanks on the beach began blasting German machine gun nests on top of a small rise, directly in back of the town. Huge spurts of brown dirt geyser up into the air. We had a grandstand seat.

German snipers continued to peck away at Allied troops along the beach, while LSTs, and LCIs continued to move into the shore. Enemy mines held up the advance for some time.

We received orders to move out and act as a defense against German "E" and "R" boats. As darkness settled, we got set for the Nazi air force, which up to this time was missing.

At twelve o'clock a Junker 88 flew between our ship and a Landing Craft, Flak. It was so low that we could not fire upon it for fear of hitting other craft nearby.

The Germans began throwing up great red tracers in an attempt to down Allied planes who were bombing the Nazi front lines. A few minutes later we saw a plane, either ours or Jerry's, in a hail of ack ack fire just off the beach. Finally hit, he plunged seaward in a great ball of orange fire.

British "Dakotas," carrying either troops or ammunition, passed over our heads every few minutes. By one o'clock the sky was full of ack ack fire and both German and Allied planes.

Ammunition dumps on shore flashed occasionally as tracers burst out from the center in all directions. The warships continued to pound the shore.

A final radio broadcast announcing only light casualties to Naval personal and assault units was gratifying news to the Royal Marines and sailors aboard this ship.

TOP Sergeant Eric E. Dawe, Royal Marines, from Plymouth, England, and Staff Sergeant James R. Kilpatrick, Marine combat photographer from Detroit, Michigan, get together after the bombardment of the German beach defenses and landing the first wave of troops ashore at Juno Beach, June 6, 1944. (USMC, photo by TSgt Richard T. Wright)

BOTTOM Royal Marine Corporal James Easton (left), of Glasgow, Scotland, and Technical Sergeant Richard T. Wright, of Arlington, Virginia, Marine combat correspondent, "jock" aboard a British landing craft after a 50-minute engagement with German shore batteries, June 6, 1944. (USMC, photo by SSgt James R. Kilpatrick)

OPPOSITE Aboard a British Landing Craft, Guns (LCG) on D-Day. British troops wait to disembark on the coast of France, June 6, 1944. (USMC, photo by SSgt James R. Kilpatrick)

Royal Marines Blast Nazi Defenses

By Technical Sergeant Richard T. Wright, US Marine Corps Combat Correspondent
June 6, 1944

Aboard a British Landing Craft, Guns – This first morning after "D-Day" at our anchorage 1,000 yards from a battered coast town in France, is far from peaceful.

The British battleships *Warspite* and *Rodney* are lobbing shells ashore with their fifteen-inch guns in an attempt to blast German strongholds eight miles inland, where a forward observer wired the range. The occasional blast of a destroyer's guns reminds us that fighting ashore is still bitter even along the coastal sectors of this beach.

The beaches at our sector are loaded with tanks, jeeps, trucks, and artillery. Equipment is being moved to the front lines as fast as possible, while LSTs by the hundreds are anchored a short distance off shore, waiting to steam in and unload their cargo of men and supplies.

At ten thirty this morning four Nazi Junker 88s peeled off and over at an LST unloading on the beach. Anti-aircraft fire shot the tail away from one plane and it crashed a rubble of dust and flames on the beach. Another Jerry crashed a short distance inland, while the two other planes took off in the distance.

Pulling along an LST bound for the United Kingdom late this afternoon, I said goodbye to a great crew of English, Scotch, Irish, and Welsh Royal Marines and sailors, after ten days as part of the ship's company.

Climbing aboard the LST I heard a deck hand exclaim, "look at that funnel, she sure caught bloody hell!" He wasn't wrong.

Aboard this ship are six RAF crewmen who were shot down off shore by Jerry ack ack last night, while towing a glider plane full of supplies. Our other guest is a German flyer, a pilot officer, who was shot down by American "lightning." He landed by parachute on the beach just as a German mine exploded alongside a British Landing Craft Tanks, and was knocked out by the blast.

Newsmen Were Closest Marines to Normandy Landings

By Herbert L. Merillat
Originally published in *Fortitudine* magazine, spring 1944

The role of US Marines on D-Day in Normandy was pretty much limited to service on battleships and cruisers that were bombarding the beaches. A crack Marine battalion that had been sent to Londonderry early in the war to help defend Northern Ireland never got into action in Europe; it was eventually dispersed among units in the Pacific. Thus it happened that the US Marines who got the closest to the Normandy beaches on that fateful June morning were a team of three combat correspondents attached to the London headquarters of the US Naval Forces in Europe. These were myself (then a captain), TSgt Richard T. Wright, and combat photographer SSgt James R. "Scotty" Kilpatrick.

I arranged with the Royal Marines and Royal Navy for the three of us to take part in D-Day proceedings on LCGs — Landing Craft, Guns. These were British tank landing craft converted to serve as floating artillery. A twin-gun turret of 4.7-inch guns was mounted on each LCG. With their shallow drafts the LCGs could get close to the shoreline, just outside the belt of underwater obstacles, and deliver direct fire against German pillboxes and other targets on the beaches – part of Hitler's Atlantic Wall – just before assault troops landed. Then they could take on targets farther inland.

The skipper of LCG-1007, in which I embarked, was Lt Hugh G. Ashworth, and the commander of the Royal Marines contingent was Lt George Hardwick, RM. The ship's company consisted of 16 seamen and 46 Royal Marines who manned the guns. We were assigned to Juno Beach in the British sector, where a Canadian division would land.

Our LCGs were part of a vast armada assembling at Portsmouth, one of the many British ports from which the cross-Channel drive was to be mounted. We joined the ships on May 28, speculating that we would shove off for Normandy about the 4th or 5th of June. Electrical engineer teams attached mysterious wires and boxes to ships' masts; we later learned they were devices to foil enemy radar. But balmy summer weather turned wet and windy. On the 4th everyone felt let down when word came that D-Day had been postponed. It was, however, rescheduled for 6 June; as we now know, it was one of Gen Eisenhower's most difficult and momentous decisions. Our flotilla set out from Portsmouth on the morning of the 5th. Shortly after noon we entered the English Channel from the Solent, the first group after the minesweepers.

That night the Channel was alive with ships – fast ones, slow ones, fighting ships of all sizes, transports, landing craft, tiny rocket boats – overtaking or falling behind according to an intricate and inflexible pattern that would get each to its proper position off the Normandy coast at dawn. As one who had taken part in the first US amphibious attack in the war, against the Japanese at Guadalcanal in August 1942, I was much impressed by the variety of new ships and boats that had been developed for such operations.

One of our main engines broke down after midnight. There were anxious minutes while it was repaired and we tried to recover our position in the formation, with the skipper peering through the gloom at numbers on buoys and other vessels. All night long the sky over the French coastline ahead was alive with German ack-ack, sweeping the skies like hoses of fire as Allied bombers roared in, wave after wave. As we later learned, some of the Allied planes carried parachutists in the early morning hours.

By 0530 it was growing light. Already the big naval guns were bombarding the shoreline of the American beaches west of us. At our beach the heavy naval guns opened fire behind us at 0600 and heavy bombers began coming over to blast the landing beaches. The shore was barely visible through smoke and dust. We closed in with the first assault wave of Canadian troops and began firing on our first designated target – a German pillbox mounting three-inch guns.

Just before the assault waves reached the beach sheets of flame rose from rocket craft astern of us. Clusters of rockets zoomed over our heads and crashed on the beach. As the Canadians went ashore, our guns were silent. Later we fired at houses in the village of Courseulles, at a strongpoint between two villages, and into the woods beyond.

In the first exchanges of fire some nearby vessels had been holed. Among them was our flotilla leader; one seaman was killed. TSgt Wright, on that LCG, joined in firing twin Oerlikon guns at beach targets. By 0930 the last German gun shelling Allied vessels from Juno beach had been silenced. Our own targets were now inland, ahead of the Canadian advance. Our ships' main work done, we watched in the afternoon as the Canadians moved slowly beyond the dunes.

The visually most spectacular events began at dusk. For hours the sky was full of Allied planes, as in the night before. First the bombers came, group after group. For half an hour the air was full of their thunder. Then the big, black transports and gliders filed over. (Later the troops landed in our sector were identified as the 6 Air Landing Brigade.) Coming low from the north amid heavy antiaircraft fire, the planes crossed the beach, wheeled, dropped their loads, and headed back. Within our field of vision one craft fell in flames in the sea, another crashed trying to land in a field, while a third, smoke trailing from an engine, swooped low, then began rising steadily and, as we all cheered, started back toward England.

The nighttime mission of our LCG was to help guard that vast assemblage of ships against possible attacks by German motor torpedo boats from bases nearby in the mouth of the Seine. It was not an E-boat but a Junkers 88 that almost got us. The German bomber dove low over the defense line shortly before midnight. It was shot down by a flak ship in our flotilla but crashed into the sea dead ahead of LCG-1007.

It was too late to reverse engines, and as we crouched on the bridge to take the shock of a possible explosion the skipper shouted down the voice pipe, "Full ahead together." Our LCG crunched into the plane, cutting it in two, and passed over the wreckage as German aviation gas drenched the gun crew in our bow.

All night the sky and the land behind the beaches were aflame with flares, bombs, artillery fire, burning buildings and planes, and great whips of German antiaircraft fire that lashed across the sky, interlacing, crisscrossing. We stayed on station for three days and nights and then returned to England. The three US Marines who had been closest to the action left their friends of the Royal Marines and Royal Navy with admiration and respect and some vivid memories. We could not claim to have contributed much if anything to the victory, but we were pleased that we had been able to witness at close quarters one of the greatest battles in history.

Author note

In the first paragraph Merillat is referencing Marine Barracks, NOB Londonderry, which was around the strength of a regiment at its highest end strength. At its peak, the Londonderry battalion had 1,600 stationed at it. However, he did not know of the unit's participation in Operation *Torch*. At the time, it is highly probable that Merillat was not knowledgeable of the

unit's activities due to the general business of the war. With so few Marines in the United Kingdom to begin with, and the secrecy involved, it is likely Merillat was ignorant of the presence of Marines on staff helping to plan the invasion.

OPPOSITE Lieutenant Hugh Ashworth, Royal Navy Volunteer Reserve, and Lieutenant George Hardwick, Royal Marines, brief Marines en route to Juno Beach, Normandy, with Captain Herbert L. Merillat and Sub Lieutenant D. B. Beyon, Royal Navy Volunteer Reserve, watching from the bridge. (USMC, photo by SSgt James R. Kilpatrick)

Marines Aboard USS *Texas* Stood by to Reinforce Rangers in Normandy

By First Lieutenant Weldon James, US Marine Corps Public Relations Officer
June 6, 1944

USS *Texas* – How Marines from the detachment of the battleship *Texas* almost took part in the land assault on Normandy in the French invasion was revealed here as 10 of the men reported to R&R Center for reassignment and 30-day furloughs.

"American Rangers were attempting to scale a 100ft cliff," said Sgt Kenneth R. Cheek of New York City. "The Germans were rolling grenades down the cliff and raking them with machine gun fire. Our 14-in. guns were plastering the enemy over the Rangers' heads, but it looked as if they were going to fail to take the cliff.

"The Marine captain on board called for volunteers to go ashore and reinforce the Rangers. We volunteered and were ready to go, but at the last minute the plan was called off. After 18 hours of fierce fighting, the Rangers took the hill.

"Maybe it was lucky we didn't go in as twenty-eight months of sea-going duty isn't the best sort of conditioning for assaulting a 100ft high [cliff]." Pfc. Adelco J. Venitelli of North Plainfield, NJ, recalled that at Normandy "five or six of us were sent out in barges to shoot out enemy flares that were lighting up the area around the *Texas*. We were armed with rifles, BARs and machine guns."

At Cherbourg, he said, Marines whose normal duties were as AA gunners were used as riflemen to pick off floating mines. The *Texas*' roughest time, in the opinion of PFC Robert C. Ogden of Endicott, NY, was during the battle for Cherbourg June 25.

"We shelled the French coast for three solid hours and the shore batteries were dropping big ones all around us," he related. "A 200mm shell crashed into the forecastle and stayed there. It was a dud – luckily – because it had come to rest in a warrant officer's cabin. Later a fire started in an ammunition stack. We had to go in and toss live ammunition over the side of the ship before it could explode. We had to run in and out between salvos from our own guns to toss the ammunition overboard and extinguish the fire."

The *Texas*' Marines were proud, too, of "victories" over our Allies. In September, 1943, said Corp Bernard J. Finnegan of Flushing, NY, the Marines defeated a British Royal Marine pistol team at Gibraltar.

"We hadn't fired pistols since boot camp," he said, "but we won pretty easily."

And PFC Clarence A. Neitzelt of Wheeling, W Va, told how the Army's championship team challenged the *Texas*' Marines to a match at Oran, North Africa. "We beat them – about 8 to 1," he grinned. Members of the detachment served as color guard at Casablanca in February, 1943, for an impressive "changing of the flags" ceremony.

Shells from German shore batteries impact around USS *Texas* the morning of June 6, 1944. (US Navy)

Slam-bang Fight of U.S.S. Texas Against Heavy Nazi Batteries Told

BATTLESHIP TEXAS IN ACTION—Smoke from her 14-inch guns hover over American warship in three-hour gun duel with German shore batteries at Cherbourg. The queen of the older Fleet received two direct hits. *(P) Wirephoto*

TOP The *Los Angeles Times*, August 14, 1944, featuring Lieutenant James's stories. Several dozen newspapers across the country republished James's stories of the sailors and Marines aboard USS *Texas* during D-Day. (LoC)

BOTTOM The *Greenville News*, August 14, 1944. (LoC)

ABOVE Second from the left is Lieutenant General Omar Bradley, then Colonel Richard H. Jeschke and on the right is Major General J. Lawton Collins. Jeschke had previously served as the commanding officer for the 8th Marine Regiment, 2nd Marine Division. In the summer of 1943, he was transferred to the Western Naval Task Force as the officer in charge of Force Marine Operations and Training located in the Mediterranean under command of Rear Admiral Henry Kent Hewitt. In his position on the task force, Jeschke helped plan Operation *Husky*, the invasion of Sicily. Omar was so impressed that following the success of Operation *Husky*, Jeschke was transferred to the First Army staff and worked directly for Bradley himself to help plan the invasion at Normandy. By D-Day, Jeschke was transferred back to the Western Naval Task Force as the assistant planning officer and joint operations officer. On D-Day, Jeschke went ashore with Bradley. Throughout the entirety of Operation *Overlord*, Jeschke made frequent trips from shore to ship with updates to help keep Admiral Alan Goodrich Kirk informed of naval gunfire effectives and provide reports on the progress of troop and logistics advancements. For his work on

D-Day, Jeschke was awarded the Legion of Merit with Combat "V" and also received the French Croix de Guerre with Gilt Star from the government of France. (MCHD)

INSET While he did not land in Normandy, Colonel William T. Clement was assigned to work on plans for the cross-Channel movements of D-Day. Shortly after Operation *Overlord*, he was transferred to the 6th Marine Division in the Pacific. (MCHD)

LEFT In June 1943, Robert O. Bare was serving with the G-3 (operations) of I Amphibious Corps when he received orders to Navy headquarters in London. After reporting in, Bare was placed as a staff officer of plans inside the Navy section working for British Admiral Sir Bertram Ramsay. Bare's work consisted of scouting training areas for Allied troops in addition to visiting command and installations to coordinate and work on combined and joint plans. Bare and other staff with him worked on much of the preliminary planning in 1943. It would not be until the very beginning of 1944 when General Dwight D. Eisenhower was named Supreme Allied Commander and Admiral Kirk and his staff arrived from the Mediterranean in March that the planning for D-Day began in earnest. Prior to D-Day, Bare requested to be attached to a British unit. As such he was attached to British Naval Force "J," which would be landing the 3rd Canadian Infantry Division. (MCHD)

BOTTOM Colonel Bare's Bronze Star Medal citation. (MCHD)

THE SECRETARY OF THE NAVY
WASHINGTON

The President of the United States takes pleasure in presenting the BRONZE STAR MEDAL to

COLONEL ROBERT O. BARE,
UNITED STATES MARINE CORPS,

for service as set forth in the following

CITATION:

"For meritorious achievement while attached to the British Assault Force J, as an Observer during the Normandy Invasion, from 29 May to 13 June 1944. Accompanying the forces through hazardous mine-infested waters as well as bomb and gunfire attacks, Colonel Bare participated in the attack by the British on the section of the Normandy coast near Courselles-sur-Mer on 6 June, observing all phases of the operation from the embarkation to the assault over the beaches until his return to England on 13 June. Compiling notes and making detailed sketches of his observations, he later incorporated these into a most valuable report. By his extraordinary initiative, keen judgment and courageous devotion to duty, Colonel Bare obtained information of great and immediate value to the United States in the successful prosecution of the war, thereby reflecting credit upon himself and the United States Naval Service."

For the President,

James Forrestal
Secretary of the Navy.

Dear Tom:

My typing will probably be worse than yours, but it's better than my handwriting.

I could write pages, and talk for hours on the planning for the Normandy landings. The year I spent in England prior to, and during the landings, were the most interesting of my career,

To go back a bit. After WW-1, it was the concensus that an Amphibious landing in the face of opposition was foolhardy, and probably impossible. A few Marine officers, and even fewer Naval officers doubted this, and began an intensive study of such operations with a view toward developing a doctrine for making such landings possible.

The majority of this work was done at the MCS, and took the form of instructional pamphlets, which in the middle 30's xxx were collected into the publication known as FTP- 167. To my knowledge, this was the first such publication in the world. At the beginning of WW-2, the Army copied it word for word, and picture for picture, and issued it as a TR. At the beginning of WW-2, the only xxx two nations in the world with an Amphibious doctrine, were the US and Japan. To illustrate how little the Army was interested in amphib operations prior to the war- when I was a student at the Army C&GS School at Leavenworth in 1938-39, the course in Amphib operations was about 6 hours, taught by a Coast Arty Lt. Col. who one day in exasperation at trying to explain Landing Schedules and Boat Diagrams, said, "If you really want to learn something about this get ahold of a good Marine Corps sergeant and have him explain it".

My belief is that the MarCorp made a major contribution to the war effort by having ready an Amphib doctrine, upon which the refinements could be built. Much the same is true for the development of close air support, and the use of the helicopter.

Now to Normandy. In June 1943, I was G-3 of the I Amphib Corps, for Gen. H.M. Smith, in San Diego. One day I received immediate orders to report to Hq. USMC for overseas assignment of an unspecified nature- even Gen Smith didn't know what nor where. On reporting to Hq I was sent to the Navy Dept. to xxxx see BG Reilly, USMC. All he would tell me was that I was going to England to be assigned to a combined staff for a period of about a year, and that I woud have to travel in civilian clothes. Ibought an old suit, shirt and tie from a friend, was processed in haste for passport and transportation, and before I came to was flying to England via Ireland, hence the civilian dress.

A Capt. Gordon Huchins, USN was on the plane with me, and after we had reported in to the Navy Hq in London, we were sent on down to Norfolk House, and reported to Lieut. Gen. Sir Frederick Morgan, ⩒ British Army. We found that he was COSSAC, the Chief of Staff to the Supreme Allied Commander, and of course at that time there wasn't any such person.
We found that for two years plans had been going on for "The return to the continent", and that the planning was definitely now to go on

THIS AND SUBSEQUENT PAGES Bare's reflection on the planning of Operation *Overlord*. (MCHD)

[9 MAY 1966?]

in a more intensive and realistic fashion. The planning was taken
out of the hands of Combined Operations, and placed in Cossacs hands.
    Incidentally, a book by Gen, Morgan entitled, "Overture to
Overlord" is excellent reading. I consider Gen. Morgan one of the
best military men I ever met.
    Cossac was composed of an Army, Navy, and Air Force section.
The Navy section was headed up by a British Admiral, and Capt.
Hutchins and I, along with eventually about 5 others, composed the
US portion of that section. After things got shaken douwn a bit,
I was designated the SOP (Staff officer,plans). It was fascinating
work, since I was in on all the most secret dope, and had an opportunity
to travel in seeking out training areas, and visiting various
military commands and installations in working out the intricate
combined plans.
    In the fall, although the Supreme Allied Commander had not been
named, the three Service Commanders were, Gen, Montgomery as ground
forces CO, Gen Sir Trafford Leigh-Mallory as Air CO, Xx and Adm.
Sir Bertram Ramsey as ANCXF (Allied Naval Commander Expeditionary
Force), and he now became our boss. He was a fine man. He had been
retired, called back, and was the man who controlled the evacuation
from Dunkirk.
    In Dec. 1943. Gen Eisenhower was Xx named as the Supreme Allied
Commander, and took charge in the middle of Jan.
    The planning all along had envisaged only landing in the area to
the west of La Havre. This mainly because of lack of forces, and
uncert nty of the outcome of some of the operations in the Med. It
now bec me apparent the the sc pe of the landings could be enlarged,
to include landings on, and at, the base of the Cotantin Peninsula.
It was decided to assign these landings to the US, and the others to
the British. I think it was about March 1944, when Adm. Kirk and his
staff came up from the Med, and the planning for the American operations
got into high gear.
    As the planning progre sed many new and wonderful ideas were
formulated, none of which can really be tied down to one man. Such
things as the artificial harbors, the pipe lines across the Channel,
the many clever diversion and deceptive plans, the swimming tanks,
and other tanks with flails to beat the mine fields, and other with
bridges attached, rocket ships, and large landing craft with large
calibre guns for close support.
    The plans for the control and movement of this huge force across
the Channel are almost unbelievable. Lanes had to be swept for
transports and NGF ships. Some ships had to leave from Scotland, and
yet be tied in with the whole force. There was the always high
prxbxbly probability that the Germans would find and hit the force
from the air. By dark of D-1 there would be some 4000 ships and
boats only about 15 miles from the landing areas. The fact is that
the Germans did not discover the huge fxrxxix force is in my mind
due to several things. An elaborate deception effort had been made
to lead the Germans to believe that the main attack would come in
the Pais de Calais, and the other the wise decision of Gen. Eisenhower
to go ahead with the attack although the weather was marginal. The
German is a land animal, and he didn't believe anyone in his right
mind would venture a landing in such bad weather.
    As the time approached, D-day that is, our Hq. moved down to
Southwich House, near Portsmouth, and I began to wonder how I was
going to get to go Normandy with the troops. Fortunately, a
dispatch came from the CMC asking that Maj. Jimmy Kerr and I be
allowed to go along as observers. Being pretty well up on US
Amphib work, I requested to go with a British force. Since Gen,

Montgomery would not allow any observers with the ground troops, it
was arrangedthat I could go with British Naval Force "J",which lifted
the 3d Canadian Inf, Div. which landed at Bernier sur Mer, and
Courseulles sur Mer. Except for a mine, which looked at that time
the size of the Lincoln Memorial, drifting on our starboard side, the
trip was uneventful. Not a German plane showed up until about 2000
on D-day, and in the ensuing 10 days I was there, there were very few
showed up. Commodore Oliver, the CO of Force "J", was good enough
to take me ashore nearly every day, beginning with the afternoon of
D-day. There hadn't been too much resistance on the beaches, but the
Canadians were hit hard as they pushed inland.

Well, Tom. give and old man a chance to talk, and he will take it.
Now, I had better answer your questions.
I was on the staff of Adm. Sir Bertram Ransey, the Allied
Naval Commander in Chief, *as Staff Officer, Plans*.
The British had an Amphib Opn book, which was not so near
compleat as ours.
Full use was taken of reports from other operations and from
observers and people engaged in them.
Other Marines involved. Maj. Jimmy Kerr, who lives near Quantico,
was in SW England with the Commander of Landing Craft and Bases US.,
and went to France with the US Naval Task Force under Adm Kirk.
Col. Johnny Clement was on the staff of the Commander Naval Forces
Europe. They were more logistical in nature and had little to do with
the overall planning. Col. Jeschke was the Marine officer on Adm,
Kirks staff. What he did, I don't know. A Col. John Anderson was
on the rather defunct Combined Ops staff.
It may sound egotistical, but, so far as I know, I am the only
US Marine officer who was on the overall planning staff. What I
contributed is doubtful, but as I said before, it was the most
interesting part of my military life, and many of the events are as
fresh now as they were 22 years ago.

As to Tex and Nancy, I will offer no comments, except to say
that she and Sandy are free from fear and continual tension. They are
up in Menlo Park today for a horse show. Sandy is crazy about horses.
Our best to you and Alyce.

Sincerely

Bob Bare

OPERATION *BUGATTI*

In preparation for the Allied landings in southern France for Operation *Dragoon*, the OSS devised Operation *Bugatti* – a mission intended to help tie down German forces, create confusion, and disrupt enemy activities behind the lines. A four-man team was assembled, consisting of one British officer, two French officers, and led by Marine Major Horace W. Fuller. Their target was the town of Tarbes, the provincial capital of the Haute-Pyrénées in southwestern France.

The Haute-Pyrénées was rich with targets of importance to the Allies. Within the area were critical sites including an aircraft engine factory, an artillery ordnance plant, a major railway yard and repair facility, and an oil refinery at Peyrouzet, just east of Tarbes. Unfortunately for Fuller's team, the region was heavily garrisoned by several German regiments.

Major Fuller was no stranger to combat. A veteran of the 1st Marine Division, he had landed on Guadalcanal in August 1942 and was wounded when a Japanese aircraft strafed his position, leaving him with a leg injury.

On the night of June 28, 1944, a B-24 Liberator took off from Blida Airfield near Algiers, carrying Fuller and his team into occupied France. After a five-hour flight, they parachuted into the countryside and linked up with local Maquis Resistance fighters. Over the following weeks, Fuller's team led the Maquis on a series of successful sabotage missions, engaging in multiple firefights with German forces. One notable clash occurred on July 17 near Arbon, where they killed 16 German soldiers without suffering a single casualty.

By July 20, Fuller and the Maquis had struck all their assigned targets and were destroying rail lines faster than the Germans could repair them. Their most significant success came when they halted the shipment of 50,000 tons of iron ore, a critical blow to the German war effort.

The team's sabotage efforts also extended to the Peyrouzet oil refinery. By manipulating the local river control valves, Fuller's operatives deprived the refinery of its water source, rendering it powerless to generate electricity and halting its fuel production.

On the night of August 14, following orders from General Charles de Gaulle for a general uprising across southern France to support Operation *Dragoon*, Fuller coordinated a large-scale Maquis offensive in the Haute-Pyrénées. Ambush teams were placed at key road junctions to disrupt and paralyze German movements, sowing chaos ahead of the Allied landings.

In the weeks that followed, Fuller's small guerrilla army swelled to nearly 5,000 fighters. Together, they executed a relentless series of

TOP Liberated French citizens gather in the center of their town to heap praise and thanks on Major Horace Fuller (center with pistol belt on, wearing light top and dark pants) in the town of Luchon, after he and his team had routed the Germans garrisoned in the town. (NARA)

CENTER Major Fuller (near center to the left of the man in the dark suit), his team, and Maquis in Tarbes, 1944. (Horace Fuller)

BOTTOM Major Fuller (third from the right back row with garrison cap on) stands with a captured German standard in Luchon. The flag was obtained after the group completed an ambush operation. Fuller, along with the French, had captured members of the elite 3rd SS Panzer Division Totenkopf. The unit was infamous in France for having committed a massacre in Le Paradis. (Horace Fuller)

Lieutenant Colonel Horace W. Fuller

CITATION:

For conspicuous gallantry and intrepidity while attached to the Office of Strategic Services, United States Naval Forces in Europe, in action against enemy forces in enemy-occupied France, from 28 June 1944 to 15 September 1944. Parachuting into the Hautes-Pyrenees Depertment of France to organize, arm and lead resistance forces personnel in sabotage and other underground activities against enemy troops and installations, Lieutenant Colonel Fuller assembled men and arms to withstand an attack, on 17 July, of over five hundred German troops, inflicting heavy casualties on the enemy without the loss of a man of his own group. Due to the heavy concentration of enemy troops in his area, he voluntarily changed to civilian clothing the better to accomplish his task, making himself liable to treatment as a spy in the event of his capture and, on 14 August, led his Maquis forces in a series of raids and ambushes to liberate Tarbes, in which over six hundred prisoners and much German equipment were taken. Throughout this entire period, he led his forces in sabotage activities, severing the rail and power lines and rendering useless the oil refinery at Peyrouzet by outing off its water supply. His courage and devotion to duty were in keeping with the highest traditions of the United States Naval Service.

ambushes along the France–Spain border, capturing more than 400 German soldiers. Operation *Bugatti* became so successful that Fuller's forces no longer needed Allied reconnaissance aircraft; they had seized several German airfields – and aircraft – allowing them to conduct their own limited air operations.

For his actions and leadership, he was awarded the Silver Star by the United States and the Croix de Guerre by the French government.

PROJECT SAFEHAVEN

By late 1944, the eventual defeat of Nazi Germany was becoming increasingly clear to Allied leadership. Although fierce fighting still lay ahead, policymakers were already focused on shaping the postwar world – and ensuring that Germany would never again pose a global threat.

Within the Foreign Economic Administration, a group of strategists launched Project Safehaven – an ambitious operation aimed at identifying and securing German assets hidden abroad. Its goals were fourfold: prevent Nazi officials from smuggling wealth out of Germany to fund future revanchist movements, restrict German economic activities outside its borders, preserve German-held assets to aid in Europe's reconstruction after the war, and block the escape of Nazi leaders already marked for postwar war crimes tribunals.

While numerous individuals and agencies contributed in different capacities, the OSS took a leading role in intelligence gathering. Among its operatives was Second Lieutenant John Mowinckel, assigned to the OSS detachment supporting the US's Third Army under General Patton. Mowinckel was tasked with spearheading OSS efforts for Project Safehaven, working deep behind enemy lines to track financial movements and identify hidden Nazi resources.

During his service, Mowinckel distinguished himself in combat as well as intelligence operations. He was awarded the Bronze Star after fighting his way out of a German ambush 15km behind enemy lines. Just nine months later, he earned the Silver Star for another daring mission, infiltrating German positions once again to establish critical contact with advancing Soviet forces.

Mowinckel's efforts – and the broader success of Project Safehaven – played an important role in disrupting the Nazis' ability to create a postwar underground network and in laying the financial groundwork for Europe's recovery.

Second Lieutenant John W. Mowinckel

CITATION:

For meritorious service in connection with military operations as Intelligence Officer, Office of Strategic Service Field Detachments, European Theater of Operations, on 15 August 1944. Second Lieutenant Mowinckel, in order to obtain intelligence, escorted French agents fifteen kilometers into enemy-held territory. While en route, they were spotted by a German machine gun crew which immediately opened fire on them. He managed to direct the jeep up a side road and by passed the German position, after which he directed the party to within a few hundred yards of the town of Morey which was strongly held by the enemy. Here the agents were dropped off and proceeded on their mission. Through second Lt. Mowinckel's devotion to duty and courageous determination, much vital information was made available to the United States Armed Forces.

Second Lieutenant John W. Mowinckel

CITATION:

The President of the United States of America takes pleasure in presenting the Silver Star to Lieutenant John W. Mowinckel, United States Marine Corps Reserve, for gallantry as a member of the Office of Strategic Services Detachment, THIRD United States Army, in action in Austria. On 3 May 1945, Lieutenant Mowinckel courageously volunteered to infiltrate through enemy lines to establish contact with Russian units in the vicinity of Perg, Austria. Accompanied by two intelligence agents, he fearlessly proceeded through the enemy lines and, although halted and interrogated by German SS personnel, succeeded in continuing his vital mission. The information this intrepid officer obtained concerning the position of the approaching Russian elements and the disposition of enemy troops was an important contribution to the success of tactical operations. Lieutenant Mowinckel's courageous actions and unswerving devotion to duty was in keeping with the highest traditions of the military service.

THE MONUMENTS MAN

Captain Marvin C. Ross served in the G-5 section of the Supreme Headquarters Allied Expeditionary Force (SHAEF) staff, representing the Monuments, Fine Arts, and Archives (MFAA) program. He, along with several hundred other Monuments Men, helped locate, salvage, and preserve Europe's irreplaceable cultural treasures amid the devastation of war.

Ross enlisted in the US Marine Corps in 1942 and later saw combat in the South Pacific, serving in New Zealand and the Solomon Islands. In February 1944, he was transferred to the MFAA Branch at SHAEF Headquarters in London, appointed deputy advisor under the leadership of renowned "Monuments Man" Colonel Geoffrey Webb. Chosen for his knowledge of military organization and procedure, Ross played a critical role in coordinating monument protection plans for both the Normandy invasion and the anticipated postwar military government in Germany.

Beyond his administrative responsibilities, Ross served as a vital link between headquarters and the Monuments Men in the field. He provided updated information critical to their operations, including captured German documents, technical manuals, lists of protected sites, intelligence on newly discovered repositories, and reports from interrogations of suspected art looters.

Ross also took on field missions himself. In December 1944, he inspected cultural repositories near Strasbourg, France, in search of looted art. At Haut-Koenigsbourg, a historic château north of Colmar in the Alsace region, he uncovered a vast cache of priceless treasures looted by the Nazis from Alsace.

Amid the disorder, Ross discovered a remarkable find: the panels of the Isenheim Altarpiece by Matthias Grünewald, hidden safely in the cellar. According to his report, the château's caretaker had taken extraordinary measures to protect the masterpiece, reinforcing it with heavy timber supports and refusing to let it out of his sight.

Ross's combination of front-line service, logistical expertise, and commitment to preserving Europe's heritage made him a figure in the success of the MFAA's efforts during and after the war.

OPERATION *DRAGOON*

Sometimes called the second D-Day, Operation *Dragoon* saw the Allies make a second major landing in France at the French Riviera just two months after Operation *Overlord*. Originally envisioned to occur at the same time as the Normandy landings, the two operations were originally named Operation *Sledgehammer* (*Overlord*) and Operation *Anvil* (*Dragoon*). However, due to equipment and ship limitations, the concurrent operations were not to be. It was decided to put everything into the northern landings at Normandy and not divert resources away from the Italian campaign.

The Allied landings were a success, seeing little resistance initially due to effective sabotage operations by French Resistance fighters and OSS operatives, Allied paratroopers securing important areas, excellent pre-bombardment targeting by Navy ships and air forces, and an already underway general retreat of German troops. The advancing Russian

Second Lieutenant Walter Taylor

CITATION:

Second Lieutenant Walter Willard Taylor, Jr. (MCSN: 0-25233), United States Marine Corps, was captured by German Forces while serving with the OSS in Europe on 24 October 1944, and was held as a Prisoner of War until returned to US Military control at the end of the war.

Marines at Operation *Dragoon*

By Technical Sergeant Richard T. Wright, Marine Corps Combat Correspondent

Aboard a US battleship, August 15, 1944 – After silencing a heavy caliber battery of German coastal guns early this morning, Sailors and Marines manning this battleship were treated to two outstanding performances by Allied units which livened up an otherwise "dull D-Day" for them during the assault on Southern France.

With the exception of the men serving below the main deck, all hands had grandstand seats to watch the work of a fighting French cruiser and an invincible group of American heavy bombers.

The snub-nosed French cruiser started off by being the first ship in this task force to open fire on the enemy – evidently it had been agreed that the honor was entirely hers.

Moving to a broadside position 7,000 yards from her target on the beach, the cruiser's guns belched flame continuously for 70 minutes.

After knocking out her target she began plastering everything in sight on the beach in an unprecedented attack of fire power which had the men on this ship wondering just when her guns would come apart.

Around ten o'clock a German heavy caliber battery 3,000 yards inland opened fire on the Frenchmen. Crew aboard this ship could see shells hitting the water a few hundred yards in back of her.

An American destroyer which had been cruising up and down the beach looking like a fox terrier in search of trouble, laid a smoke screen around the French cruiser which concealed her immediately.

Five minutes later the French sailors got their revenge.

Contacting a spotting plane which gave them the range of their target, the Frenchmen opened up with everything they had. Blasting at rapid fire she dumped salvo after salvo on the Nazi battery up in the hills. Finally, the order came through: "Cease firing, target destroyed."

Sailors and Marines were surprised to find that this was not enough for the French cruiser. Seconds later she opened up again, this time with broadside salvo, as German targets continued to "take it" from the Frenchies.

"Those Frenchmen are making up for a lot of lost time," a Leatherneck aboard this ship stated.

Having attacked heavy German shore batteries from point-blank range before H-Hour, Southern France, this ship's 12 big guns so completely saturated beach defenses that there was no answering fire from the Germans ashore.

Sailors and Marines were convinced that the pounding they gave the Germans was quite a performance – that is until 1:15 this afternoon.

Cruising slowly some 5,000 yards offshore, crewmen on this ship watched a group of B-24 bombers soar in from a southwesterly direction, to bomb beach installations along a particularly troublesome sector which the "Jerry" still held on the South coast of France.

Waiting for the inevitable bang as the bombs hit, Sailors and Marines were completely awed by the terrific blasts which shook the ground as great scoops of dust and debris geysered into the air. The bombs burst like great firecrackers and appeared to hit beach and installations only a few yards apart in an area not exceeding five hundred yards in length.

So convincing was the attack that several men shied away from the beach as the blockbusters found their mark.

August 17 – "I'm doggone glad I'm playing for this team," one Marine remarked, while a sailor was heard to comment: "I'd hate like hell to be a German in there right now."

The aerial attack was so perfect that not a single bomb dropped into the water, which would have been evidenced by a large splash.

Dust concealed the bombed area for 30 minutes afterwards and it was the consensus that if there were anything living on that beach sector, it was a miracle.

The sailors and Marines aboard this battleship were so completely surprised by the effect of the bombing that several made statements to the effect that "we can get those Jerries out of holes those bombs can't hit. But I'm telling you we could fire for 48 hours and not do as much damage as those babies did in 30 seconds."

August 17 – United States Marines were again perched high in the mainmasts of American warships today watching for enemy mines to destroy with their rifles, as Allied warships plastered German shore batteries in the assault against the Southern Coast of France.

Army, coupled with the Allied landings at Normandy just months before, had placed incredible strains on the German Army.

Again, Marines from ship detachments would take part in defending the skies. But, in one of the few instances during World War II, a large group of Marines would come face to face with German troops.

A 70-man landing party comprised of Marines from aboard USS *Augusta* and USS *Philadelphia* landed on the islands of Ratonneau, Pomègues, and Château d'If off the coast of southern France at the end of August. While there, they took into custody 700 German soldiers. A few weeks later, Marines from USS *Philadelphia* would take part in liberation ceremonies in the town of Toulon, France.

While the Marine detachments were gathering prisoners, some Marines were ashore behind enemy lines. Marine Second Lieutenant Walter W. Taylor and Corporal James S. Sweeney were attached to the headquarters element of the US Army 36th Infantry Division. Taylor was captured by a German patrol in October in Saint Cézaire, France, while on a reconnaissance mission. He would not be freed until April 1945. Taylor was no rookie working behind enemy lines. Just a few months prior from March to July, he had been a part of a small OSS team that carried out raids and recon missions on the island of Corsica, infiltrating Italian intelligence networks.

A Mediterranean Port

August 6 (Delayed)

United States servicemen stationed near this city have initiated one of the strangest "leave systems" in existence – that of reciprocal liberty parties.

On their first liberty ashore, Marines and sailors aboard this battleship soon found that the combination of steaming mid-summer heat and a white-hot sun were not conducive to pleasant liberties. The town has practically nothing to offer servicemen, and even the most consistent "liberty hounds" agreed that it was worse liberty than Norfolk, Virginia.

However, it took the Marines and sailors only one day to remedy the situation.

Their own battleship, which is anchored in the harbor here, Benito Mussolini's "West Point" of the air, recently occupied by a heavy bombardment group of the 15th Army Air Corps, and some Stateside beer, provided the essentials.

Few Marines and sailors have ever flown in a B-24 Liberator bomber. Battleship duty for the Army Air Corps men has been confined to watching maneuvers in news reels.

The second day in this port a group of Marines and sailors made their first jaunt to a dusty camp located a few miles outside the city where the 15th Air Force made their headquarters.

After a short motor launch ride over choppy bay waters to the dock, khaki clad Leathernecks and sailors were wearing summer whites, headed for the main road leading out of the city. They hitched a ride on an Army truck which was going to the airport.

Bumping along the narrow Italian roads which were lined with swarthy men and brown skinned women and children, walking and driving carts laden with everything from sheep to furniture, the Marines and sailors got their first view of Italian rural life as the truck miraculously dodged in and out between the horse drawn carts.

Passing row after row of grape vines was inspiration enough for two Marines who thought it might be an opportune moment to pilfer a few clusters, until a Leatherneck Sergeant suggested that such action might be a bad taste.

Arriving at the camp, the liberty party was impressed with the remains of two large hangars which had been bombed during the Italian blitz last year. All that remained were gutted struts and crumpled operations buildings. B-24 bombers dotted the field as great clouds of dust geysered into the air while Liberators roared down the strip on the takeoff.

The liberty party was met by Technical Sergeant James E. Wiess, of 1117 East Third Street, Pine Bluff, Arkansas. An aerial photographer, Jimmy had just completed his 39th mission over enemy territory.

Several other soldiers put in an appearance and the next hour was spent getting acquainted and asking questions.

"Where's the water fountain Sarge," a chief asked a private in the Army.

"Are you kidding, chief?" was the reply. The chief had to be satisfied with a canteen full of luke warm water.

Marines and Sailors soon found that the cramped quarters on the battleship weren't so bad after all. The soldiers slept in tents. Their bunks were covered in mosquito netting as protection against malaria-carrying insects. The field is dry here. There is plenty of dust, and you take a bath from a bucket.

Several cans of beer found their maker and a trip to operations was next in order for a long-awaited trip in a B-24 Liberator.

Jimmy split the groups up and the men thronged over an Army truck which took the Marines and sailors out to their respective planes which were warming up.

After inspecting the dashboard in the cockpit, Marine Sergeant Major Charles B. Widestrom, of 12 West 95th Street, New York City, came to this conclusion: "Brother, it would take me a month of Sundays to learn what all those gadgets mean." The sergeant major has spent 13 years in the Corps.

An hour and a half low-level flight over the surrounding countryside followed. Chief Boilermaker Jack Lee, USN, of Jupiter, Florida, stated "Well doggone, I never thought I'd see the Adriatic Ocean – especially from 4,000 feet."

A veteran of 26 years in the Navy, Chief Commissary Steward White, of 630 County Street, Portsmouth, Va was most impressed with the ball turret.

"Stu" weighs 225 pounds and has amazed bartenders the world over by placing his magnificent stomach on a bar and telling the bartender to "fill'er up mac." His muscled "tummy" proved a nemesis in a futile attempt to fit into the ball turret which was built for little guys in the first place.

Marine Gunnery Sergeant John H. Chittick, of 17 Earlemoor Blvd, Pontiac, Mich, was surprised at the Lieutenant pilots. "Those guys sure are young," he stated. "One of them looks like he just started to shave but he can certainly fly the hell out of this plane." Gunnery Sergeant Chittick is 24.

After landing, Soldiers, Sailors and Marines retired to the Club 69 located on the top floor of Mussolini's ex-control tower. The front of the building is air conditioned, having caught a 500-pound bomb right in the front door somewhere in the distant past.

Sergeants, Chiefs, Privates, Apprentice Seamen – all enjoyed more beer, wild stories about memorable liberties, politics, sex, and Hitler. The soldiers told about bombing raids over Ploesti, Toulon, and Marseilles. Marines and sailors told how their battleship out-shot other battlewagons in the invasion of Normandy, and the shelling of Cherbourg.

A good chow, much good-natured clowning, and finally time to call it a day came all too soon. Sailors and Leathernecks said good night to their Air Corps buddies and departed amidst much revelry and thanks from the Navy men, including an invitation for the soldiers to visit the ship the next day.

At four o'clock the following day, Jimmy and a group of his friends walked up the gangway of their first battleship.

"A tour of the ship proved to Jimmy that, a B-24 is the simplest ship on earth after looking at the engine room and the bridge instruments."

The soldiers went everywhere on the ship. From the boiler room where the temperature hovers around 130 degrees, to the mainmasts where they looked down on the 12" guns which blasted German shore batteries at Normandy and Cherbourg.

Ice cream, plenty of cold water, and a movie up on deck rounded out another swell liberty for everybody.

"You know, it gets me," Jimmy stated as he prepared to enter the motor launch which would transport them to the shore, "in the States we never had much to do with sailors and Marines, but I sure have a different idea of things after the past few days."

He expressed the sentiments of all soldiers, sailors and Marines at this station.

Aboard the USS *Arkansas*

August 10, 1944 (Delayed)

United States Marines serving on this battleship agree that a woman called Midge is one of the war's greatest "bum dope artists."

This new idol of the air lanes used to be a beauty parlor operator in Boston, Mass. Now she is one of Adolf Hitler's pet stooges, much to the amusement of the Allied troops serving in the European Theater.

Her present activities are confined to regular propaganda radio programs which are designed by Dr. Goebbels for the purpose of making Allied troops homesick.

Marines serving aboard ships in this area take great delight in tuning in on Midge's daily radio program. Her smooth, dreamy voice jams the air lanes in this vicinity between ten o'clock in the morning and two in the afternoon.

Midge plays all the latest recordings. Harry James's music, Bing Crosby's crooning, and Frank Sinatra's swooning, are among her repertoire of musical offerings designed to play on the sympathies of the servicemen.

She philosophizes and she attempts to prophesy. As far as these Leathernecks are concerned, "It's the greatest four hours of corn in radio, but we love it."

Recently Midge honored the men aboard the Navy ships in this area with a few timely remarks. She stated: "Hello, all you Marines and sailors of Uncle Sam's Navy. I often wonder if you people know what you are fighting for. Just think, back in the states tonight I'll bet there's a big yellow moon. Your beautiful girl is probably out with some 4-F, but don't worry, she'll be there when you get back, but she won't be the same old gal."

Midge seems to have all the inside dope on all military operations in this section. Her daily report occasionally reads: "Ahoy Gyrenes and Sailors – German torpedo bombers sank two destroyers and five freighters this afternoon. That's pretty bad news, isn't it? Boy I bet you'd like to be home drinking nice, cool American beer after a swell movie with your girl. Let's listen to Tommy Dorsey's recording of 'Somebody Else Is Taking My Place.' Think it over boys."

Too bad, but we know there haven't been any sinkings.

Among her recent broadcasts was an offering to United States Marines guarding the Naval base in Londonderry, Northern Ireland. The gist of her program was about the same:

"Don't you Marines get tired of the rain and cold up there? If you were home now you could be enjoying a comfortable evening at home with your wife. How is she by the way? Hear from her lately? I hope so." This is always followed by a very nasty, throaty laugh.

Even Admiral Harold R. Stark, Commanding Naval Forces in Europe, comes in for his share of comment: "We've got a flying bomb over here with your name on it Admiral Stark. Your London command has been lucky so far, but you're next. Watch out you square boys."

Midge prophesized the invasion about seven times. She can tell you what weather will be like tomorrow, what the latest Broadway shows are, when the end of the war will come, and occasionally, she comes across with a few, too few, baseball scores.

The consensus among sea-going Marines over here is that without Midge, things might get very dull at times.

"They can kill all the Germans they want fast," one Leatherneck stated, "but I hope they save Midge because I'd like to see what the old bag looks like."

Aboard a Command Ship, Off Southern France

August 15, 1944

Attempting to make personal contact with any particular craft in the maze of shipping off the Southern coast of France this evening was like looking for a needle in a haystack.

The small "landing craft, personnel" which moved away from our command ship around 6:30 this evening carried a crew of three Coast Guardsmen, one American officer who was intent upon finding an LCI, and an English officer who wished to be landed on one of the beaches which had been secured early this morning.

Moving through the smooth blue waters the coxswain steered us in and out between transports, LSTs, LCTs, and other landing craft in search for the officer's LCI. Unable to find the craft in our sector we were forced to move along a hostile beach area which had not been completely freed from German shore batteries and infantry troops.

After traveling for some 5,000 yards, we finally found the LCI, dispatched the officer and headed back from our beach where the English officer had pressing business.

And that's when the trouble started.

One of the oldest and scrappiest ships in the United States Navy, with a combat record second to none, chose that moment to bombard a German shore battery not more than 1,500 yards from our landing craft.

The cruisers' guns belched a broadside of death which we watched explode a little to the right of the Germans who were perched on a lofty crag a few hundred yards up a wooded hill.

Sharp reports followed this assault as the Nazis fired back over our heads in an attempt to sink the cruiser. Evidently their position had been unnoticed by the warships and they had been waiting for an Allied man-of-war to come in close enough to blow it out of the water. There was plenty of other smaller shipping that they could have fired upon.

At this point we saw two tiny blue puffs of smoke blowing toward us from the side of the battery. Two minutes later we were convinced our guesswork was correct as two bullets flicked the water next to the boat while one hit the steel rack in front and richocheted off into space. All hands hit the deck, except the coxswain who remained exposed.

Almost immediately, we heard the cruisers' guns thunder, and the German shore battery went up in flames from a direct hit. Fires licked at the trees and what was left of the gun and control house. The German sniper who was firing at us also joined his comrades.

The coxswain steered our boat in between two LSTs that were unloading on the beach. They seemed comforting in a protective way. The English officer gave our coxswain the order to stand by for 20 minutes and that's just what we wanted to hear.

We walked ashore and watched American Army MPs herd a batch of 150 German prisoners into an LST. It did our hearts good to see a husky private first class very firmly showing the Nazis the right way to go when their feet became twisted.

They were a very arrogant looking group of Poles, Czechs, and what appeared to be low-grade of German youth. They all smoked cigarettes and seemed hot and stuffy in their blue-grey heavy winter uniforms. The Nazis moved into the LST in a manner which gave the impression that they were quite glad to get the thing over with.

We talked to two GIs who wore the red cross arm banner which designates Army "medics" in the American Army. They showed us the front lines from the top of a small hill and we watched American artillery pound German positions two and half miles inland. They also showed us two dead soldiers who had stepped on a mine.

The area was a mass of bomb craters where both Naval bombardment and Allied bombings had sealed many a Nazi's lips forever.

It was growing dark and after kidding with an Army lieutenant who suggested we take a "Molotov Cocktail" back with us for a souvenir, we headed back for the boat where we were ordered to shove off without the English officer who was remaining ashore.

As we moved out past the LST we heard the "red alert" piped over the loud speaker system. That was all the Coxswain needed. Our ship lay two miles out and speed was urgent, but we didn't quite make it before the Jerry put in an appearance.

To our left we could plainly see two JU-88s moving in to the area, completely ringed by a cluster of red tracers. Every ship opened fire at the Junker and we suddenly felt very lonely in the boat with thousands of bullets shooting skyward all around us. We seemed to be right in the middle.

A terrific explosion shook the shore line and a great sheet of flame rose into the air. Looking back we observed a bomb hit on one of the LSTs which we had left not more than six minutes before.

The flames leaped high into the air and we wondered how our army acquaintances on the beach had fared. It wasn't a nice feeling lying out there and not being able to help.

After the firing ceased and the Junker 88s passed over, we found our ship and were hoisted aboard.

Aboard a US Battleship, Off Southern France

August 15 (Delayed)

Marine Sergeant Major Charles Billy Widestrom, whose wife, Violet, resides at 12 West 95th Street, New York City, was aboard this fighting ship which shelled German shore batteries in the initial assault on the coast of Southern France.

Sergeant Major Widestrom, who is the Marine detachment administrative first sergeant on this warship, was at his post in the mainmast as control officer for 20mm anti-aircraft batteries, which are manned by Leathernecks.

A veteran of the Normandy invasion, and the shelling of Cherbourg, the sergeant major found this "D-Day" quite a bit different from the June 6 engagement.

"I'm not at all unhappy because we weren't fired at by German shore batteries," he stated. "Those big shells bursting all around us off Cherbourg will do me for some time to come."

A veteran of 13 years' service in the Marine Corps, Sergeant Major Widestrom was born in Boden, Sweden.

His battery of anti-aircraft guns were credited with downing two Junker 88s off the coast of France.

Late this evening a trio of the same type of planes flew in over shipping in this area. Again the Sergeant Major's sharpshooters sighted in on the German planes, which flew over very high and very fast. No hits were observed, but as the sergeant major puts it "we'll probably get a few before this engagement is over if the Nazis can get any planes past our air support groups – those Allied planes this morning were a comforting sight."

The sergeant major of Marines has served on two other battleships and has also done duty in the Pacific prior to this war. His other posts include Panama, Cuba, Puerto Rico, Haiti, and United States Naval bases.

Sergeant Major Widestrom was formerly a bank teller with the First National Bank, Portland, Oregon.

Aboard a US Battleship, Off Southern France

Marine First Lieutenant Hurley Edward Fuller Jr. son of Army Colonel Hurley E. Fuller, 208 Luther Drive, San Antonio, Texas participated in the invasion of Southern France as assistant air defense officer on this ship.

The 25-year-old Marine officer commands the Leatherneck detachment aboard this battlewagon.

During the D-Day landing operations in Northern France, this ship gave close support to troops commanded by his father, Colonel Fuller who landed with a unit of Army troops on D-Day. Lieutenant Fuller was also with this ship when German shore batteries were plastered by Navy vessels off Cherbourg.

Lieutenant Fuller found things a little easier on this invasion, than the operations in Northern France.

"Of course, our Marine job on this ship is primarily concerned with shooting down German planes, but I am glad that our big guns silenced the Nazi coastal guns. They can be rather unpleasant at times," he said.

Lieutenant Fuller has a hobby of collecting ammunition shells of different types. He has high hopes that his father, who is still in Normandy, can collect some new types.

The Texas Leatherneck is a regular in the Marines, and intends to make a career of the Corps. He enlisted August 15, 1942.

Lieutenant Fuller attended Louisiana State University, and recently completed a course of instruction at the Armored Force School, Fort Knox, Kentucky.

Aboard a US Battleship, Off Southern France

August 15 (Delayed)

Marine Second Lieutenant Charles A. Meyer, the son of Mrs. S. L. Meyer, 605 Highland Avenue, Aliquippa, participated in the invasion of Southern France on this ship as an anti-aircraft control officer.

The 25-year-old Marine Lieutenant could not work up much enthusiasm over this D-Day.

After a lull in the firing of the heavy guns, he came to the conclusion that "judging from the sound those bombs are making from the planes, I guess the Jerries find it more convenient to

hide in a hole somewhere until it's over – then maybe we'll get a crack at them."

Lieutenant Meyer enlisted in the Marines May 29, 1942. He served as a drill instructor, earned a platoon sergeant's rate, and entered Officer Candidates' School in November 1943.

The husky Leatherneck attended Duquesne University and worked for Jones and Laughlin Steel Corporation in Aliquippa as an electrician specialist prior to joining the Marine Corps.

TOP Marines with the Marine Detachment aboard USS *Nevada* receive a refresher class from Gunnery Sgt David M. Bynun (far left) prior to taking part in Operation *Dragoon*, August 11, 1945. Other Marines in the photo from left to right are: Privates First Class Charles G. Montrose and Elmer R. Zimmerman, Field Musician First Class John H. Merriman, Privates First Class Ludvik Kristofik, Emil Barbosa, William G. Griffin, and John L. Cuomo. (USMC, photo by SSgt William J. Kilpatrick)

BOTTOM From left to right are Private First Class Frances D. Hubbell of Milwaukee, Wisconsin, Corporal Robert L. Serman of Berkeley, California, and Corporal David W. Springer, of Grinnell, Iowa, stationed aboard USS *Nevada*. They are keeping lookout for enemy sea mines off the southern coast of France, August 11, 1944. (USMC, photo by SSgt William J. Kilpatrick)

TOP Marines from USS *Augusta* leaving the ship for the islands of Ratonneau, Pomègues, and Château d'If off the coast of southern France to guard prisoners after the surrender of the islands on August 29, 1944. (US Navy)

BOTTOM USS *Augusta* Marines transferring from a minesweeper to a whale boat on their way to the beach on August 29, 1944. (US Navy)

TOP Marines from USS *Philadelphia* who landed on the islands of Ratonneau and Château d'If in Marseilles Harbor, August 29, 1944. (USMC, photo by Sgt Yeager)

BOTTOM A Marine checks the uniform of a German Army corporal during the capture of Ratonneau Island, August 29, 1944. (US Navy)

TOP Marine Detachment from USS *Philadelphia* commanded by First Lieutenant R. A. Thompson immediately after landing on Ratonneau Island. (US Navy)

BOTTOM Marines from USS *Philadelphia* carrying supplies on Ratonneau Island. Supplies were brought by motor whale boat, which can be seen in the background speeding away. Two German boats are moored to a pole in the foreground. (US Navy)

TOP Two Marines and a sailor from USS *Philadelphia* work with German prisoners to account for weapons and supplies on Ratonneau Island. (US Navy)

BOTTOM German prisoners, guarded by Marines from USS *Philadelphia*, wait to be loaded aboard US landing craft and be taken to a prisoner-of-war camp. (US Navy)

TOP German prisoners are closely guarded by Marines. (US Navy)

BOTTOM A conference held on August 30, 1944 to discuss disposition of hospital assistance. On the left are Captain Schlesinger and Captain Fullgrabe. On the right is Lieutenant Reck, USNR. (US Navy)

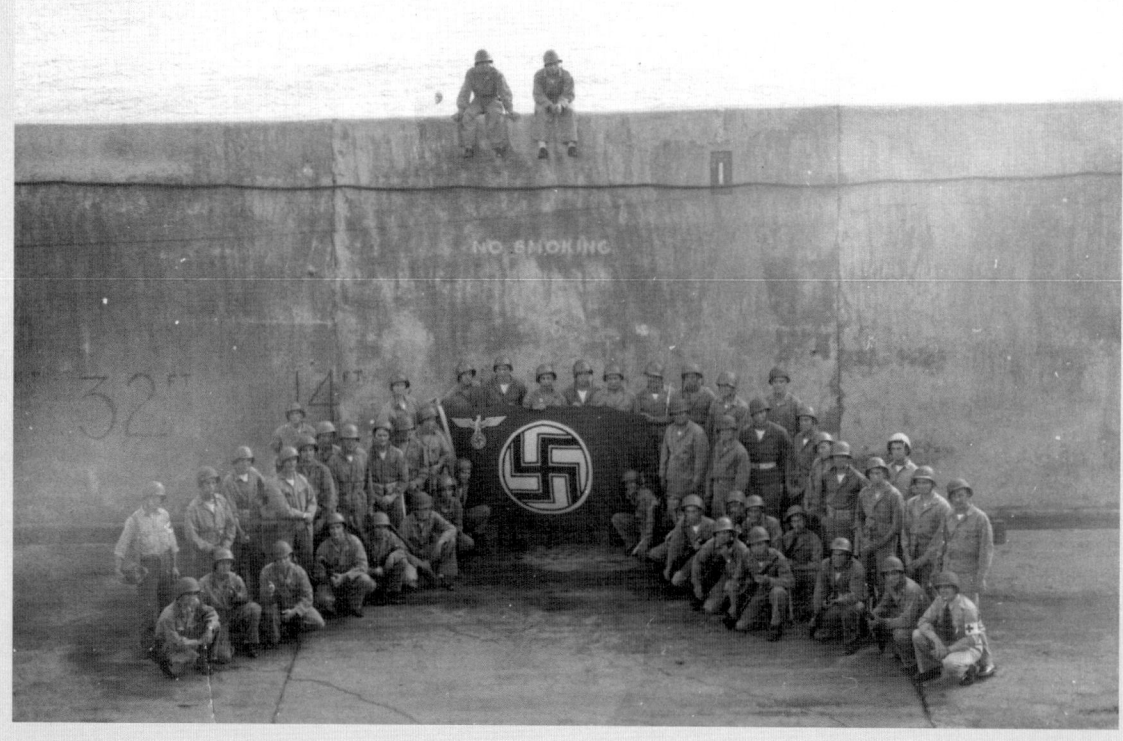

down and brought back to Admiral Davidson. The Marines embarked on a sub-chaser and transferred to an L.C.I. at sea. The L.C.I.'s were underway all night for the area where the prisoners were to be landed. Prisoners were landed at first light on the morning of August 31.

The detachment reported aboard the AUGUSTA at about 0730 on the morning of August 31, 1944.

FRANCIS R. SCHLESINGER

John H. Magruder III was assigned as a US liaison officer to the British Army. He had grown up in Holland due to his father being a naval liaison officer in his adolescence. Being familiar with the Netherlands, and fluent in the Dutch language, he was assigned to British General Bernard Montgomery's 21st Army Group during the liberation of Holland. For his work the Netherlands awarded him the Order of Orange-Nassau. It can be seen on the bottom right of his ribbon stack. (USMC)

Marines from the ship detachment aboard the USS *Augusta* stand at attention during a welcoming ceremony for King George VI and the President while the ship in in port in Plymouth, England, August 1945. (US Navy)

Aboard USS *Nevada* off Toulon

August 23, 1944

For seven hours today this 29-year-old battleship, veteran of Attu, Normandy, Cherbourg, and the Riviera, blasted at a concentration of German guns guarding the approaches to Toulon.

It began this morning when the *Nevada* was nosing in toward Toulon, now besieged by French and American troops, with a chip on her shoulder. Big Willie knocked the chip off at 9:22 by the clock, and there was hardly a let-up until 4:30 this afternoon, when the "Cheer-Up Maru" had fired 354 shells, each weighing well over half a ton, at the challengers.

Big Willie is really a twin. The name refers to either of two long range naval guns, removed by the Jerries from French battleship *Provence* and set up on a point of land outside the harbor entrance. This peninsula forms the southern boundary of Toulon Harbor. This peninsula dwindles into a narrow hook of land commanding the approaches to the naval base. That hook is the home of Big Willie and his satellite batteries of lesser guns, including anti-aircraft guns. They are the biggest thing in these parts, well protected by thick turrets, and very hard customers to deal with, as any Allied ship will attest, and which has come within range of them the past few days.

Just before the fireworks started HMS *Aurora*, a British cruiser, flashed a signal: "Please give Big Willie a poke in the kisser for me. Have a grudge against him since yesterday." A few minutes later a big column of water splashing up 500 yards from the *Nevada* and the roar of a bursting shell announced that Willie had got in the first poke. Our escorting destroyers, USS *Madison*, USS *Gleaves*, and HMS *Lookout*, immediately began darting about us laying protective screens of smoke. Two more splashes from German shells rose out of the water nearby while the *Nevada* maneuvered into position

to begin her firing run and then the day-long bombardment began.

It looked for a few minutes as though this might be another Cherbourg, when the *Nevada*, *Texas* and *Arkansas*, and American and British cruisers and destroyers had played tag for three hours with German shells, but Big Willie didn't come very close the rest of the day. He found closer targets when he was able to fire at all.

A few days ago, the *Nevada*'s chief engineer, Lieutenant Commander W. J. Buckley, knew what speed this battleship could make in her hey-day, thinking that her speed record had probably been set up many years ago. "Her hey-day," said the commander, "was June 25 off Cherbourg. Today we were lucky and didn't have to try to beat the record set up then."

From 9:30 the battleship's big turrets pounded the hook of land incessantly. As the blast of our own guns sprung shell lockers open, tore off ladders, and kicked us in the stomach, we began to feel a little sorry for the enemy gunners caught on that neck of land as ton after ton of steel and high explosive crashed among them.

At the halfway point in the day's firing, the new cruiser USS *Quincy*, who herself has had some brushes with Willie in recent days, passed nearby and signaled through the smoke: "Your shooting is beautiful, captain, keep it up."

The half-ton bullets lasted until almost 4:30. When our allowance of ammunition was fully expended, our spotting plane swooped down over the peninsula for a last look, found no signs of activity, blast damage everywhere, hits in the target area, and damage over a wide area. As we steamed away, Big Willie was silent. Whether he will remain silent can't be said. If he comes back after this pounding, on top of bombings and shellings of earlier days, we must take our hats off to him.

Marines and sailors from USS *Philadelphia* and sailors from French cruiser *Montcalm* go ashore in southern France after D-Day. The landing craft carrying them is British. (USMC, photo by Pfc Donald Passoth)

Marines from USS *Philadelphia* and USS *Augusta* stand in formation and accept the formal surrender of German forces in Toulon, France, September 14, 1944. (USMC, photo by Pfc Donald Passoth)

Ceremonies in Toulon celebrating the liberation of France, featuring Marines and sailors from USS *Philadelphia*. (US Navy)

Allied naval units take part in the victory parade in Toulon to celebrate the return of the French fleet to the port. Taken from the USS *Catoctin* (AGC-5). (US Navy)

TOP Marines of the battleship *Texas* are inspected by one of their officers during a guard mount on the dock at Oran, Algeria, July 27, 1945. The Marines are in tropical uniform. (USMC, photo by Cpl William R. Gibbon)

BOTTOM Marines chat about their experiences a few days after the invasion, August 15, 1944. In the background is the city of Algiers. From left to right are Privates First Class Herman J. Determan, of Glendale, New York; Private First Class Clarence Neitzelt, of Wheeling, West Virginia; and Private First Class John T. McLaughlin and John P. Pawley, of Philadelphia, Pennsylvania. (USMC, photo by Cpl William R. Gibbon)

ELSEWHERE **IN 1944**

JULY 10: Marines and sailors reconnoiter beaches on Tinian

JULY 21: The 3rd Marine Division lands on Guam

JULY 24: The 4th Marine Division lands on Tinian

JULY 26: President Roosevelt meets with Navy leadership in Hawaii. One topic they discuss is bypassing the Philippines in favor of Formosa (Taiwan)

AUGUST 9: Aslito Airfield on Saipan becomes operational for B-24s

SEPTEMBER 8: The Joint Chiefs of Staff issue a directive for the invasion of the Philippines

SEPTEMBER 15: The 1st Marine Division lands on Peleliu

OCTOBER 2: Military leadership meet in San Francisco and decide to land and take Okinawa instead of Formosa

OCTOBER 9: Major General Holland Smith receives orders directing the seizure of Iwo Jima

OCTOBER 10: A task force of fast carriers from the Third Fleet strike Okinawa while also capturing photographs for intelligence

NOVEMBER 24: Saipan-based B-29s bomb Tokyo. This is the first land-based aircraft attack on the Japanese capital

---

First Lieutenant Edward T. Dickinson, Jr

Author note

Not to be forgotten is First Lieutenant Edward T. Dickinson, Jr. While he never landed during Operation *Overlord*, his impact was immense. As an expert in factories, and with intelligence from behind German lines and gathered from reconnaissance planes, Dickinson was entrusted with and tasked to develop plans for the sabotage of key industrial facilities and chose targets for resistance fighters across Europe.

CITATION:

For meritorious service in connection with military operations while serving with the Office of Strategic Service, European Theater of Operations, from 7 March 1944 to 30 November 1944. First Lieutenant Dickinson, because of his foresight in estimation, appraisement, and execution, accomplished with signal success the difficult task set before him. He contributed greatly to the success of operations which were of such vital assistance to the Allied Forces prior to the subsequent invasion of the continent of Europe. His services during this period reflect high credit upon himself and the armed forces of the United States.

BATTLE OF THE BULGE

From December 1944 to January 1945, Hitler made a last-ditch attempt to push Allied forces back in the Ardennes Forest between Belgium and Luxembourg. During this time, Marine Second Lieutenant Peter Viertel and First Lieutenant Charles A. Muecke were attached to the US Army's Seventh Army as intelligence officers. Viertel received a Bronze Star and Silver Star for his participation and efforts in Europe. He would go on to become a successful Hollywood screenwriter after World War II.

OPERATION *UNION II*

Following the success of Operation *Union I*, a second one was immediately put into planning upon the return of Major Peter Ortiz and his team to the United Kingdom. In August 1944, after D-Day, Ortiz led an even larger team to France. The team of six US Marines, one US Army soldier, and one French Resistance fighter dropped into Haute-Savoie in France to carry out Operation *Union II*.

On the morning of August 1, 1944, B-17s from the 338th Bomber Squadron, 96th Bomber Group, from Knettishall Army Airfield, came in several hundred feet over the French Alps to drop the OSS team. Over the course of the next several days, they dropped more than 1,000 canisters to give to the French fighters. Despite the good weather and ideal drop zone, the mission began on a tragic note.

The team was using British-style parachutes, which had no reserve parachute and utilized metal straps to pull the chutes out of their packs, unlike the American parachutes that used fabric straps. As the team jumped, Sergeant Charles Perry's parachute cable snapped and he tragically fell to his death.

Desperately needed supplies were parachuted into occupied France to equip and replenish the Resistance's weapons, ammunition, and medical stores during Operation *Union II*. Located 8,000ft above sea level in the French Alps, near Col-des-Saisies in the Savoie Province, a fleet of 100 B-17 Flying Fortresses delivered the OSS team of *Union II*, along with vital supplies and munitions to the Maquis. (USMC)

The team carried weapons, ammunition, and money and was directed to not only sabotage, but also when possible, seize key installations to prevent the destruction of critical infrastructure by retreating Germans who were fleeing the Allied advance from Operation *Dragoon* or slow down additional units heading to the front to reinforce German garrisons.

After a burial ceremony for Perry, the remaining members set out to train the nearly 3,000 French Resistance fighters in weapons handling, patrolling, and sabotaging. However, once they moved past the immediate hillside, German forces moved in, having heard rumors of Allied troops in the area from a local shepherd who was a German informant.

On August 16, 1944, *Union II* members were making their way outside of the town of Montgirod when German soldiers from the 157th Alpine Reserve Division unexpectedly arrived with trucks full of soldiers. Catching the Marines walking across a street, the Germans dismounted from their trucks and began to engage the Americans and some French Resistance fighters. The team retreated, being vastly outnumbered by the Germans. They took cover in the town of Centron. By now Captain Francis Coolidge had been shot in the leg. He and Sergeant Frederick Brunner made their way to the bank of the Isere River and made their way across.

Major Ortiz and Sergeants John Bodnar and Jack Risler continued to fight the Germans. However, knowing how ruthless the Germans were, the townsfolk implored the Marines to surrender to spare their lives after news had spread that the Germans had massacred a nearby town looking for the Allied troops.

At first, Ortiz attempted to surrender just himself; however, two of the *Union II* Marines who had been separated with him, Risler and Bodnar, refused to leave without Ortiz and surrendered with him. Ortiz and the two sergeants were captured and taken into custody and sent to the prisoner-of-war camp Marinelager-Nord in northern Germany by mid-September. They would remain there until the camp was liberated by British troops of the 7th Guards Armoured Division on April 27, 1945.

Upon being liberated, the Marines attempted to attach themselves to a nearby Royal Marine Commando unit to continue fighting. But they were refused and ordered to return to England. Every Marine in Operation *Union II*, including Perry, was awarded a Silver Star for their involvement in the operation, except for Ortiz. He was awarded the Navy Cross, his second that year after receiving a Navy Cross for leading *Union I*.

Sergeant Charles R. Perry

CITATION:

The President of the United States of America takes pride in presenting the Silver Star (Posthumously) to Sergeant Charles R. Perry (MCSN: 324308), United States Marine Corps, for conspicuous gallantry and intrepidity in connection with military operations in German occupied territory on 1 August 1944. Volunteering for the extremely hazardous duty of entering enemy controlled territory for the purpose of serving as weapons instructor to resistance groups located in the Savoie Department of France, Sergeant Perry, with the full knowledge that he was undertaking additional risks in accompanying an officer who was known to the Gestapo because of his former resistance activities, courageously initiated his perilous mission by being parachuted from one of the seventy-two Flying Fortresses flying in formation at high speed. Although killed instantly in the jump, Sergeant Perry, by his resoluteness of purpose and fearless determination to serve despite all danger upheld the highest traditions of the United States Naval Service. He gallantly gave his life for his country.

Here, Captain Ortiz and his team render honors at Perry's grave. From left to right: Captain Ortiz; Captain Francis Coolidge, US Army; Gunnery Sergeant Robert E. Lasalle; Sergeant John P. Bodnar; Sergeant Frederick I. Brunner; and Sergeant Jack Risler. (USMC)

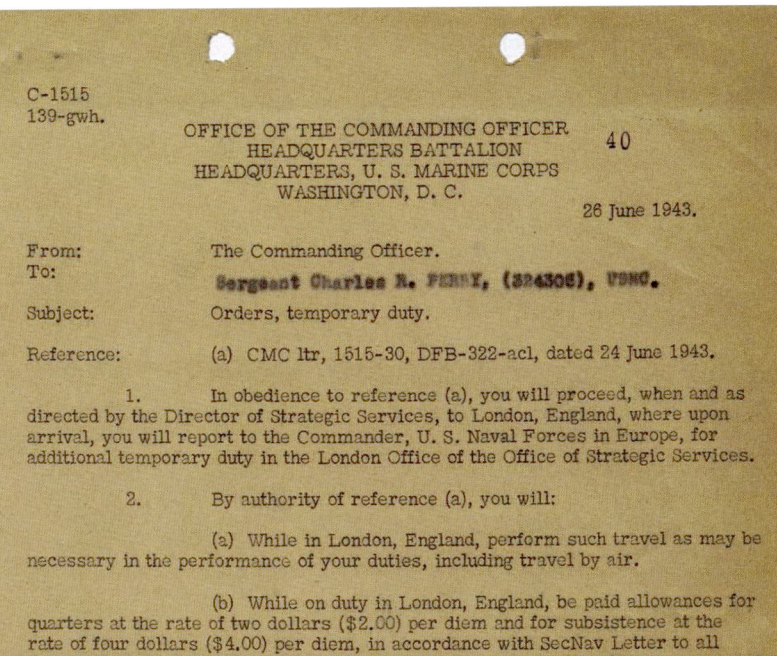

C-1515
139-gwh.

OFFICE OF THE COMMANDING OFFICER
HEADQUARTERS BATTALION
HEADQUARTERS, U. S. MARINE CORPS
WASHINGTON, D. C.

40

26 June 1943.

From: The Commanding Officer.
To: Sergeant Charles R. PERRY, (324306), USMC.

Subject: Orders, temporary duty.

Reference: (a) CMC ltr, 1515-30, DFB-322-acl, dated 24 June 1943.

1.   In obedience to reference (a), you will proceed, when and as directed by the Director of Strategic Services, to London, England, where upon arrival, you will report to the Commander, U. S. Naval Forces in Europe, for additional temporary duty in the London Office of the Office of Strategic Services.

2.   By authority of reference (a), you will:

(a) While in London, England, perform such travel as may be necessary in the performance of your duties, including travel by air.

(b) While on duty in London, England, be paid allowances for quarters at the rate of two dollars ($2.00) per diem and for subsistence at the rate of four dollars ($4.00) per diem, in accordance with SecNav Letter to all Ships and Stations of 30 April 1943, provided that quarters and subsistence are not furnished to you.

(c) For all travel by air in connection with the performance of your duties be allowed a per diem of six dollars ($6.00) in accordance with Article 24-119, Marine Corps Manual.

3.   Your staff returns are entrusted to you for delivery to the Commanding Officer, Marine Detachment, American Embassy, London, England.

4.   The cost of the travel involved in the execution of these orders is chargeable to "Pay, Marine Corps", except when you are in a travel status other than by air, when the charge will be made to "General Expenses, Marine Corps".

5.   The travel herein enjoined is necessary in the public service.

OFFICIAL COPY

E. E. BARDE,
Major, U. S. Marine Corps,
Commanding.

Copies to: The Paymaster and Quartermaster.
            Commander, U.S. Naval Forces in Europe.
            Director of Strategic Services, Washington, D. C.
            Office of Naval Intelligence.

FILE

Charles Perry's original transfer orders to the Marine Detachment in London. Administratively, many Marines were assigned to the London detachment on paper to track their general whereabouts. However, most Marines in the European Theater of Operations did not work at the detachment in London. (LoC)

First report of
Sergeant Perry's
death. (NARA)

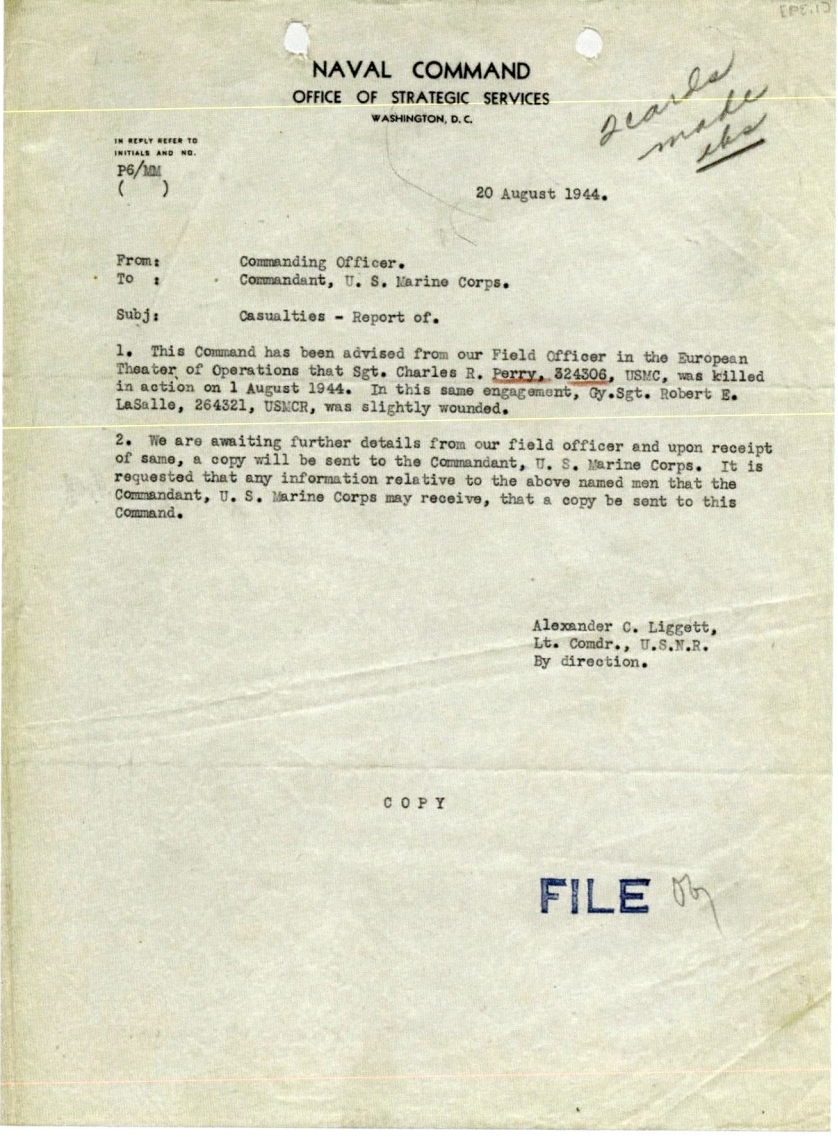

NAVAL COMMAND
OFFICE OF STRATEGIC SERVICES
WASHINGTON, D. C.

IN REPLY REFER TO
INITIALS AND NO.

P6/MM
(   )

20 August 1944.

From: Commanding Officer.
To :   Commandant, U. S. Marine Corps.

Subj: Casualties - Report of.

1. This Command has been advised from our Field Officer in the European
Theater of Operations that Sgt. Charles R. Perry, 324306, USMC, was killed
in action on 1 August 1944. In this same engagement, Gy.Sgt. Robert E.
LaSalle, 264321, USMCR, was slightly wounded.

2. We are awaiting further details from our field officer and upon receipt
of same, a copy will be sent to the Commandant, U. S. Marine Corps. It is
requested that any information relative to the above named men that the
Commandant, U. S. Marine Corps may receive, that a copy be sent to this
Command.

                                        Alexander C. Liggett,
                                        Lt. Comdr., U.S.N.R.
                                        By direction.

                    C O P Y

                                        FILE

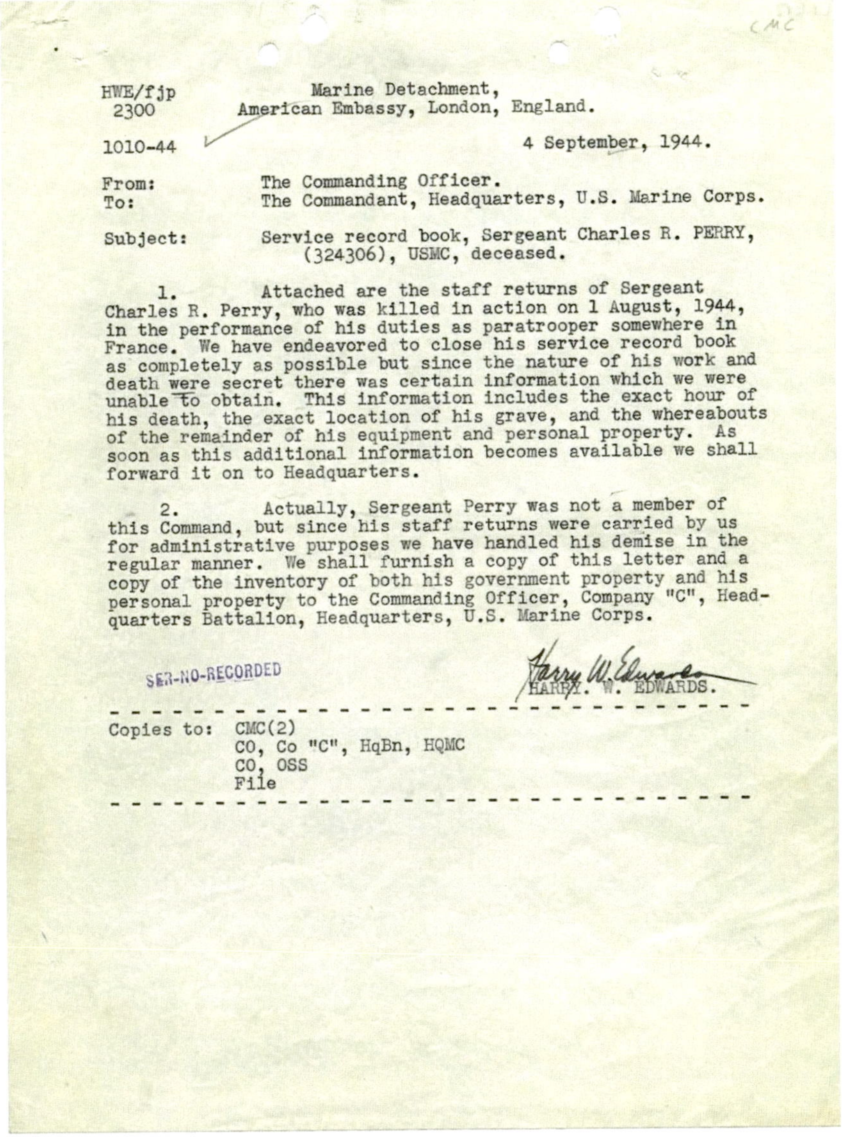

HWE/fjp
2300

Marine Detachment,
American Embassy, London, England.

1010-44

4 September, 1944.

From: The Commanding Officer.
To: The Commandant, Headquarters, U.S. Marine Corps.

Subject: Service record book, Sergeant Charles R. PERRY,
               (324306), USMC, deceased.

     1.   Attached are the staff returns of Sergeant
Charles R. Perry, who was killed in action on 1 August, 1944,
in the performance of his duties as paratrooper somewhere in
France. We have endeavored to close his service record book
as completely as possible but since the nature of his work and
death were secret there was certain information which we were
unable to obtain. This information includes the exact hour of
his death, the exact location of his grave, and the whereabouts
of the remainder of his equipment and personal property. As
soon as this additional information becomes available we shall
forward it on to Headquarters.

     2.   Actually, Sergeant Perry was not a member of
this Command, but since his staff returns were carried by us
for administrative purposes we have handled his demise in the
regular manner. We shall furnish a copy of this letter and a
copy of the inventory of both his government property and his
personal property to the Commanding Officer, Company "C", Headquarters Battalion, Headquarters, U.S. Marine Corps.

SER-NO-RECORDED

Harry W. Edwards
HARRY. W. EDWARDS.

- -

Copies to: CMC(2)
             CO, Co "C", HqBn, HQMC
             CO, OSS
             File

- -

Report from the London Marine Detachment commander to Headquarters Marine Corps on the notification of Sergeant Perry's death. (NARA)

TOP Sergeant Bodnar (left), Sergeant Brunner (center), and Sergeant Risler are shown paying their last respects to Sergeant Perry. Sergeant Brunner was killed March 19, 1945 when the A-26 bomber he was riding in for an OSS mission crashed near Bramsche, Germany. (USMC)

CENTER Sergeants Risler and Bodnar, a member of the French Maquis, and Gunnery Sergeant Lasalle shortly after their mission parachute drop in Col-des-Saisies, France. (USMC)

BOTTOM LEFT Bodnar shortly after parachuting into France, August 1944. (USMC)

BOTTOM RIGHT Sergeants Risler (left) and Bodnar in Paris shortly after being released from a prisoner-of-war camp in Germany, May 1945. They are looking at orders assigning a priority flight for them to be flown back to the United States by commercial airlines. (USMC)

Sergeant Risler, Gunnery Sergeant Lasalle, Major Ortiz, and Sergeant Bodnar were reunited at the OSS Headquarters in Washington DC, June 1945. Lasalle sustained a broken back during a parachute jump into Savoy, France, was evacuated to Italy, and finally flown back to London. Ortiz, Bodnar, and Risler were later captured by the German Army and lost contact with Lasalle until they were liberated a year later. (USMC)

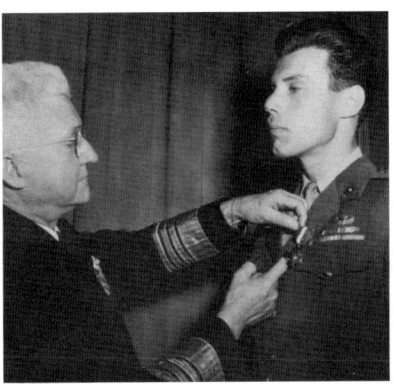

LEFT Peter Ortiz being awarded his second Navy Cross by Admiral Stark after his release from the German prisoner-of-war camp. (USMC)

RIGHT Ortiz portrait, late 1945. (MCHD)

Major Peter J. Ortiz

The Commander, United States TWELFTH Fleet, in the name of the President of the United States awards a Gold Star in lieu of Second Navy Cross to:
Major Peter J. Ortiz
United States Marine Corps Reserve

CITATION:

For extraordinary heroism and devotion to duty in the performance of outstanding service in connection with military operations against an armed enemy in enemy occupied territory, from 1 August 1944 to 27 April 1945.

After having been parachuted into the Savoie Department of France in a region where his past Resistance activities had made him an object of search by the Gestapo, Major Ortiz, with extraordinary courage and resourcefulness, continued his work of coordinating and leading Resistance groups in the section. On 16 August in the conduct of a special mission detained to immobilize enemy reinforcement in the area, Major Ortiz and his team were attacked and surrounded. Disregarding the possibility of escape, which course of action would most certainly have caused severe reprisal to be taken upon the villagers, Major Ortiz surrendered, and the townspeople were thereby spared. The story of the self-sacrifice of Major Ortiz and his group has become a brilliant legend in that section of France where acts of bravery were considered commonplace.

Subsequently imprisoned and subjected to numerous interrogations, he divulged nothing.

The heroic conduct throughout his dangerous mission reflects great credit upon himself and are in keeping with the highest tradition of the United States Marines Corps.

H. K. Hewitt
Admiral, US Navy
Commander, TWELFTH Fleet

MARINE CORPS SPECIAL OPERATIONS IN AFRICA

Marines were involved in Africa up until the very end of the war. Marine Colonel William A. Eddy led numerous OSS activities throughout the war in North Africa and was at several key events such as when President Roosevelt met numerous leaders in the Middle East.

Emperor Haile Selassie of Ethiopia boards USS *Quincy* on the Suez Canal near Cairo, February 13, 1945. He is escorted by US Navy Fleet Admiral William D. Leahy. Note the Marine captain at the bottom right of the photo, likely the commanding officer for the ships' Marine Detachment. (US Army)

TOP King Ibn Saud, surrounded by Commander Bernard A. Smith, commanding officer of USS *Murphy*, Colonel Eddy, minister to Saudi Arabia, and Captain John S. Keating, commodore, Destroyer Squadron 17, aboard *Murphy* (DD-603) en route to Great Bitter Lake near Cairo to meet USS *Quincy* with President Franklin D. Roosevelt aboard, February 1945. (US Army)

CENTER Admiral William D. Leahy, and Marines and sailors from the USS *Quincy*, salute as King Ibn Saud of Saudi Arabia arrives from USS *Murphy*. A Marine can be seen near the bottom right with the ship's Detachment patch. (US Army)

BOTTOM Admiral Leahy looks on as King Saud speaks to Eddy, who is interpreting. (US Navy)

King Ibn Saud (on the President's left) was received by President Roosevelt aboard USS *Quincy* amid pomp and colorful ceremonies. It was the first time in his life that King Saud had left his country's soil. The meeting took place at Great Bitter Lake, near Cairo, after the monarch had traveled more than 800 miles. King Saud and President Roosevelt are shown seated on the deck of the ship that brought him from the "Big Three" conference at Yalta, Crimea, February 14, 1945. Colonel Eddy is shown to the left of King Saud, utilizing his Arabic skills to fill in as an interpreter. An unnamed Marine is seen at the top left corner between two men in white. (US Army)

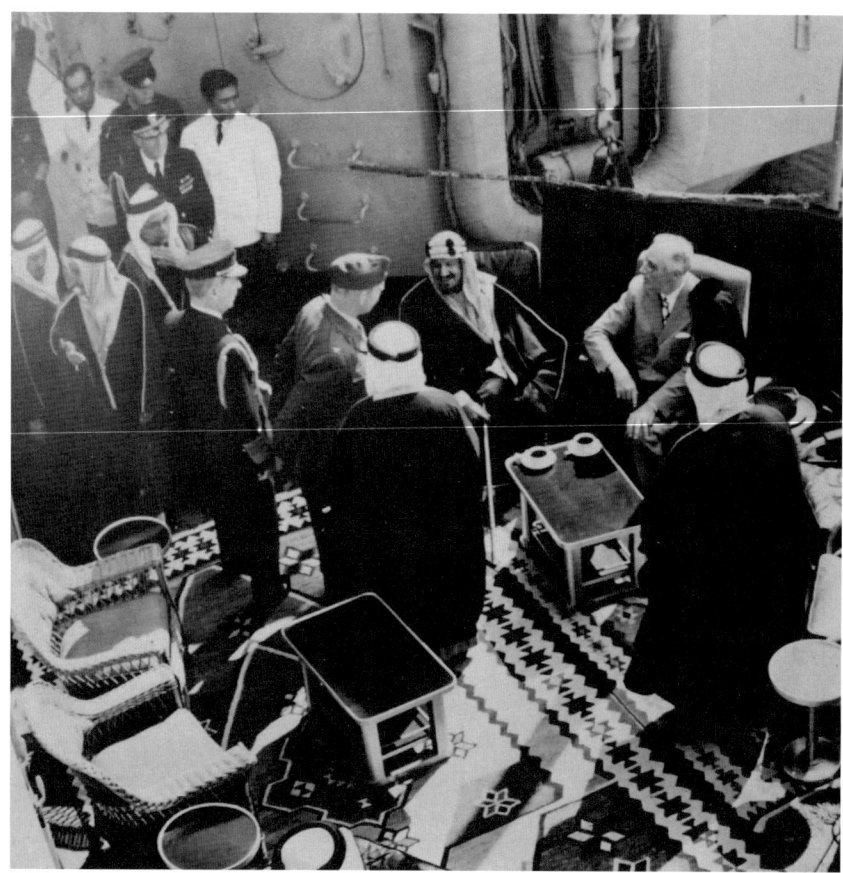

MARINES CONFIRMED TO HAVE SERVED IN THE OFFICE OF STRATEGIC SERVICES

NAME OF MARINE	AREA OF SERVICE
Colonel William A. Eddy	North Africa
Lieutenant Colonel Horace W. Fuller	France and China
Lieutenant Colonel Franklin P. Holcomb	Morocco, Algiers, and France
Lieutenant Colonel Peter J. Ortiz	North Africa and France
Major William G. Hamilton	England and France
Major Albert F. Moe	France and China
Major James T. Patterson	England and France
Captain William F. Grell	France
Captain William L. Cary	Romania, Yugoslavia, and Italy
Captain Joseph E. Charles	England, France, and Germany
Captain Gordon A. Craig	West Africa and Algiers
Captain Gerald F. Else	Cairo, Greece, and Liberia

Captain Leon Grell	England
Captain William F. A. Grell	England and France
Captain Sterling Hayden	Egypt, Italy, Yugoslavia, Albania, France, and Germany
Captain Elmer Harris	Tunisia, Corsica (France), Italy, and China
Captain William A. Holmin	Algeria, Italy
Captain Emil M. Krieger	France and Germany
Captain Walter R. Mansfield	England, Yugoslavia, and China
Captain George H. Owen	Algeria, Egypt, Burma, and Italy
Captain Sebastian Passanessi	Algiers, Italy
Captain Winthrop Rutherford Jr.	Tunisia, France, and Germany
1st Lieutenant Joseph F. Campisi	London and Italy
1st Lieutenant Edward T. Dickinson Jr.	London, Sweden, France
1st Lieutenant Harry H. Harper	Egypt, Bulgaria
1st Lieutenant George M. Hearn	Italy
1st Lieutenant Rolfe Kingsley Jr.	Egypt, Italy, Austria
1st Lieutenant William B. Macomber	France, Burma
1st Lieutenant Alan K. Magary	London, France
1st Lieutenant John J. Meilly	London
1st Lieutenant John W. Mowinckel	France, Germany, Austria
1st Lieutenant Charles A. Muecke	France, Germany
1st Lieutenant Robert Rubin	London
1st Lieutenant George S. Seabury	Egypt, Sri Lanka, Malaysia, Burma
1st Lieutenant Michael Shaughnessy	London
1st Lieutenant Edward E. Weismiller	France
1st Lieutenant Richard D. Wylly	France
2nd Lieutenant Nicholas R. Cooky	Italy and Albania
2nd Lieutenant Walter W. Taylor	Corsica, Italy
2nd Lieutenant Peter Viertel	France, Germany
Warrant Officer Thomas L. Curtis	Greece and China
Warrant Officer John L. Richardson	Washington DC, England, and Sri Lanka
Gunnery Sergeant Thomas L. Curtis	Egypt and Greece
Gunnery Sergeant John Harnicher	France and Germany
Gunnery Sergeant Robert LaSalle	France and Germany
Gunnery Sergeant Larry Elder	North Africa
Sergeant Charles Perry	France

Sergeant John Bodnar	France and Germany
Sergeant Fred Brunner	Germany
Sergeant Jack Risler	France and Germany
Corporal James S. Sweeney	Washington DC and England

A MARINE IN RUSSIA

Originally ordered to Moscow on December 10, 1943 as an assistant US naval attaché, Major John M. Maury, Jr.'s orders were changed and his assignment in Murmansk, Russia, began when he arrived there on February 29, 1944. Shortly after his arrival, he was promoted to the rank of lieutenant colonel. As a naval attaché, Maury carried out duties such as collecting intelligence, offering advice to the US War Shipping Administration (WSA), administrative duties concerning the Lend-Lease shipments to the Soviet Union, and provided oversight for repairs to US vessels. Maury wrote many reports and journal entries which detailed the Russian economy, bureaucracy, industry, and attitudes toward the West. Maury was detached from the WSA and left Russia on November 18, 1945.

LEFT Maury stands with a Russian barrage balloon crew in Murmansk, Russia, June 1944. (USMC)

RIGHT Maury (left) with his host Russian officer and his family in Murmansk, Russia, June 1944. (USMC)

CHAPTER 4

THE TIMES IT ALMOST HAPPENED

World War II is full of "what if" possibilities. These range from what if Hitler had waited a few more years before attacking the Allies to allow his scientists time to mature emerging technologies, to what if the Allies had skipped Okinawa and invaded Taiwan instead, or not dropped the atomic bombs at all. The following are four major times US Marines were almost deployed and would have caused a major shift in World War II as we know it.

MARINES INVADE THE AZORES

Located approximately 950 miles west of Portugal in the Atlantic Ocean lie the nine islands that make up the Azores. On May 22, 1941, President Roosevelt directed the Army and Navy to draft plans for the occupation of the Azores. A week later, the proposed plan was approved by the Joint Board and called War Plan Gray. It would call for a 28,000-troop landing force, 14,000 of which would be Marines.

It was calculated that at least 41 transport ships would be required to move the forces. The naval component would be led by Admiral King, Commander in Chief, Atlantic Fleet, and the landing force by Brigadier General Holland M. Smith, commander of the 1st Marine Division. In addition to the Azores expedition, plans were made to send Marines and soldiers to the south to the Canary Islands and Madeira Island if the British requested assistance.

Initially, planners had wanted to send nine Marine combat landing teams, and three Army ones, to Puerto Rico for joint amphibious training. However, this was canceled due to a lack of troop transports able to ferry troops from the continental US to Puerto Rico. The expedition to the Azores was approved by the Joint Board on May 29, 1941, but it was not approved in time by President Roosevelt, who had already left for a trip to New York.

During a trip to his hometown of Hyde Park, Roosevelt weighed the benefits, capabilities, and potential outcomes of the US involvement throughout the Atlantic. On June 4, plans were approved for both the Azores expedition and an already considered occupation of Iceland. However, once Army planners began the overarching planning for both expeditions that would occur simultaneously, it was decided not enough transports existed for both expeditions. On June 5, 1941, Roosevelt announced the redirected movements of Marines from War Plan Gray to Iceland to relieve the British garrison there until the Army was able to move adequate forces to Iceland.

MARINES INVADE BRAZIL

With the surprise attack on Pearl Harbor hurling the United States into war with Japan, and then the declaration of war on the US by Germany, the US mindset immediately changed from a reactive to proactive stance. In February 1942 Washington planners elaborated on Rainbow 5 with the creation of the *Joint Basic Plan for the Occupation of Northeast Brazil.* The Marine Corps' contribution would be called Plan Rubber.

Plan Rubber called for landings in Natal, Fortaleza, and Recife followed by additional landings at Salvador, Belém, and Fernando de Noronha Island. With its strategic geographic position, Campo Parnamerin Airport in Natal was considered to be the most important of all the locations.

From the onset, there were significant geographic concerns for the invasion due to tides and hydrography, among other factors. Despite these, it was decided to carry out the invasion. The Atlantic Fleet would provide naval bombardment spearheaded by USS *Texas* alongside air cover and close air support from USS *Ranger*. Rubber's plans included having Marine Corps aircraft squadrons tasked with providing close air support in addition to the aircraft already embarked on the *Ranger*. The newly created 1st Marine Division and the Army's newly created 9th Infantry Division were tasked with carrying out the invasion. Both units began training for the expected amphibious assault in January 1942. Initially, exercises planners had hoped to have the practice landings in the southern part of the US in either Florida, Georgia, or the Carolinas. However, due to sightings of German submarines off the coast of the southern US, planners had to settle for Cape Henry, Virginia.

The training exercises exposed several major issues. Navigation of the landing crafts from ship-to-shore landing zones proved to be particularly difficult. Troops were too dispersed on the beach, there was a lack of naval gunfire support, pilots were untrained in how to cooperate with ground troops for close air support, and command and control on the beaches broke down significantly. The training exercise was deemed a tactical failure by Marine Brigadier General Holland M. Smith despite the landing force having a 4:1 numerical advantage. It exposed how incompetent the US military was at carrying out a joint amphibious operation – all this despite the efforts that went on during FLEX. Unfortunately, some lessons were not learned, and the command-and-control issues would reappear in Operation *Torch* a few months later. The lack of organizational learning from the FLEX experiments demonstrates how limited communication capabilities were during the era – institutional knowledge was not easily shared.

However, the amphibious assault on the coast of Brazil was not to be. There were major diplomatic efforts behind the scenes to persuade President Vargas to allow US troops into the country, leading to several years of US Marines in Brazil.

OPERATION *CROSSBOW* – THE PLAN FOR MARINE AVIATORS TO ATTACK V-1 SITES

In early 1943, Allied bombing efforts were dealing devastating blows to Hitler. By May, Allied High Command was beginning to lay the groundwork for an amphibious assault in France, codenamed Operation *Overlord*. During aerial reconnaissance missions for this planning, Allied intelligence discovered the construction of numerous secret facilities in Germany, France, Belgium, and several other countries. Reconnaissance flights, and intelligence gathered on the ground by Resistance fighters and spies, uncovered 96 small launch sites for V-1s with another six launch sites for V-2s alongside numerous logistics facilities for the rockets.

Fearing an advanced technological weapon that would give Germany an edge, Winston Churchill's War Cabinet leaped into action and ordered Operation *Hydra*, the bombing of the Peenemunde facility, in

August 1943. *Hydra* became the first in a series of continuous bombings of V-1 and V-2 sites wrapped under what would become Operation *Crossbow*.

Realizing the demoralizing effects the German rocket attacks would have on the British public, the War Cabinet requested General Eisenhower place priority on destroying the launch sites. Eisenhower granted the request in June 1944, stating "with respect to *Crossbow* targets, these targets are to take first priority over everything except the urgent requirements of the *Overlord* battle."

While bomber crews and Allied leadership created new tactics for bombing the heavily fortified launch sites, several other new technologies were brought to bear to help eliminate the V-rocket threat – one of which utilized Marine Corps aviators.

In support of Eisenhower's directive of the rocket launch sites becoming a priority, Naval Air Atlantic staff speculated on ways to assist. Navy Commander Thomas H. Moorer created the idea of arming the newly fielded F4U Corsair with guided Tiny Tim rockets, a brand-new type of munition. Moorer created his plan, codenamed Project Danny, and with the permission of his leadership was able to assign Marine Aircraft Group 51 (MAG-51) to USS *Gilbert Islands* (CVE-107) for travel to Europe.

As a testament to the urgency to rid the Germans of the rocket sites, the *Gilbert Islands* had just recently been commissioned and put to sea on July 20, 1944. Project Danny would be the shakedown cruise for the ship, an event typically completed prior to a ship entering full service.

Stood up in February 1944, MAG-51 was stationed at Marine Corps Auxiliary Air Facility (MCAAF) Oak Grove, a smaller auxiliary field near Cherry Point, North Carolina. MAG-51 consisted of Marine Fighter Squadrons 511, 512, 513, and 514. Around May 1944, Marine Observation Squadron 351 (VMO-351) would be added to MAG-51. VMO-351 would retain its observation designation for a few more months, although the squadron had already been fielded with Corsairs and was organized as a fighter squadron like the others in the MAG.

While MAG-51 was making preparations to embark aboard the *Gilbert Islands*, Moorer was sent to the newly created Pentagon building to brief US strategic planners.

Project Danny would have seen USS *Gilbert Islands* take up residence in the North Sea, just off the coast, and attack V-1 and V-2 launch sites in Germany, the Netherlands, and Belgium. By the time Moorer arrived at the Pentagon, the Marines' departure was all but complete. Logistics issues had been sorted out, deployment orders approved and dispatched to

Marines, and training was in progress for Marine pilots on how to attack the launch sites. The plan called for Marines to fire the newly fielded Tiny Tim rockets. The 500lb rockets were 11ft long and approximately 1ft in diameter and had a semi-armor-piercing warhead.

Unfortunately for the Marine Corps and Commander Moorer, one of the attendees of the brief was none other than General George C. Marshall, US Army. Marshall was a staunch opposer of the existence of the Marine Corps due to the Marine Corps receiving much fanfare from journalists during both World Wars. Marshall's animosity toward the Corps was not unfounded. The Marine Corps had a knack for sucking up media attention and receiving much glory in the news, sometimes receiving exclusive credit even when Army units were side by side with Marines.

Upon hearing Marine aviators would be taking part in Project Danny, Marshall stood up, walked to the door, and stated, "that's the end of this briefing. As long as I'm in charge of our armed forces, there will never be a Marine in Europe." And with that, Project Danny came to a close.

So close was the deployment of MAG-51 on German sites that Marine Corps equipment, supplies, and personal effects had already been sent to Norfolk starting July 11 and loaded onto the *Gilbert Islands*. Project Danny was canceled on July 30. The Marines of MAG-51 would eventually get retasked and sent to the Pacific and would take part in battles at Okinawa, Japan, and Balikpapan, Indonesia.

Although inter-service rivalry played a part in the canceled deployment to Europe, the Allied advance across Europe proceeded at a much quicker pace than was originally forecasted and German launch sites were eliminated faster than anticipated. Marshall inadvertently ended up helping the Allies by causing the redirection of the *Gilbert Islands* and its planes to the Pacific ahead of schedule.

US ARMY REQUEST FOR 100,000 MARINES IN EUROPE

Almost lost entirely to history is the fact that General George C. Marshall considered asking the Marine Corps for help. While Marshall may have had much disdain for the Marine Corps, he did realize the Marine Corps had a considerable amount of manpower. The US Army and Allied militaries had taken sizeable losses in the infantry ranks. The fighting across Europe after landing at Normandy and the German counteroffensive at the Ardennes (the Battle of the Bulge) had racked up significant losses. The irony of this was that it occurred when the number of soldiers in the

US Army stood at its largest point in the history of the country, with more than 11 million wearing the Army uniform at the end of 1944. Infantry soldiers were already in such short supply for the Army that Eisenhower had ordered rear units to look for ways to thin out their ranks and free up men for front-line duty.

(Eisenhower's instructions to look for rear-echelon personnel for front-line duty was intentional. It would be easier to move men in stateside garrison roles to the front lines versus pulling support personnel in Europe to the front line. This is due to the fact that the support and sustainment work must still be carried out during combat operations. To remove troops from their support jobs would increase the workload of those left behind, creating a backlog of supplies to move with front-line units eventually feeling the pain of not receiving food, water, medical supplies, or fuel due to lack of supply personnel.)

Allied military situations were equally as bad, if not worse. British forces had been taking alarming losses due to worldwide commitments of defending an empire. While the French had men to train, precious equipment and supplies to create the divisions and turn civilians into professional soldiers were needed to sustain front-line units already engaged in combat operations. Belgium and Poland had similar issues to the French after having been decimated at the beginning of the war by the German war machine. Hitler's winter offensive of 1944 had forced the Allies to reexamine their resources across the board.

As Allied and German forces engaged in fighting at the Ardennes, the Joint Chiefs of Staff in the US moved up the sailing date of three infantry divisions, one airborne division, and three armored divisions. Originally scheduled to depart the US in the spring of 1945, their sailing dates were moved up to January and February. Additionally, two infantry divisions that were originally slated for service in the Pacific were reallocated to Europe upon Eisenhower's request and were now scheduled to depart for Europe in mid-February. While these movements were occurring, Marshall also issued instructions for senior leaders to look through defense units stationed in Alaska and the Caribbean and see what men could be cut and redirected for service in Europe.

Meanwhile, Eisenhower and his staff contemplated more ways to ease the manpower shortage in Europe. Four more possibilities for the US were considered:

1. Convincing the Russians to commit to another major offensive in the east to stop the Germans from transferring troops from the Eastern Front to the west.

2. Shifting troops from Italy to western Europe.
3. Utilizing black soldiers as front-line troops.
4. As a last result, asking the Marines for men.

Marshall suggested to Eisenhower to request 100,000 Marines be diverted from the Pacific to the Atlantic for the final push into Germany. Marshall may have thought the idea had merit due to the thought that the United States had made its unofficial deal with the United Kingdom to knock Germany out of the war first before concentrating on Japan.

Through correspondence between Eisenhower and Marshall, it was decided that even if the Marine Corps were willing to help the Army in Europe, it simply could not. At its peak in World War II, the Marine Corps reached 475,604 Marines at the end of 1944. Compare that to the 7,994,750 serving in the Army at the same time. A 21 percent request of the entire Marine Corps simply could not have occurred in a timely fashion no matter how urgent the need. Even if the logistics network existed to transport and sustain a movement of 100,000 Marines from one side of the world to the other, the Marines would have arrived too late to Europe to have had any measurable impact. The Allies had advanced at a much faster than anticipated pace, forcing the surrender of Germany less than a year after D-Day.

Original memo from Marshall to Eisenhower, S-74003, January 7, 1945, page 2. "Maybe the Marines would like to turn over a hundred thousand to us" is in the list of "several things [that] could help us." (Eisenhower Presidential Library)

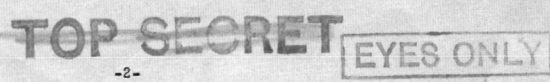

TOP SECRET

EYES ONLY

CONSEQUENCES FROM WITHOUT. THE GERMANS ARE CONVINCED THEY ARE FIGHTING FOR THEIR VERY EXISTENCE AND THEIR BATTLE ACTION REFLECTS THIS SPIRIT. SEVERAL THINGS COULD HELP US: (a) CERTAINTY THAT THE RUSSIANS ARE GOING QUICKLY TO BEGIN A SUSTAINED/MAJOR OFFENSIVE REQUIRING GERMAN RESOURCES TO REVERSE THEIR FLOW.

(b) SUFFICIENTLY GREAT STRENGTH HERE SO THAT I COULD KEEP SOME FEW DIVISIONS IN SHAEF RESERVE TO MEET EMERGENCIES, AND GIVING ME A SMALL POOL THROUGH WHICH TO ROTATE TIRED DIVISIONS FOR RE-FITTING. IN THIS CONNECTION I THINK THE ITALIAN FRONT SHOULD BE STUDIED TO DETERMINE CONDITIONS UNDER WHICH ADDITIONAL DIVISIONS SHOULD BE BROUGHT HERE, AND TO HAVE MEANS READY FOR IMPLEMENTATION OF ANY PLANS ADOPTED. ANY UNALLOCATED DIVISIONS AT HOME OR ANY THAT COULD BE OBTAINED IF PERMITTED BY OVERALL STRATEGIC PLANS BY POSTPONING ACTION ELSEWHERE, SHOULD BE SENT HERE AS SOON AS POSSIBLE. (c) IMMEDIATE AND DRASTIC COMB-OUT HERE OF ABLE
                    IF POSSIBLE
BODIED MEN. (d)/INCREASE ARMY CEILING AT LEAST TO EXTENT OF SUBTRACTING DETACHMENTS OF PATIENTS FROM THE TOTAL ALLOWED, SO AS TO PROVIDE A GREATER FLOW OF REPLACEMENTS. (MAYBE THE MARINES WOULD LIKE TO TURN OVER A HUNDRED THOUSAND TO US.) (e) CONTINUOUS EFFORT TO EXPEDITE FLOW OF CRITICAL AMMUNITION TYPES AND TIRES. (f) SPEED UP DEVELOPMENT OF FRENCH DIVISIONS. PARAGRAPH. I AM CONVINCED
                                              U.S.
THAT WE CANNOT RESORT TO CANNIBALIZATION OF DIVISIONS BECAUSE OF THE STRENGTH NEEDED ON THIS LONG FRONT. THE ENEMY ENJOYS THE ADVANTAGE OF SHORT COMMUNICATIONS, FORTIFIED DEFENSE ZONES AND TOTAL MOBILIZATION AND OUR ONLY ANSWER IS SUFFICIENT DIVISIONAL STRENGTH, FULLY MAINTAINED. PARAGRAPH. I BELIEVE THAT GASSER'S WORK WILL DO MUCH TOWARD GETTING US RIGHT DOWN TO BEDROCK IN REACHING DEFINITE AND ACCURATE CONCLUSIONS. PARAGRAPH. IN THE MATTER OF COMBING OUT ABLE BODIED MEN

TOP SECRET EYES ONLY

-2-

CHAPTER 5

FACES BEHIND THE LENSES AND STORIES

Captain Herbert L. Merillat, Marine public relations officer for Leatherneck units in the British Islands, tries a Royal Marine beret on for size, May 10, 1944. The Royal Marine beret was given to Captain Merillat during a tour of British Leatherneck bases. The US Marine Corps device fits on a patch of red, while the beret itself is navy blue. Merillat, a former attorney and press analyst for the US Treasury Department, was the public relations officer for the 1st Marine Division, reinforced during the fight for Guadalcanal from August 7 to December 10, 1942. He held degrees from the University of Arizona and Oxford University in England. (USMC, photo by SSgt James Kilpatrick)

TOP First Lieutenant Weldon Bernard James, United States Marine Corps Reserve, a public relations officer with Marine units in the British Isles. A former London correspondent for *PM*, First Lieutenant James served in the European Theater from August 1942 to December 1944. Originally from St. Charles, South Carolina, Lieutenant James covered the wars in China and Spain as a newspaper correspondent, and was on the USS *Panay* when it was sunk in December 1937. James was aboard USS *Texas* on D-Day and landed on Omaha Beach later in the day to help coordinate naval gunfire. Photo dated May 10, 1944. (USMC, photo by SSgt James Kilpatrick)

BOTTOM LEFT Second Lieutenant Robert H. Rubin, of New York City, reported for duty with the Commander, US Naval Forces in Europe. He led a special field photographic unit that was there for action. Rubin attended St. Paul's School and Yale University and was employed by Metro-Goldwyn-Mayer Corporation before he was commissioned in the Marine Corps in December 1942. (USMC, photo by SSgt Weldon L. Keating, August 1943)

BOTTOM RIGHT Technical Sergeant Richard Thomas Wright, United States Marine Corps combat correspondent. A native of Arlington, Virginia, Technical Sergeant Wright was the first Marine correspondent sent into the Pacific area, where he served at various bases including Samoa, Funafuti, and Australia. He was an alumnus of Washington and Lee University, at Lexington, Virginia, and a former reporter for the *Philadelphia Evening Bulletin*. Wright landed at Juno Beach with British and Canadian forces and made subsequent visits to Juno in the coming days to chronicle the invasion. Photo dated May 10, 1944. (USMC, photo by SSgt James Kilpatrick)

TOP Gunnery Sergeant Raymond T. Kaiser, center, and other Marines stand with captured German military items in September 1944 aboard USS *Augusta*. (MCHD)

OPPOSITE TOP German prisoners on Ratonneau Island off the southern coast of France are closely guarded by Marines from USS *Philadelphia*. (US Navy)

OPPOSITE BOTTOM Marines and sailors from USS *Augusta* pose with a captured Nazi flag taken from the German garrison, which was presented to the Commandant of the Marine Corps. (MCHD)

CA31/A16-3
(09/)

U.S.S. AUGUSTA,
c/o Fleet Post Office,
New York, New York.
6 September 1944.

C-O-N-F-I-D-E-N-T-I-A-L

From: Commanding Officer.
To: Commandant of the Marine Corps.

Subject: Landing Party.

Reference: (a) Article 721 (4), U.S. Navy Regulations.

    1.   In accordance with reference (a), the following
information is submitted:

                On 29 August 1944 the below named officers
and men landed on the Ile d'If as temporary
garrison troops and to take charge of prisoners
of war on the island. The party returned to
this vessel on 31 August 1944.

    2.   The below named officers and men were the
members of the landing party:

Officers - Francis R. Schlesinger, Captain, U.S.M.C.
           Henry D. Reck, Lieutenant, D-V(S), U.S.N.R.
           William H. McDaniel, 1st Lieutenant, U.S.M.C.

Navy   - WIRTH, Benjamin F., 295 51 03, CPhM(AA), USN.
           BEAUREGARD, Leo L., 202 24 86, PhM1c, USN.
           WEBER, Raymond, 642 01 80, PhoM1c,V-6, USNR.
           NOLAN, Philip, M., 207 37 61, RM2c, USN.
           DUFFY, John E., 300 69 72, PhoM2c, USN.
           THOMAS, Robert E., 208 79 21, SM3c, USN.
           KRUGER, A.F., 905 57 34, S2c,V-6,SV, USNR.

Marines - SMITH, Memory H., (256338), 1st.Sgt., USMC.
           KAISER, Raymond T., (204110), Gy.Sgt., USMC.
           WALKER, Leonard A., (211849), Gy.Sgt., USMC.
           WOODS, Eugene S., (277525), Pl.Sgt., USMC.
           FETT, Bernard P., (315993), Sgt., USMC.
           PASSOTH, Donald W., (398387), Sgt., USMCR.
           PIERGIOVANNI, Henry, (316968), Sgt., USMCR.
           CHRISTOFELS, Adrian L., (263554), Corp., USMC.
           DAVIS, Harry J., (403981), Corp., USMC
           EVANS, Donald G., (444163), Corp., USMCR.
           HUMMEL, George E., (313481, Corp., USMC.
           LOGSDON, Jack B., (390107), Corp., USMCR.
           NOVAK, John L., (398437), Corp., USMCR.
           SEVENE, James G., (359403), Corp., USMC.
           TEMPEST, Reid W., (318531), Corp., USMC.
           WESSINGER, Frank, (368647), Corp., USMC.
           ADLER, Stanley R., (450938), Pfc., USMCR.
           ANTCZAK, Walter J., (885665), Pfc., USMCR.
           BARTLEY, William J., jr., ((450168), Pfc., USMCR.
           BAYLOR, Richard P., (895934), Pfc.,,USMCR.
           BOREN, William V., (491529), Pfc., USMCR.
           BUTALA, Bruce V., (551243), Pfc, USMCR.
           CATANIA, Cosmo, (862884), Pfc, USMCR.
           COLE, Joseph A., (539119), Pfc., USMCR.
           CONKLIN, Daniel D., (855324), Pfc., USMCR.
           D'AGATA, Anthony, jr., (390545), Pfc., USMC
           DOUGHERTY, James MacD., (459735), Pfc.,USMCR.

CA31/A16-3

U.S.S. AUGUSTA,
c/o Fleet Post Office,
New York, New York.
6 September 1944.

C-O-N-F-I-D-E-N-T-I-A-L

Subject: Landing Party.

- -

ELLENBERGER, Victor M., (448342), Pfc., USMCR.
FLATI, Henry M., (512030), Pfc., Pfc., USMCR.
GARBACKI, Anthony A., (403997), Pfc., USMCR.
GOBIN, Charles H., jr., (398558), Pfc., USMC.
GREENE, Charles V., (347894), Pfc., USMCR.
GLEASON, Franklin J., (527297), Pfc., USMCR.
HACKMAN, George S., jr., (505321), Pfc., USMCR.
HIRLEMAN, James W., (867693), Pfc., USMCR.
JACOBS, Alfred A., (857078), Pfc., USMCR.
JUDICE, Frank D., (846068), Pfc., USMCR.
LONERGAN, Thomas J., jr., (432106), Pfc., USMCR.
MAGNONE, Elbert L., (804831), Pfc., USMC.
MARLEY, James W., (281167), Pfc., USMC.
MOSS, Delbert, (411844), Pfc., USMC.
MULGREW, William, J.P., (469602), Pfc, USMCR.
REGAN, Joseph T., jr., (880297), Pfc, USMCR.
RICHMAN, Harold M., (870161), Pfc., USMCR.
RING, William G., (457909), Pfc., USMCR.
SMITH, Richard D., (487220), Pfc., USMCR.
WENTSKOWSKI, John jr., (403659), Pfc., USMC.
WOKOWSKY, Joseph M., (392331), Pfc., USMC.
MACLEAN, Robert G., (539130), Pvt., USMC.
JARZYNIECKI, Sylvester J., (319807), FMCorp., USMC.

3.   A detailed report of this landing is being
forwarded via official channels to the Commandant of the
Marine Corps.

4.   A certified copy of this letter is being
appended to each of the above named officer's individual
files and men's service records.

E. H. JONES.

- -

Copy to: Chief of Naval Personnel.

ABOVE AND OPPOSITE Parts of an after action report written by the US Navy on the Marine Corps landing party. (MCHD)

3 ptember, 1944

From: Captain, Francis R. Schlesinger, U.S Marine Corps.
To: Captain, E.H. Jones, U.S. Navy.

Subject: Operations of Augusta Marine Detachment on August
          29, 30, and 31.

1.   At midnight on the night of August 28-29, Rear Admiral Davidson called me to his cabin and explained to me the operation plan for the following day. On the Islands of Ratonneau, D'if and Pomegues, in the harbor of Marsielles, there were 850 Germans who were manning coast artillery and flak batteries. These Germans had refused to surrender but that plans were underway to negotiate a surrender with them. The plan in brief was to send Captain Ansel close to the islands in a destroyer for transfer to a mine sweeper, an officer interpreter, Lieutenant Nuelsen, in his company would meet a German boat from the islands and negotiate the surrender. The entire U.S.S. AUGUSTA Marine Detachment, minus 6 men who were to remain aboard ship as orderlies, were to land, occupy the islands, disarm the enemy and garrison the islands until the prisoners would be taken off. The U.S.S. PHILADELPHIA Marine Detachment was to land in company. The Marine Detachment was to land with sufficient supplies to last four days. Charts, aerial photographs were furnished after the brief.

2.   At 1200 on August 29 the detachment with full equipment disembarked from the AUGUSTA and embarked on Y.M.S. #28. The AUGUSTA and PHILADELPHIA followed the mine sweepers as close to the mine fields as possible to give fire support if necessary. Y.M.S. #28 with two other mine sweepers and the destroyer Madison #425 carefully maneuvered through the mine fields and lay off the island of Ratonneau. At about 1440 a German boat flying a white flag stood out from the breakwater and went along side the minesweeper on which Captain Ansel was embarked. The surrender was formally accomplished and at about 1550 the landing was made on Ratonneau.

3.   It's Thompson and Cable with 17 men were directed to land on the Island of D'if and occupy and disarm the enemy. The Commanding Officer of the German garrison was directed to tell his men that they would immediately surrender all their arms and stack them in a designated area. A large warehouse which was surrounded by barbed wire was used as a stockade for the 700 prisoners on Ratonneau. Prior to sunset a patrol was sent to scout the ridges surrounding the dock area where the prisoners were being searched and confined in the stockade. The same patrol was to occupy the ridge in the vicinity of the enemy batteries during our first night on the island. A curfew was established at 2030 after which there was to be no movement of the prisoners from their assembly area. Before sunset approximately 600 prisoners were rounded up in the stockade. The remainder were confined in barracks near the flak batteries. The wounded and German doctors were allowed to remain in a cave which was being used as a hospital.

4.   On the morning of August 30, the remainder of the 700 Germans on Ratonneau were placed in the stockade and all the prisoners on D'if were interned. The Germans on Pomegues surrendered on Ratonneau. About 1000 four L.C.I. stood into the small harbor on Ratonneau and one L.C.I. moored alongside D'if. The wounded and 11 women were embarked on the first of the L.C.I.'s. By late afternoon all prisoners were embarked on the five L.C.I.'s. The white surrender flag which was flying from a hill over looking the harbor on the island of Ratonneau was taken

ABOVE AND OPPOSITE Pages from the August Marine Detachment Commanding Officer After Action Report. (MCHD)

TOP Not much is known about Staff Sergeant James R. Kilpatrick, combat photographer. He also landed with British and Canadian troops at Juno Beach. (USMC, photo by TSgt Richard T. Wright)

BOTTOM LEFT Staff Sergeant Weldon L. Keating, of New Orleans, Louisiana, Marine Corps combat correspondent and combat photographer. Before enlisting in the Corps in 1938, Keating graduated from Our Lady of Holy Cross College, New Orleans. (USMC, photo by 1st Lt Weldon James)

BOTTOM RIGHT Corporal William Ross Gibbon, United States Marine Corps combat photographer, of Columbus, Ohio. Corporal Gibbon enlisted in the Corps in March 1942, and attended Miami University in Oxford, Ohio, prior to enlisting. Gibbon was aboard USS *Texas* and chronicled the ship's activities during the attacks along the Normandy coast. Photo dated May 1944. (USMC, photo by SSgt James Kilpatrick)

TOP Sergeant Robert Davis, Marine combat correspondent. (USMC, photo by Cpl William Gibbon)

CENTER Sergeant Andrew B. Knight of Washington DC, Marine Corps combat photographer. (USMC, photo by Pvt William Ostoich)

BOTTOM Sergeant Allen A. Sommers, Marine Corps combat correspondent. Sommers was a native of Philadelphia, Pennsylvania, and married to Ruth Sommers. (USMC, photo by Sgt Allen Knight)

INDEX

Page numbers in **bold** refer to illustrations and their captions, page numbers in *italic* refer to contemporary accounts